speak fiction and poetry!

speak fiction
and poetry!

*the best of BOMB magazine's
interviews with writers*

edited by betsy sussler

with suzan sherman and ronalde shavers

G + B Arts International

Australia • Canada • China • France • Germany • India • Japan • Luxembourg
• Malaysia • The Netherlands • Russia • Singapore • Switzerland • Thailand

Amsteldijk 166
1st Floor
1079 LH Amsterdam
The Netherlands

British Library Cataloguing in Publication Data
Speak fiction and poetry! : the best of Bomb magazine's
     interviews with writers
     1. Authors, American—20th century—Interviews 2. Authors,
     English—20th century—Interviews 3. Authorship—
     Philosophy
     I. Sussler, Betsy
     810.9'0054

ISBN 90-5701-351-7

for

Patrick McGrath,
Lynne Tillman,
Gary Indiana,
and in memoriam for our poetry editor, poet, and translator
David Rattray.

contents

This book would not exist without the aid and support of some of our earliest contributing editors, Lynne Tillman, Patrick McGrath, and Gary Indiana. Their insights and literary vision helped establish the criteria for choosing the writers who have spoken in BOMB: humor, daring, and a passion for language. While their fiction has appeared regularly in the magazine, we decided that as contributing editors it would be inappropriate for them to be interviewed at length in its pages. It seems strange now, not to have them featured here as the groundbreaking writers they are. All the more since many of the writers interviewed in these pages were so enthusiastic about the process—speaking face to face with respected colleagues, the opportunity to rewrite the spoken word, the intimacy and the revelations— that they in turn interviewed writers who enthralled them, and as a consequence became contributing editors. Patrick McGrath single-handedly opened our pages to British writers. He interviewed Graham Swift, who interviewed Caryl Phillips, who interviewed American writer Melanie Rae Thon. Deborah Eisenberg interviewed Francine Prose, who interviewed Lydia Davis. This is the way our masthead has grown from five to twenty-two contributing editors in fiction and poetry, and our pages have filled with writers from all continents.

Writing, like love, as Michael Ondaatje has so memorably stated, has no fixed borders. It is a mysterious process, and mysteries—the oldest sort, the mythic ones, should remain so. That is their power, they demand an act of faith, and writing is an act of faith. However, circling the mystery is a never ending source of fascination that for me, eavesdropping as I have on the transcripts of all our interviews, is also a great privilege. There was a section of Luisa Valenzuela's interview that for one reason or another was cut. And yet it has stayed with me for years: Luisa couldn't figure out the ending to one of her stories and decided that a stroll through the park would clear her mind. While she was in the park, a stranger, a man from the provinces, approached her. Annoyed because she was trying to concentrate on the problem at hand, she shooed him away, but he kept insisting he had something to tell her. Finally, she listened to him, and he told her the end of her story. This is not, I might add, an unusual occurrence; small miracles accompany every act of creation.

Betsy Sussler

acknowledgments

Ameena Meer, Lawrence Chua, and Jenifer Berman, all writers, were BOMB's managing editors between 1986 and 1996 when most of these interviews were made, and their suggestions and expertise were and still are invaluable. Editors Suzan Sherman and Rone Shavers edited this volume with me; no one could hope to find better sounding boards or voluble opinionators. Interns Ashley Fantz, Stacey Green, Rachel Lipton, Maria Mackinney, and Mara Nelson aided in the production and proofing with admirable patience and diligence. Interns Amanda Junkin, Corinne Pierce, Leah Quin, Brandt Rumble, Matthew Simpson, and Chad Woolums read through early interviews. And as always, our contributing editors deserve a deep bow of gratitude and affection: April Bernard, Tom Bolt, Peter Carey, Thulani Davis, Deborah Eisenberg, Jessica Hagedorn, Amy Hempel, A.M. Homes, Kelvin Christopher James, Gary Indiana, Roland Legiardi-Laura, Patrick McGrath, Ameena Meer, Caryl Phillips, Robert Polito, Francine Prose, Lynne Tillman, Graham Swift, David L. Ulin, Benjamin Weissman, Bruce Wolmer, and Linda Yablonsky.

Saul Ostrow, our Associate Art Editor, Fred van der Marck, Publisher, and our agent Dan Mandel are responsible for each and every volume. Stewart Cauley and Skúta Helgason have come up with a better design vision than I ever hoped for. Sharon Gallagher at D.A.P. and everyone at Gordon & Breach have paved the way with enthusiasm and support—Thank you all.

This is a book for writers, for those who want to be writers, and for those who want to know what writers are like. What are writers like? Split personalities, for a start. Ariel Dorfman: "I fluctuate between two conditions all the time. I'm exiled and at the same time I'm obsessed with my country. I feel very much alive while at the same time I'm a ghost. I love the mass media and I detest the mass media. Fortunately, I'm a writer. Otherwise I'd probably be in an asylum." Writers are obsessed with making sense of things. Melanie Rae Thon: "There's always a risk: how far will I go, and how long will it take me to come back? But the alternative is to willfully ignore what's in front of me. I can't. To live that way would be like being dead."

Writers are opinionated and ruthless. Jeanette Winterson: "I think it's rude to write long books." Padgett Powell: "There's this notion that writers become drunks. That's not the case at all. Drunks become writers." James Merrill: "Poetry siphons off into harmless backwaters hundreds, perhaps thousands, of young people whom it will fulfill and civilize without their really amounting to much." Luisa Valenzuela: "When I write I become a vampire. I suck cold blood from anything for a novel."

Writers muddle along in the dark. Francine Prose: "Why do these things belong in the same story? I never understand what they are, or what they mean, or why anyone is doing the things that they're doing. But I don't in real life either."

In fact, based on this quite extraordinary cross-section of mostly American writers, we are almost anything you can imagine; except, that is, incurious, inarticulate, literal, conventional, detached, abstract, humble, or demure. There is a truly broad spectrum of writers represented here, and in a sense the only thing they have in common is that at one time or another all were interviewed for BOMB magazine. Yet certain themes emerge again and again as they talk about their work. Form. Inspiration. Film. Academe. Power, or the politics of race, class, gender, and culture. Language, of course. Danger and failure. Roots, exile, self. Curiously, there is not a lot of talk about sex, nor about money, the publishingindustry, or each other's careers, all of which are the other major staples of writers' informal conversation. So there are few ripe indiscretions here, no envy, and only occasional displays of swagger. Instead these conversations go for the broad picture, and what emerges most strikingly is a portrait of the writer as social barometer: taking a reading, getting the weather right, maintaining the instrument, knowing how it works. Art and politics, for the most part.

Take art first. All writers agree on this at least, that what we do is very, very difficult. Why doesn't it get any easier? John Edgar Wideman and Tobias Wolff are both good on this. Wideman: "I'm always working against my limitations. And I wonder, is it ever going to get any better, because it's me talking to me, what do I know? So you need that infusion from somewhere else, whether you call it the muse, or the unconscious, or whatever. It has to swing in, you have to be visited." Wolff: "You're always trying to top yourself. You don't want to do what you did before again and again. You get tired of certain conventions. You want to do other things, so you're creating the difficulties as the very condition of your art." It's precisely this sort of self-imposed frustration that makes writers want to top themselves in the other sense. They usually destroy their work instead.

Another question that almost all these writers are asked in one form or another is where they get their ideas. Jeanette Winterson says: "For me the point has always been to take people who are exiled or come at life at an angle, who are slightly askew to the mainstream vision of the world—which, let's face it, most of us are—and then to use the glorious power of art, the power of language, to really elevate these lives." Paul Auster started a novel after an odd thing happened to him. "One night the telephone rang and the person on the other end asked for the Pinkerton Detective Agency. I told him he had the wrong number, but the same person called back the next night with the same question. When I hung up the phone the second time, I asked myself what would have happened if I had said yes." Brad Morrow, when asked how one of his books got started, replies: "Insomnia." He was in New Mexico, and late one night noticed "these amber twinkling lights in a long string up along the western mesas at the foot of the Jemez mountains. They were entrancing." He discovered the next day they were the lights of Los Alamos, where the atom bomb was invented. A novel was born.

There is much more in these pages about the business of conception and gestation, process and technique, the shifting and editing and combing that goes on, the long weary haul from that first tantalizing glimpse of possibility to the glorious day you abandon it to the world or, as Ariel Dorfman says, it abandons you. And what we see here clearly is that no two writers think about these things in the same way, and when they do, they find entirely different and entirely idiosyncratic ways to talk about them.

Many of the writers here in some way see their work as a means of giving expression to the voice and experience of those not invited to the feast. These are some of the most passionate and engaged conversations in the book. Caryl Phillips says: "Reading and writing equals power. Once you have a language you are dangerous." bell hooks says: "Masses of black people suffer from internalized racism, and our intellectual work will never impact on their lives if we do not move it out of the academy." And this: "I had to give people something that allowed them to identify with what I was saying, and not just offer some abstract idea that might not have any relevance to their lives. That is all about the function of story." Whereas Walter Mosley says: "Very often, in black art and literature, the mistake is made that the correct political stance makes good art, when indeed the correct political stance has nothing to do with good art. Nothing. The only issue for me is good writing."

Nor is racism the only form of oppression engaged with here. Ariel Dorfman and Luisa Valenzuela, from Chile and Argentina respectively, talk about the military juntas they knew, the torture and disappearance of their friends, the need as Dorfman states, to remember lest the past be repeated, the need "to create an imaginary world which gives an alternative meaning to the fate that has been imposed on us."

Class in America is a preoccupation of Russell Banks, particularly in respect to working-class kids, whose options, he says, are closed off in this country by the age of ten. Peter Carey is very funny on the sort of cultural colonialism imposed by America on practically everywhere else in the world: "I started to imagine a country where figures like Mickey and Minnie Mouse were the decadent flowering of a heretical Protestant sect. It was like drawing a cause-and-effect line connecting Mickey and the Mayflower."

Jeanette Winterson is scathing about gender stereotyping and much else. "I am not interested in writing about women who are not in control and not strong. I'm quite prepared to display their vulnerabilities and their questionings and conflicts, but I don't believe women are weak. I hope to bring together a different kind of fiction that makes space within it for the female voice in all its complexity." Sheila Bosworth talks of the anger that was the source of a novel: "Southern women are taught that they're always going to be protected by someone—Daddy's going to protect you, or big brother is going to protect you, or your husband's going to protect you—and God of course is the greatest protector of all. And it just isn't true. You're not protected by any of these people. The grand silence reigns."

There are no grand silences in these pages, but many grand topics. Edmund White, resident in Paris, talks about Genet, Beckett, Giacometti, and America. Frederic Tuten talks about history, irony, revolution, and aesthetics: "Trite to say, but beauty is politics and a hedge against vulgarity." Honor Moore talks about her grandmother, the painter Margarett Sargent, and Suzannah Lessard talks about her great-grandfather, the architect Stanford White. The conversation with these two biographers sweeps us into the lives and times of two eminent American families and their doomed, brilliant black sheep.

There is much more in this book that could be quoted as a fascinating instance of a serious writer reflecting on his enterprise. Graham Swift's wry linkage of history, superstition and storytelling. Sapphire's intensely vivid picture of her community, her Harlem, what's wrong with it, what needs doing, what's being done. Michael Ondaatje's account of that most prickly ordeal for a writer, the adaptation of a complicated novel to the screen, and much else that is fascinating, particularly the connection between writing and acting. Lucy Brock-Broido on writing by night and the composition of a noctuary.

How to sum up? One idea that few of these contentious people would dispute, I submit, is that the imagination exists, that it can be nourished, that it can mature and grow strong, and that it can change the way a segment of the world is perceived and thus, perhaps, change that segment of the world. Not much art for art's sake here. John Edgar Wideman, who claims in these pages that he became a writer because (a) he didn't grow tall enough for pro basketball, and (b) because writers don't have bosses, says this: "If there is any threat to our humanity, it's the threat that somehow our imaginations will be squashed, will become obsolete. And writing is one way to keep that idea of imagination alive. In my best days I see that as the primary enterprise I'm involved in. Saying that whatever is in your head has some meaning. So I welcome people who are on a different track. We're on our little boat, ship of fools, and there we are. It's nice to have company."

Meet the company.

Patrick McGrath

Michael Ondaatje, © Christina Hartling. Courtesy Knopf.

MICHAEL ONDAATJE   willem dafoe

Michael Ondaatje's *The English Patient* is a novel cherished by readers for its lush, subliminal prose. At the end of World War II, four characters find themselves in the remains of a deserted Italian villa. The enigmatic English patient, burned beyond recognition, speaks through a morphine haze. His young nurse, Hana, suffers from her own emotional shell shock. Kip, a Sikh soldier in the British army, dismantles bombs left by the Germans. And Caravaggio, a thief turned spy for the British, sets out to reveal the English patient's true identity. While the book's imagery lends itself to film—a plane crashing, its pilot falling from a desert sky in flames; Kip hoisting himself up a rope, lighting flare after flare to gaze at a fresco of Solomon and the Queen of Sheba; Hana playing the piano in a bombed out room—the narrative in the desert, the time at the villa, back-stories told in flashbacks, and the English patient's diary are the stuff of literature. Therefore, it is with great anticipation, and some cynicism, that the novel's readers, all of us enamored, await the film version.

Willem Dafoe met Michael Ondaatje on the film's set in Rome during the first few days of production. It was important to Willem, being one of those enamored readers, that the film and his being cast as Caravaggio in the film, had Michael's blessing. Willem said, "I don't pretend to know him, but we had some wonderful walks in Rome where we would wander . . . into a church or a café for coffee. They were long walks and it was great to have Michael on the set." They met this past October in New York to discuss the novel's transformation to film. They're both, by the way, very happy with the film, not because it replicates the novel, but because it has become its own story.

BOMB # 58, Winter 1997

willem dafoe Let's start with *The English Patient*. Why didn't you want to do the film script?

MICHAEL ONDAATJE I spent six years writing the book, the last two years of which were spent creating the only structure I thought it could have. So to turn around and dismantle that structure and put the head where the tail was . . . There's no way I could have been objective and known what should go, what should stay.

wd Were you involved in the initial script development?

MO Quite a lot. Anthony Minghella, Saul Zaentz, and I met every time there was a draft, and I think we worked well and adventurously together. The script felt "new," and was not a "shadow" of the book. Because all three of us were working on something new it was a much more exciting project. I was amazed, right from the beginning, how Anthony got the voices, when Barnes meets Katherine and says, "Of course, I know your mother," that sense of class knowledge of each other was caught perfectly. In any case, each time there was a new draft, we would meet up. It was a real education in terms of how a script gets tighter and tighter. Film is much tougher. I don't think I could write a great chapter and then give it up because of the book's overall time limitations, as you sometimes must do with entire scenes in film. That's like a bad joke for a writer.

wd I run into so many people who, when they hear I'm involved with the film, say, "Oh, I loved the book." And I get this sinking feeling, not out of disrespect to the movie, but that somehow they're not going to see the book, not even a version of the book. They'll see something that grew out of it.

MO I feel the film has become something quite distinct, with its own DNA.

wd It's a book that people have very personal reactions to. People either sat down and read from page one to the end, or it was so rich for them that they could only read three pages at a time. I was the three pages at a time guy. Are some of the things that struck you about the process of working on the film still percolating in your head?

MO I have made a couple of documentary films. I edited those films, and that was what I really enjoyed. The precision of twenty-four frames a second—you can cut it at frame seven, or frame twenty-one. I really enjoyed that kind of microscopic timing.

wd How is that different than working with words? Particularly in poetry.

MO I *do* do that in poetry, and coming out of poetry—which is what I wrote before I wrote novels—I try to edit novels the same way, obsessively—taking a sentence from over here, and putting it over there, so the whole thing topples over into new suggestiveness.

wd Is there anything you consistently notice about a piece when it's done? How do you know when to stop working? I read your novels before your poetry, and when I went to the poetry, it was so precise. When you talk about this long editing process with the novel, I can't imagine it.

MO I do take very much care. Once I finish a story, which takes around four or five years, it's all over the place. The order is not necessarily the order it ends up in. So the editing stage then begins, shaving it down, until you've got a cleaner line of the story. What more can you remove without losing the story? I have a tendency to remove more and more in the process of editing. Often I'll write the first chapter last, because it sets up the story. The last thing I wrote in *Coming Through Slaughter* was "His Geography," almost like a big landscape shot, with buried clues you can pick up later.

wd As you edit, how much does it shift around? Particularly *The English Patient*, where you're dealing with so many points of view. How much do you fall in love with different characters? Or do you discipline yourself to maintain an overview right away?

MO I go wherever it takes me. I try everything. I completely test it, jostle it, so I'm not locked into the rhetoric, or the order I wrote it in. In a way this is what Anthony and Walter Murch did in the last stages of the film, taking a visual from one scene and putting it in another scene and creating something different. It is collaging and piecing.

wd Do you usually start out with a few rough ideas, central images?

MO I don't have a rough idea. It's usually an image.

wd Reading the book was a revelation. And when we were shooting, I felt it deeply in my body, my mind, and my soul. When I was in a room shooting with the other characters,

Kip, Hana, the English patient, and my character, Caravaggio, I thought, what a great story that can possibly contain all these people. It's a very special world.

MO There's something about that story— half of me wants it to be a long, nine-hour TV thing: thirty years of Caravaggio's history and twenty years of Hana's history, and they all come together in that moment in the room. The book began with the plane crashing, and it began with Caravaggio. In fact, the very first thing I wrote was where he steals the photograph of himself in the dark room. And Hana was there. Hana, Caravaggio and the English patient, but I didn't know how they were linked.

wd And Hana comes from any place in particular?

MO Hana was in one of my previous novels, *In the Skin of a Lion*. But the nurse in *The English Patient* was there before I discovered she was Hana. I don't like repeating characters, but Hana seemed so different, like a new character.

wd Does the process of flushing out a fantasy become somewhat personal, a self-revelatory process? Even if it's not about you, it's about your taste, what you're attracted to. So you've got this wonderful mask . . .

MO Yeah, and that's a sort of costume. It's what you have as an actor as well, this ability to reveal yourself through the character much more amazingly than you could by yourself.

wd Absolutely.

MO I can do things in fiction that I couldn't do in a poem, for that reason.

wd I'm getting to the point where I only really love films from other cultures, and the classics, much more than any film that comes from my culture, these speak to me. I think it's because I'm dealing with them through such a heavy mask. The irony is that the story hits me all the harder, because it's not about me. I'm like some schoolboy that's drawn to the exotic, to the other. And I find myself there, almost to the degree that I project myself as that. I feel it so deeply, it's better than any movie or place I've ever seen in my life.

MO It is a learning process. It's why I'd rather read a book that is completely unlike something I could do, in the way it's written, than read a book that's very similar to my habits or style or subject. William Maxwell—I couldn't write like him if I had a gun to my head, but I love a book such as *So Long, See You Tomorrow*.

wd This is embarrassingly academic, but what's the connection—is writing really an extension of reading? Why did you want to start writing, did that desire come out of what you were reading?

MO The reason I'm a writer is that I read like mad all through my teens. And I'm sure it was mostly trash that I was reading.

wd And the first things you wrote, were

you imitating what you'd read?

MO No, it kicked in when I went to university, when I started to study poetry. I had just arrived in Canada, I was living alone, I was starting a new life. After reading Robert Browning I started writing these dramatic monologues. And that was it. It wasn't really connected with the reading I had done, that reading kicked in later on, as some sort of influence. There's a huge connection, but I don't know how it in fact literally influences you.

wd But when you started writing, did you have the impression that this was how you were going to live your life?

MO No, no, it was a private, secret act. I never really admitted to anyone in the real world that I was a writer. It took a long time to get over that . . . thing. So I wrote, got involved with small literary magazines where you could fall flat on your face and no one would notice. If I had been Jay McInerney who had such huge success with his first published work, *Bright Lights, Big City*, I would have been completely fucked up.

wd Look, I'm amazed at anybody with terrific literary success, that they can write another good book.

MO Yeah, well, I went into a tailspin after *The Collected Works of Billy the Kid*. I won an award for it in Canada and I went into this hole. So I wrote *Coming Through Slaughter*, which was a huge fury about fame. It was on a very small scale, but it was big enough. I mean, the thing is to continue to avoid being self-conscious. To write and forget that you wrote other books. Because I don't think it becomes any easier, it becomes more difficult.

wd And you're reading the same author—you.

MO Yeah, that's probably why I don't reread my books once they're published.

wd I never see a film once I finish it. I see it when it goes to press so I can talk about it, but after that, there's no real reason to go back. And particularly for that reason you don't want to be self-conscious, you don't want to reflect on it. You've made the gesture and there's no taking it back. But my memory is so bad about how stuff happens, and in the end, the only thing that matters publicly is the performance that people see. Everything else is deep dark secrets that I will only access if I'm forced to.

MO In that last editing stage, I am outside myself. I'm looking at it much more clinically and saying, okay, get out of this scene quicker. There's that element of technique and dramatics and timing and "lighting" in those last stages. Punctuation and paragraph. But I don't at any point say: What is this book really about? It's unsaid. I worry instead that it's cloudy over here or the brambles need clearing. And there are links between the books. There's a scene in *In the Skin of a Lion* where Ambrose dies, it's only about half a paragraph long, and perhaps that is really the germ for *The English*

Patient's plot in one half page. I just recently realized that each book is a rewriting of what you didn't quite get to in the previous book.

wd That's charming. . . . Yeah, I think so.

MO I saw a documentary about a New York artist, and when he had almost finished a painting he had someone hold up these boards at the edge of the painting, so he could see where the painting might possibly end, as opposed to where it did end.

wd Just framing what he did differently.

MO Yes. Recognizing a new arc. That goes on a lot in the final editing of a book. And watching how Walter Murch and Anthony Minghella edited the film, you could see it there too.

When you came on to the set as Caravaggio, for *The English Patient*, how much of your character was prepared before you got there?

wd Very little. You meet something that isn't you half way, and you make a third thing. That's always the process of finding what you're doing. Ideally you want stuff to work through you, and you believe that you're an everyman; and framed properly, in good faith, you put yourself in a place where you can receive the adventure, then the character makes itself, I think. That's the philosophy. Practically, there's stuff that you have to do, impressions you may have to make; things you may have to accentuate or play down about what comes off of you as a separate persona—because you've seen pictures of yourself, and you recognize certain innate talents or deficiencies. But as far as finding the character, it's all pretty mysterious. And really, it's all pretending. It sounds a little cute and glib, but you can't prepare entirely for that. Preparation only gives you the confidence, the authority, to do the pretending. Because philosophically, you are all things, all things are in you, right? If you buy into that as an actor, and I do, then it's about making yourself available to the story, and the story will use you. It's the way you participate when you read a poem.

MO When I was writing *The English Patient*, what became really interesting was how the patient evolved. At first, I didn't know if I liked him at all. I wasn't sure if he was a villain or what. And after about three years, I discovered a voice for him, and once he had a voice . . . I guess, with acting, you were doing things, as I was with writing, that you were not at all aware were in you. At one point, the patient talks about an aerodrome, as opposed to an airport, and, bang, I realized I was in another era, writing alongside him. So, a simple word like that, or a gesture, throws you into the character.

wd What are you working on now? Various things, or one thing?

MO I'm working on, I guess, a novel. I hedge my bets as long as I can. I'm working on poems as well. I really

wanted to go back to writing poetry again after finishing *The English Patient*.

wd There are different demands, right? You don't have to live with a poem all the time, you can keep revisiting it, you can do your work and then you can go away. But I imagine writing a novel stays with you all the time.

MO Also, in the last stages of a novel, the last couple years of writing a novel, you're writing at a different level, you're shaping it, you're aware of a scene in the context of this big arc. You are not just creating a moment. And you cannot write lyrics when your mind is like that. So I had to get away from that huge thematic thing, into something that was just a moment. Describing an emotion, seven lines long, or ten lines long. That was important for me, to get back to writing the small scene. Because that's how my novels get written. Small scenes that build and merge, and then you recognize the larger context.

wd And in that last process, does the story complete itself for you, and then it becomes an obligation to order it properly so you can have other people read the story?

MO There is this stepping back so you can see it as someone who doesn't know the story. That's why I give it to others to read, to get that kind of reaction, which is often quite simple, like, "What happened to this guy? He was very interesting and he doesn't appear for a hundred pages?" Those are very real problems, as opposed to the "theme," which I don't think about.

wd People really look for interpretation, particularly if you do personally charismatic and mysterious work. *The English Patient* is mysterious, partly because of how it's structured, and partly because it's so rich and the narrative is fragmented. Because you jump around, people want to be reassured that their reaction is all right. I think so much of, even criticism, involves that impulse. And the extension of that is wanting to find out who you are, so they can interpret the work through your personality.

MO Some things are too important to share. It's not even about protecting myself, it would just be spoiling the book.

wd So you don't complete it, you leave enough air for that participation from the reader we were talking about. That mystery is so important. In a puritanical, Western culture, there's a prejudice that if it's not a familiar form, or if it can't be reduced to a certain kind of meaning for everybody, then it's obtuse. That's the prejudice against art.

MO Yeah.

wd Now you're going to be the guy who wrote the book that this movie came from. How's that feel?

MO I feel responsible for what's out there, and yet I'm not responsible for it.

wd It happens to actors all the time, of course. You're not an actor, you're that guy from *NYPD Blue*. It will be interesting to see how the movie affects you.

MO It's a great guard for me. Now people ask me about the movie. And that's fine. I say, "Well they're in Italy, they're in Tunisia."

wd Are you collecting stuff for a novel?

MO Yeah, well . . .

wd From *The English Patient*, to *Coming Through Slaughter*, and *In the Skin of a Lion*, I have this fantasy of you taking trips, going places to get a historical perspective. And then you rip on into the writing.

MO That is what I do. I live a life where I go to work in one era, or place, or historical moment, and at the end of the day return to another. It's schizophrenic, but it's a constant thing. I'm often uncertain about what I'm trying to make. The clarity doesn't click in until somewhere near the end. Let me ask you, the career you have as an actor on stage, and the career you have as an actor on film—is there any parallel between that and say, my thing with poetry and fiction?

wd One's more public, one has more cachet; the two are in different places in society. One's lonelier, one's more celebrated. The biggest difference, particularly working in theater with The Wooster Group, is that my responsibilities are so different than they are in a film. In film, one is constantly interrupted, it's so fragmented although the activity is basically the same. And the big thing about theater is of course the timing. Do you perform your poetry much?

MO Yeah . . .

wd Do you enjoy that?

MO Yes, I do. But Willem, you obviously like this kind of theater. It keeps you very sane in some ways.

wd The theater work predates film for me, and I don't have a lot of control over film because it is a collaboration with many more people, and often I do it with strangers. I love doing films, but because of the theater, for better and for worse, I feel outside the system, which always raises the question you're cheating both worlds. You should make some sort of decision. Often people envy me, being able to go between the two. It's weirdly lonely that way, because you're a man without a country. And I admit, I can only do it because the people in The Wooster Group allow me to leave and come back. It's a good situation. Things take a natural balance, you know. It's the old story, the grass is greener. When you're working on a film, towards the end, you long for that different experience of performing in a theater and vice versa.

The English Patient was quite a huge success. . . . Do you feel the pressure of that, meeting people who say, "Michael! When's your next one coming? We're starving baby. Loved your latest. Come on, get on with it brother. What's wrong . . .?"

MO Yeah, that happens a lot.

wd It's awful, isn't it? I mean, some truck driver will pull up, who's seen an action picture two or three years ago, and he'll say, "Hey baby, what's happened to you, don't you make movies anymore?" And I'm like, yeah, Tom and Viv.

MO Well, in the book trade, there are these guys who finish a book, and they're on to the next one the next weekend. I am completely exhausted by a book, and I have to take a major break and change my vocabulary. My role models are those writers who take seventeen years between books. Truly.

wd But that's a different kind of activity when people turn out books like that. It's like an actor I know, he's a good actor, but he works all the time, and I think his power is diminished by his availability. It doesn't have the same kind of gravity because you see him so much. That transforming magic takes a little while. You've got to go away to come back. That's what I tell myself.

MO I know who that actor is.

wd Do you? [tape recorder shut off]

wd You went back and forth on the shoot. What were you doing when you were on the set? Were you just hanging out?

MO I was very interested in how it worked, not so much in what the words were saying, but the blocking and the lighting and how things were put together. The director is creating the thread between actors, how someone feels, an emotional state. I haven't necessarily written that. And so, although film is done in little bits and pieces, what you're really watching is how the points are joined to make another kind of thematic sense. I find it fascinating.

wd How quickly do you give over to that transformation? As a writer, you've given your character a face, and you know that face. Then to have an actor come, and have it radically changed. Can you accept that pretty quickly? Do you forget the old face?

MO I don't have a face for people I write. I'm *inside* Hana's head. I don't know what Hana or Caravaggio really look like.

wd Can't you not help but see them in the world? Or have a model for them? Or not really, because you're inventing the world.

MO During script development and in rehearsal I got a sense that we were all on the same wavelength about what qualities there were to the characters. What was very interesting to me as a writer was what happened in the screenwriting. For instance, the patient needed a scene where he talked about the desert. And I said, "I think he has to have an aria, where he explains the desert to Katherine. . . . It's got to happen right here. . . . ."

And Anthony took off, and then wrote a scene that was not point M, but at point C, and about something completely different but that solved that problem. He was very good at not hitting everything on the nose, but he was able to solve it, subtly.

wd You work from a central idea, or image, and it sounds like you do a certain amount of research. How does research lead to invention and where does it get in the way of invention?

MO That's still a very difficult thing to know. You can always fuck up by having too much research. You can paint yourself into a corner by finding out everything about 1926. Or you can hear someone on a bus say something that happened to somebody, and that's enough to keep you going for fifty pages. It's difficult to know what's right and wrong. The kind of research I do, as a result, is quite intentionally random.

wd But do you go when you feel the need to? Oh, I've got to take a trip to North Africa, or do you say, Oohhh, I'm going to get a good atlas and look up the names?

MO Yes . . . [*laughter*]

wd I always think of this writer, a very popular German guy who wrote novels about the American West. He never went there. And many a German boy grew up learning about the American West from him. He wrote these terrifically detailed stories, and he got all his information, as I understand it, from other books, [*laughter*] and just making it up.

MO And there are those great spaghetti Westerns by Sergio Leone. On the first novel, *Coming Through Slaughter*, I couldn't afford to go anywhere. I was stuck in London, Ontario; sending off letters at that time to archival libraries. Often what happens with research is that what you really want to find out cannot be found. You can't find the photograph or the person you want to find. So then you invent the photographs and the photographer. Often the best stuff comes out of staring at a brick wall.

wd In theater pieces, all our greatest creative things come out of practical solutions for getting stuff on its feet.

MO Sometimes it's not real research, but an invented research. With *The English Patient*, I did go to the Royal Geographic Society but I didn't spend that long there, a couple of afternoons actually. They weren't very friendly. "What specifically do you want?" they asked, and I didn't know what I specifically wanted. I went away and came back and said I want to find out about something or other in the desert in 1935, and then they let me in. And once I was in, then I could look around in a more random way. It is a defensive kind of research, I don't want to know everything about the desert in 1935. I needed space to invent, choreograph. Similarly, I limited myself to knowledge of bomb disposal up to about 1941. That was the early period, where they were literally

using hammers and ropes. In this way you're writing and learning at the same time, and that's the best for me. You're writing about building the bridge and you're also reading about how the bridge was built, with how much concrete and wood and mortar. So it's a simultaneous learning about it and getting it down fast.

wd Where did you get the central image of the plane crash, do you even remember?

MO I just got the image, and it was there. The artist, Joseph Beuys, was in a plane crash in the far north, not in the desert, but I already had this image in my head. It was one of those things where I'd heard about Beuys and his obsession with felt and that worked its way in too. That was enough. I didn't need to know anymore. The medicine man . . .

wd Yes, where did that come from?

MO That was an adaptation of something I'd seen in Cairo. I was there in 1978. You pick up a gesture or an image from a long time ago. You put yourself in a position where you come up with those more subliminal references. You have to keep writing in order to find those sorts of things.

wd Were there ever points in the actual filming, let's say something like the man with the bottles, that did not jive with what you had in mind?

MO The art direction was interesting to witness because while most of it seemed dead on, it was more dead on than the book. It really bugged me when I heard from the art department that they had gone to the Royal Geographic Society and were welcomed with open arms. I said, "Weren't they difficult?" And they said, "No, they were so nice."

What's interesting is if I'm writing a scene in the patient's room and it's from Hana's point of view, I see about three feet, as if with a small light. She's reading a book and she sees the floor. And the patient's over here and Caravaggio is over there. But I never really get a sense of the whole room and everything in it. It's almost black and white spotlights in an odd way. Suddenly I was in that set, and the whole room, the exact kind of stone floor that would be right for that period or a fresco that was created. Everything was there. That was a shock to me.

wd That's not decided in your head when you're writing, it remains liquid and instinctive.

MO I build the aspects of the room as I write over a period of years. And then there's a stage when you're editing when you start erasing stuff. You have dressed the room completely, but it might be getting in the way of the story. So how much can you remove of the background so that the reader is concentrating on Hana's emotional state? I think a lot of historical novels get too involved with art direction. If it's set in Germany in 1943 they know the exact kind of cigarettes that were smoked and the length of the leather jackets. But what we were talking

about earlier on, where everything is liquid, where any aspect can come into the story . . . I don't write with a plan. Most people do write with a plan, but I tend not to. I tend to . . .

wd . . . feel your way around.

MO It's an emotional thing when you're writing. The problem for me with novels is when I sense the writer's talking down to me. Like a puppeteer. Too sure of what is about to happen.

I thought Juliette Binoche was wonderfully instinctive as an actress, she allowed things to come out of the blue in the middle of a scene. When you were both in the kitchen and she started weeping in the middle of your speech. It was quite wonderful, I don't know what it would be like for an actor to work against that.

wd It doesn't matter. It's happening.

MO I love those moments—a curtain opens for a second. You get a further glimpse into a truth.

wd People have this notion that in writing, or any other art form, you get better, you improve, that it's cumulative. And it's just not true.

MO In fact, it's more difficult to write the eighth book than the first book.

wd Have you ever started something and then had to finish it where the spirit wasn't really quite with you?

mo No, but I've stopped books like that. When I wrote *In the Skin of a Lion* I began it from the point of view of the millionaire, it was about what happened to him when he disappeared. I wrote two hundred pages of the thing and realized I hated the guy. I was just plodding, I was forcing myself to write. It was dead. So I stopped and left it for a couple of years. And went back to the minor characters who were just starting to emerge and they became the main characters. I think people want to believe that artists know what they're doing, and that there's a solution at the end of all that. But when I write a book, I'm sitting down to discover what the story is, as opposed to telling the story. I don't have that story yet.

wd **I feel that so much as an actor. As I get older I feel more and more shamed by opinion. I believe more and more in stuff happening, and I participate as things happen. As an actor, it's the fundamental difference between doing things and showing them. On the other hand, if you've been doing something long enough you accumulate, you revisit certain things enough that you get an instinct that almost becomes a technique. But it isn't necessarily connected to cognitive intent.**

MO In terms of skill, I'm never sure that I've learned anything. And I don't think about "style" when I'm writing. Writing is a kind of tunneling, that's what it feels like.

wd **How did you come upon Herodotus?**

MO I had already read some of him. Then there was a reference to him in one of the explorer's desert journals; one guy who said, "I was responsible for our

library on one of our expeditions. But our library was only one book, Herodotus." And I thought that was great, because Herodotus was a historian writing about a place where these guys return to many hundreds of years later. The idea of a contemporary history and an ancient history that links up . . . These explorers in the 1930s were out of time. I love the idea of them checking out sand dune formations. I love historical obsessives. And I kept thinking of writers like Charles Olson and Robert Creeley in some odd way. Creeley in his toughness, brittleness and lovely guarded lyricism was a clue for me about the patient, Almazy. And this wonderful, heroic era of exploration that was then ignored, while the twentieth century became more mercenary or mercantile. Also Herodotus' sense of history is great because it's very much based on rumor. If he heard a story in the desert, he wrote it down. Anyway, I liked the sense of people reading books within the novel; that there is a library in the villa. And then the other thing that came up was the Rebecca spy code. I originally found out about Almazy through a friend of mine's parents who were in Cairo during the war. Rommel had sent a spy to Cairo to send information back to the Germans. And he used a copy of *Rebecca* by Daphne du Maurier as the code book. Ken Follet wrote a book about it called *The Key to Rebecca*. The spy was finally captured by the British, and my friend's parents were involved with his capture. So I was asking them about it. And in a nonfiction book about the episode, there was this paragraph of how the spy got to Cairo. He was taken across the desert by Almazy, an explorer. Almazy seemed much more interesting to me than the spy. Who was this guy? What was he doing there? So I found out more about him.

wd **Writing not in contemporary times frees you up a lot.**

MO Yeah, it's wearing that mask.

wd **Particularly if it takes you six years to finish a book.** [*laughter*] **A country in Africa may change its name before you finish. Sorry.**

MO I know, I know. So that's how I got interested in this man. And it opened up a whole world of explorers, and a way of seeing the world. What was useful in the Royal Geographic was not so much the information, as it was their manner of writing; very low-key, not at all self-aggrandizing, or chest beating, or beautiful sunsets or flies. No complaints. No praise. It was just, you had to get from here to there . . . so many kilometers. There's a water-hole here. That kind of laconic Robert Creeley voice. But these were all fragments I collected or wrote down over a five-year period. One gets really interested in mapmaking or bomb disposal, this relationship here, you're constantly learning and you're not quite sure if it will hold together, if there's a whole ship.

John Edgar Wideman, © Stephen B. Long. Courtesy UMass Photographic Services.

JOHN EDGAR WIDEMAN   caryl phillips

Woottons Bookshop, Amherst, Massachusetts, March 29, 1994; for a live audience.

John Edgar Wideman, like any great storyteller, discovers the truth by telling the tale. Every story is a journey, unexpected and frightening, a deep plunge into the unconscious minds of those he has dared to commune with. One reads John Wideman knowing that one is in the presence of an author who moves intuitively, and courageously, an author who plunges below the surface, an author who might not find his way back to the surface, but in the struggle for light and air, he is discovering meaning and hope, and truth, in the midst of chaos. It has been said that he is an author who asks us to come with him, but an author who makes no promises.

John Edgar Wideman has been a Franklin scholar, a Rhodes Scholar and a Thuron Fellow. His teaching career has taken him from Howard University in Washington D.C. to the University of Pennsylvania, where he was a Professor of English, Director of *the African American* Studies Program and an assistant basketball coach. In 1974 he moved west, to the University of Wyoming, Laramie, and in 1986 he moved back east, to the University of Massachusetts at Amherst where he took up his current position as Professor of English.

But it is as a writer that John Edgar Wideman is best known, a writer who seems at ease in both the novel and short story forms. His seven novels are: *A Glance Away* (1967), *Hurry Home* (1970), *The Lynchers* (1973), *Hiding Place* (1981), *Sent for You Yesterday* (1983), *Ruben* (1987), and *Philadelphia Fire* (1990). His three collections of short stories are *Damballah* (1981), *Fever* (1989), and *All Stories Are True* (1992). He is also the author of a very moving memoir, *Brothers and Keepers* (1984) and recently, *Fatheralong* (Pantheon, 1994).

Some years ago, the French critic, Michel Fabre, wrote, "John Edgar Wideman is one of the few novelists who emerged in the Black Power era without sacrificing the demands of art to the persuasions of radical militancy. Possibly as a result of his commitment to his craft, his sizeable fictional production has attracted increasing attention and he is now considered as one of the best American writers of the younger generation." This observation needs updating. John Wideman is not one of the best American writers of the younger generation, he is one of the best American writers of *any* generation. His work is not limited by traditional conventions of storytelling. His narrative is, and John will love this word, post-Joycean, his sensibility often Faulknerian. He is a consummate ventriloquist, able to appropriate the voice of a murdered baby with the same facility with which he speaks from the point of view of a child, or an American jazz singer in a Nazi death camp. The prose is elliptical and dense, but always elegant and, at its best, it hits us with the force of prayer—or perhaps more appropriately—gospel.

His awards and fellowships are too numerous to mention. I will, however, mention the PEN/ Faulkner Award in 1984 for his novel, *Sent for You Yesterday*, for it seems appropriate that John should have an award named for Faulkner. And last year he received a much-deserved MacArthur Fellowship.

caryl phillips I want to begin by asking you, John, about that moment, if there was such a moment, when you first decided that you wanted to write.

JOHN EDGAR WIDEMAN There are probably many moments. And what I'll do now is tell a story, hopefully slightly entertaining and with some bearing on the truth, although I wouldn't claim for it any veracity beyond that. My father was a reader and I have a very strong image of him right now: I remember him sitting in our living room, which was also our dining room, [*laughter*] which was also our kitchen, which was mostly the whole house. I remember him sitting in a chair, tired from work, and he would pick up these pulp novels, westerns mostly, like Zane Grey, and he'd read these things as a kind of sleeping pill. He was a big man, so these books were always small in his hands and his legs would be stretched out in front of him, and gradually, his eyes would start to drop and the legs would get more and more slack and then he'd fall off to sleep and I'd hear "plunk," the book would hit the floor. They were pretty trashy, tacky books, but I read them because that's what was around. And I began to see that there were certain formulas in these books which weren't too difficult to figure out. And I thought, well, hell, I could do that. These things aren't hard to write: the guy rides into town, he sees a beautiful lady, something is at stake, he figures out a way to help her, et cetera, et cetera. And I thought, you know, this would be fun to do, easy to do. So, that's when I had this glimmer that I could, maybe, become a writer. The other part of it comes from another direction and has nothing to do with books and writing and reading but it has to do with listening. I was lucky enough to grow up in a family full of storytellers. It was particularly the women's province, and I grew up listening to women's voices tell stories—my aunts and my mother, my grandmother and their friends. And I loved to listen to these stories. And they created a world for me. Not only did they create a world, but they created a kind of sensibility—something to measure myself against. And the more I listened, the more the act of storytelling penetrated my consciousness. It was something I wanted to partake of. The reading was easy. Anybody could do the stuff that Zane Grey was doing, but telling the stories the way the women in my family told the stories was something that I could only wish I could do, hope I could do. That was the real comparison, that's what I wanted to be able to make—the kind of energy and eloquence, and the funny, crazy stuff that was in the stories women told. So those were my two models and as far back as I can remember, they were the models that I strove to emulate.

cp So, by the time you went to the University of Pennsylvania, did you embark on a degree in English with the notion that you wanted to write, or teach, or both?

JW Well, what I did was embark on a degree in experimental psychology. And I did that because I thought the idea of reading people's minds was kind of groovy. You know, to read people's minds and anticipate what they were going to say and do, that was a great power trip. And Penn was the center of experimental psychology. I lasted about a month, because I found out that, rather than reading Freud and getting into orgone boxes, what

you do is count the number of times rats walk through this maze and pick up a pellet in an hour if you zap them with electricity.

cp We haven't talked about it, but did you know that I began in experimental psychology and [*laughter*] I switched after three months?

JW Well, there's something about it that has an appeal. But anyway. In college, I worked very hard to figure out a way that I could live the rest of my life and not have a job. To that end, I was a jock, I played basketball. I figured that I would play basketball and make a lot of money. Anything that I could do that would enable me to have my cake and eat it too; that is, to have this sort of pseudo-job but have a good life, and have the good things, that's what I wanted to accomplish. So, basketball was the first thought. And then I didn't grow the extra foot I needed to grow as an undergraduate and so I decided well, what's the next best thing. I can't play ball, writing seems like a pretty good gig. Writers don't have bosses, they don't have to go and punch clocks. So that's the reason I thought to maybe try writing.

cp You ended up going across the water to Oxford. What influence did Oxford have on you as a writer, and as an American? And as a black person finding yourself at Oxford in the mid 1960s?

JW Yeah, [*laughter*] in any order. Well, going to Oxford, for me, was an exciting opportunity. In fact, I went there consciously because I had made the choice to be a writer. I had never been out of the country—and I knew, or I thought that, in order to be a writer, you had to be down and out in Paris or Rome. And since Mom and Dad were not going to send me to Paris or Rome, I had to figure a way to get there on my own, and the Rhodes seemed ideal. So, it was important in the sense that I had begun to identify with a kind of vocation and I was making big choices, major choices that would facilitate this writing business. What happened there? First of all, I heard the language spoken in a different way. People there take the language seriously in a way that we don't. You read a box of tea and it says, "Wait until the water boils furiously." [laughter] This is the kind of eloquence on a teabox that I didn't get from my professors at Penn. So that was exciting. And also the time at Oxford was an interesting time, because these were the early sixties. So, I left an America in tremendous ferment and found myself in a kind of catbird's seat across the water looking back on all this stuff that was happening. And that was, for me, a little frustrating. It's almost like the people you've heard about who never went to war and wondered, well what kind of person would I be if I actually had that wartime experience? I didn't have the civil rights experience. The only march I ever went on was back in 1967 in Iowa City—a protest march—and by that time, it was no big deal. I still wonder . . . how my life would have changed if I were in America and had decided to go south during the Freedom Summer to ride the buses or join a radical organization. It would have been a

different life. But I discovered that I liked that distance. I liked that angle, the oblique angle. The vantage point of seeing this business from England and having to put it together in my imagination on the basis of headlines and letters and spot visits back to the United States. So I found myself getting a lot of practice being an outsider. England was changing a lot at that time as well. The first wave of people from the so-called third world were making their voices felt at Oxford. People who went back to Africa and became prime ministers of their countries, people who went back to the West Indies and became political powers, artists, et cetera. So, I had a firsthand look at this ferment: people of color who were unlike anybody I had ever known in the states. Now it may be hard for some of you to believe but, the degree to which black people—and all of us—were kept ignorant—and still are for that matter—in the sixties, it was appalling. Politically I was uneducated, unsophisticated, I could feel that race was a problem in the South, but as long as I kept my nose clean I could kind of make my own way in the North. I was very naive. So, England was a way of getting a perspective on a lot of these received attitudes. And in that sense, it was very important. It was a political renaissance. It was, for me, growing up.

cp You began to write, pretty soon after you got back from Oxford.

JW Well, I began to write there. I did do the tour of Europe and I began to keep notebooks. And by the time I got back, I had most of my first book finished.

CP In 1988, you made this statement: "At a certain point in my writing career, after I had done three books, I made a decision, I wanted to reach out to readers that the earlier works had perhaps excluded. I wanted to get everybody's ear." Those three books were written in the late sixties and early seventies. Can you explain what it was about those first three books that you felt excluded certain people, and who were the people being excluded?

JW I would second-guess that statement. It's too simplistic because, for one thing, it served critics who have written about my work since, as a point of departure. And I think it's unfair. I believe if I look closely, objectively, at what I've done, the themes and the concerns and the centering in an African American world have been there from the beginning. What I sensed was a lack of fluidity in a vernacular voice that I wanted to change. We're talking shop, we're talking about a writer's ability to use various registers and communities of the language in a way that feels natural. I feel that in my first three books, as is the case with many writers, I had models, I had examples of eloquence, examples of people who I felt captured something special in their vision, in their themes, et cetera. And so, as I tried to get my own feet under me, I was imitating, I was enthralled, I had stars. And I realized, the more I wrote, that that kind of looking outside of myself for models was insufficient, that, as good as the stuff was that I had been reading, it missed whole levels, whole realms of experience

that were personal, that were mine. I could not simply take my experience and put it in this language that I had received—as a graduate student and as an undergraduate—as the language of literature.

CP Who were the models and the stars?

JW Certainly, T. S. Eliot was one: his poetry, the blending of levels of language that's in his work, his concern with time, his concern with history, his use of classic sources, his ability to speak to, not only other writers, but other epochs, his sense. . . . This was probably unconscious—but one thing that appealed to me was the West African notion of "great time" that is part of Eliot's writing, that is not time as a linear flow but as a great sea. And if you read "Prufrock," Eliot is operating in "great time." People who lived a thousand years ago speak to people who live now. They bump up against each other: Take a boat ride in the Thames and you might run into Queen Mary. All that appealed to me. I didn't know exactly why. Also, as a young writer particularly, anything that was strange, that I didn't quite understand, presented a challenge. So I had to go after it. I had to master it and figure it out.

CP Many writers have cited other art forms, perhaps most commonly painting and music, as influences upon them. When I was reading your second novel, *Hurry Home*, I was struck by the character Cecil who sees a relationship between his experience and what he sees when he looks at a painting by Hieronymous Bosch. Does one need some understanding of Bosch to get at the heart of this novel? And, to what extent, if at all, have other art forms influenced your writing?

JW Hmm. What has been very useful to me—and simply fun for me—is to find that, through the medium of writing, I could think about things that were important to me. It's actually a means of thinking. I was very moved and excited by the paintings of Hieronymous Bosch. I didn't exactly know why, but then my handle on understanding him came intuitively. It wasn't a question of going out and reading a lot about Bosch. Although I did make it my business to travel to cities where there were Bosch paintings so I could see the originals. I had a kind of craziness about him, an obsession. On the other hand, it didn't drive me to the library. I began to see these black faces in Bosch, black people in his paintings, sometimes at the edges, sometimes at the center. . . Particularly the Bosch painting which contains the Annunciation and the wise men on the lefthand panel, in the Adoration of the Magi. And one of those magi was a black person. I guess I can make this kind of simple. When you're traveling through Europe as an African American, and you see an image of yourself, it's rare, and you do get excited. I understood something very crucial about Bosch through the way that he depicted this African personality. Why was the African dressed so down, compared to these dowdy wise men? Why did he stand in a certain ele-

gant way, with his limbs supported in a particular fashion? Why was his waist more narrow? Why was there a certain luxuriousness and splendor in his garments? What was this medieval lowlander seeing in these African people? And why was what he saw so much of what people saw in Pittsburgh and in New York about contemporary African Americans? Why was there that kind of continuity? Jesus! And, through the character of Cecil, I sort of worked those thoughts out. So, Bosch comes into the novel. And no, you don't necessarily have to know a lot about Hieronymous Bosch, but if you listen to the questions I ask in the book then I would hope maybe you would become interested in Bosch and become interested in the whole idea of representation in Western art and where we fit in it and how we've influenced it from the very beginning.

cp Okay, let's just go back to that quote of yours from '88. I picked it up from a piece you wrote for the *New York Times*. The title of the piece was, "The Black Writer and the Magic of the Word." Let me play devil's advocate for a minute and ask you: Do you think of yourself as a black writer?

JW [*pause*] No, because the word, like so many words, has been totally. . . raped of meaning, it's been destroyed, it's a tool, it's a kind of tong, something to pick up people without touching them. And that aspect of the word, unfortunately, hits me when I hear it. I don't like it. And it has a very vexed history, that word. Those two words.

On the other hand, in my own mind, there's something very much like the word "black" that resonates and is crucially important to me. I might lexify it with the term, African American, but I have no doubt that I represent and am part of a very specific culture. And that culture has its roots in Africa and across the ocean; and some of you, fortunately, know the story of how African cultural traits were retained and transmogrified and met Europe. And so, I see myself in that cultural strain and it's crucial to me. And the more I understand about those roots, the closer I get to what's important in the voice that I have.

cp You mentioned, in a short interview in the *New York Times,* how over 20 years ago you were approached by students at Penn and asked to teach a black literature class. I quote from John Wideman, "I gave them the jive reply that it wasn't my field. I was one of the few black faculty members at Penn; they came to me for all kinds of soulful reasons and I gave them the stock academic reply, which was true. But I felt so ashamed that I got back in touch with some of them, then agreed to teach the course—and then began my second education." Can you characterize the nature of that second education?

jw Well, very specifically, I spent the summer in the Schomburg Library, reading books that had been written by people of African descent. Of course,

we're all of African descent if we believe the latest anthropological bulletin. But, people of the African diaspora—I read those books, and then I made it my business to begin to interview and talk to and make a connection with other black writers. And I organized a course in Afro-American lit. And since that point, I've been reading everything I possibly can. As I learned more, I found out what I needed to understand, what African-American culture might be. It led me into linguistics, it led me into a study of the language. And that was a very fruitful part of it. I mean, once I was in Germany, giving a lecture on the black voice, of all things, black speech, and, at the end of the lecture—I was speaking English, I only know two German words, to an audience who supposedly understood English—and a fräulein raised her hand and said—(I had been talking for an hour about black speech)—"Herr Professor Videman, vould you speak some of that black English for us?" [*laughter*] So, you're me up at the podium, what do you say? "Hey, baby, what's happenin'?" [*laughter*] I didn't know what to say. It stunned me. This was a nitty-gritty question. One answer is, "Hey, I'm an African American and I've been talking for the last hour. You've been listening to African American speech." And I think that is something which is the beginning of the real answer: there is no single register of African-American speech. And it's not words and intonations, it's a whole attitude about speech that has historical rooting. It's not a phenomenon that you can isolate and reduce to linguistic characteristics. It has to do with the way a culture conceives of the people inside of that culture. It has to do with a whole, complicated protocol of silences and speech, and how you use speech in ways other than directly to communicate information. And it has to do with, certainly, the experiences that the people in the speech situation bring into the encounter. What's fascinating to me about African American speech is its spontaneity, the requirement that you not simply have a repertoire of vocabulary or syntactical devices/constructions, but that you come prepared to do something with that repertoire, those structures, and do something in an attempt to meet the person on a level that both uses the language, mocks the language, and recreates the language. It's a very active exchange. But at the same time as I say that, the silences and the refusal to speak is just as much a part, in another way, of African American speech.

cp Okay. I want to take a left turn now and ask you a few questions about your actual process of writing. You move with equal facility, it seems to me, between the short story form and the novel. What criteria, for you, defines whether an idea is better suited to a novel or a short story? Is there one?

JW Only the practical working out of it. I still think the story, "Fever," is a novel. But one of the reasons it works well, and I'm happy with it as a short story is because, somehow, the novel is

in there, and it's pushing to get out. And I think that gives it some of the resonance that it has. A novel is certainly not a single idea and sometimes a story can be. But I would hesitate to think that there are any absolute cues, because I know that things in my experience that have started as stories became novels. And vice versa.

cp Let me ask you about the story form, specifically the short story "Everybody Knew Bubba Riff," from your last collection, *All Stories Are True*. It reads as though it has been composed in one sitting. It is like a long modernist cry—almost like a long note blown by a jazz trumpeter—was it composed at one sitting?

JW About half of the body was composed in one sitting. But that particular text that came out of that one sitting, which is half the story. . . you'd probably have a hard time finding it in the published version, because the way I work is to work and work and to rewrite.

cp Which half answers my next question. Are you a man who painstakingly revises loose drafts, or are you a man who crafts slowly and deliberately, almost chiseling into stone words, phrases, that are already finely tuned?

JW Well, I hate to cop out, but it's always a combination. Some things come easily.

cp Right.

JW And if some didn't come easily, I would change professions. [*laughter*]. You have to have that gift every now and again. And when the gift comes, you open yourself to it and the words just flow and you love it and that's what the whole process is about. It's really a way of going outside of myself. The sculpting and the chiseling and the work is more of a different discipline altogether. And I get tired of myself. I'm too aware of my limitations there and I'm always working against my limitations. So it's claustrophobic for a while. And I wonder, is it ever going to get any better, because it's me talking to me, what do I know? So you need that infusion from somewhere else, whether you call it the muse, or the unconscious, or whatever. It has to swing in, you have to be visited, I think. At least this writer does.

cp I want to ask you about your role as a teacher of writing. Two questions: firstly, has teaching affected your writing in any disturbing way? And do you feel inspired when you read the work of students?

JW Hmm. [*pause, laughter*] This is not a commercial, I assure you. [*laughter*] Well unless you're a total hypocrite, if you sit around and your job is to tell people, "Hey, look at this, this isn't right, you can do better. Here's something, change this. Write something beautiful. Write something strong," if that's your job. . . I take those messages home with me. When I sit down at my own stuff that shrewish voice which I hope is not shrewish too often, but that voice talks to me about my own stuff. So that's one answer.

Am I inspired. . . ?

cp Or encouraged by who is particularly good.

JW Bring it down a few pegs. [*laughter*]

cp Interested?

JW [*laughter*] Alert. [*laughter*] I'm very lucky. Because we have an extraordinary group of writers at U Mass. And I am in fact inspired by some of their work. Inspired that this whole activity of writing is still alive. Some people are still hooked into it, hooked on it, and willing to take the chances and willing to push themselves. And willing to go a little crazy and willing to confront demons. And I see that activity as absolutely rare and crucial because what it does is sustain the whole notion of imagination in the culture. If there is any threat to our humanity, it's the threat that somehow our imaginations will be squashed, will become obsolete. It will become redundant, useless. And writing is one way to keep that idea of imagination alive. In my best days I see that as the primary enterprise I'm involved in. Simulating the imagination. Foregrounding it, saying that it counts. Saying that whatever is in your head has some meaning. And I think most of the messages in the culture are saying that it doesn't have meaning, that it doesn't matter what's inside your head. Fuck you, ya know. Get in line. So I welcome people who are on a different track. We're on our little boat, ship of fools, and there we are. It's nice to have company.

LUCIE BROCK-BROIDO carole maso

I see her from a distance in the last of summer. She has waist-length blonde hair and is wearing a diaphanous white dress. From across the quad she is an improbable figure: wafting as she is toward me, enveloped in blue cigarette smoke. Even though it is only the first day, she is already followed by a cloud of students and they are speaking passionately of poetry.

Three years ago, Lucie Brock-Broido and I were hired to join the permanent faculty of the Graduate Writing Program at Columbia University. Along with classes and meetings, our afternoons would consist of endless cappuccinos and forbidden cigarettes, talk of Emily Dickinson and Maine Coon kittens. Such was the bliss of our short time together. Alas, I would only last one year at Columbia, but our friendship during that time became indelible. It is the kind of friendship I cherish most—based, as it is, on a deep respect for Lucie's work.

I had found her first book, *A Hunger*, to be a mesmerizing and riotous rhetorical celebration and could not wait to see what would follow. Over the next seven years the intriguing *Master Letter* poems would slowly begin to appear in various magazines. Yet nothing could prepare me for the impact of the final text. It is a rigorous and dizzying book. A book of rage and renunciations and acute praise. A book of dark concoctions, of strange, gorgeous potions: Lamb's Blood and Chant, Crave and Ruin. A Book of Swoon and Fever and Goodbye. A Book of Mysterious Elusive Universe.

BOMB # 53, Fall 1995

carole maso Every time I open a page of your work I see another one of these words: "corvid," "rubricant," "lubricious," "noctuary." Are you a collector of words?

LUCIE BROCK-BROIDO Oh, yes. Another word that's in the works is "ichor"—it's the ethereal fluid that runs through the veins of the gods instead of blood. I got it from one of my great heroes, now dead, someone I never met, the poet Thomas James. The night was my ichor, flowing. . .

cm You seem to write with night in your veins, your pen seems dipped in night. I think of charm and magic and fetish and talisman when I think of this book. Do you work at night?

LBB In the night, in the evening of the year. I have a peculiar, and reliable, and renewable pattern of writing. Every year I forsake writing for at least six or seven months. Each October, I begin again.

cm It's like a bulb that has to be put away so that it can bloom again, come its season.

LBB Only it's the antiseason.

cm How did you find your place as a seasonal and nocturnal writer?

LBB It must have happened as a child; I had some recurrent dread of returning to school, and the noises of late August, of the cicada, or whatever that low noise is that comes into the world that heralds the end of the summer. I dreaded returning to school. My theory is that a poem is troubled into its making. It's not like a thing that blooms; it's a thing that wounds. I had a terror I could tell to none, as Dickinson would say.

cm What was the origin of *The Master Letters*? You've got such a lovely description of the project in your preamble, could you talk about the original letters and your intention?

LBB Seven summers ago, to the day, no doubt, I began this project (unwittingly—I didn't know it would be a Project) after reading Emily Dickinson's three letters to her Master. I had always turned away from Dickinson's poems, I thought she was precious; I didn't get it.

Then I began to read her letters. These I fathomed. And if there were such things as visitations, then I would have had them. Though, just for the record, no one has appeared in a white dress by my fireplace.

cm Can you relate to her poems now, as well?

LBB Not so much, no. But I think the one perfect poem ever written in English is Dickinson's number 341, which begins, "After great pain, a formal feeling comes. . . ." But it's still her surviving letters which are the Rorschach to her psyche. Among Emily Dickinson's 1,049 letters, there are three "Master Letters": one addressed to a recipient unknown, one addressed to "Master," and one addressed to "Dear Master." They're very strange documents. I'm quite sure they're real, although there is no evidence that they were ever posted. I'm certain they were composed in earnest, though Dickinson was capable of playing any number of games. I keep thinking that somewhere in New England, there's one small humpbacked trunk that has what's left, what's still missing of her work. These three were found in a box by her sister Lavinia, sometime in late May of 1886, just after Dickinson had died. They were tied separately from the fascicles of Dickinson's poems. The letters were suppressed, of course, for a long time, because they're really peculiar, chilling. They are sexy, and they take the pose of a woman addressing what's clearly, in her mind, a male god figure, whom she calls "master" or "sir." The theories about the letters have been infinite and

unresolvable. Were they to a real person? Were they to God? A lover? A
woman? A man? No scholar thinks
that the master is Thomas Wentworth
Higginson—and, of course, the letters
predated her correspondence with
him—but in my mind they are closest
to the tone that she uses on the page
with him. He was the editor of the
Atlantic, in an obvious position of
power, and to whom she was sending
out her first verses, and she lied ram-
pantly, and coyly, to him in their correspondence. He was about to reject the
poems, pat her on the head and say,
these are sweet, have you written
much? And she wrote back: "Thank
you for the surgery."—he had edited
her verse—and then: "It was not so
painful as I supposed . . . You asked me
how old I was? I made no verse—but
one or two—until this winter—Sir—."
It was April of 1862 and already
Dickinson had composed at least six-
hundred poems. She was on the brink
of her most fertile, furtive time.

In late August of 1988, my book,
A Hunger, was published. I had gone
to visit Stanley Kunitz, who was my
prophet-teacher, and told him,
"That's it for me, I have nothing
more." And he said, though the well is
dry it will replenish itself, and to just
let it go for now.

cm How lovely, so Stanley.
LBB The letters, then, were a catalyst, a
provocation. I thought, I'm going to
go home and write a little triptych in
homage to these three Dickinson letters. There are now fifty-two poems in
the book.

The Polish poet, Zbigniew Herbert,
says there are two kinds of writers:
cats and oxen. The ox is plodding and
deliberate, and goes back and forth
and back and forth and line by line,
and dutifully plows his acre by the
light of day. And then there's the
cat—who's sleek and nocturnal and
furtive and has sporadic leaps at writing. I am one of those.

Through the seven years, though
I've written over ninety master letter
poems, I've killed off half of them. By
the time those seven years were over, I
had been through many, many forms.
Though my letters originated in
prose, eventually I found the present
coupleted form. That's my great
addiction. I can't ever imagine writing
in another form. Every stanza has an
absolute beginning and an absolute
end. And no middle. I decided that it
was my dream to write short poems,
so I began writing what I call
American sonnets.

cm Will you talk about the evolution
of the master?
LBB The master began as what I call a
"fixed star."

cm What happened next?
LBB He became . . . not a force of light,
but a force of sublimation, subordina-
tion. He became an unfixed star; he
became a constellation—of ideas, a
widening gyre.

cm It's a very courageous move. One
feels that sense of supplication all
the way through, that kind of
ruined worship.

LBB There are a lot of times when the speaker, quite nastily, speaks of the master's hand, which she says is "concaved around her mouth." In other words, it is his will to temper or tamper with her . . . languages. But the speaker always surfaces again and says, "You have the catchweed of quiet on your tongue, I have the power of speech."

cm The struggle all the way through is one of speech and silence. And master and speaker. What about the evolution of the speaker? Because the speaker changes and constantly evolves and transforms as well.

LBB As the idea of the master got larger and larger, more encompassing over the seven years, the speaker, who began—not as a fixed star but as a whole little galaxy—an Andromeda of women with Dickinson at the center, her peculiar swooning syntax, her diction, her coy subservience, her voice. Around her was everyone and her sister, the beloved and the not so beloved.

cm You do hear a polyphony of voices.

LBB She, then, became more and more hungry, and narrow and slim and lean, and muscled.

cm Particular.

LBB During the fourth year into the project, I had a student at Harvard named Ravi who became gravely ill during the course of the semester, and his handling of his illness was so brilliant and miraculous and honorable and brave that I wrote a letter, because

of him, called, "I Don't Know Who It Is That Sings, Nor Did I, Would I Tell." This was the great answer in Dickinson's words to the question Who is the master, after all. I signed this poem, Bliss Is Unnatural—Your L. And at that moment, I'm the speaker—not Akhmatova, not Plath, not Dickinson. That opened up a whole new realm of possibility. Though as the project became more and more cruel and autobiographical, I gave myself complete legal freedom to lie, as always, for the sake of the poem.

cm You have a very complicated relationship to other texts in *The Master Letters*—in dialogue with other voices, in reverence, in all sorts of things; but, in fact, you do finally feel that L. is our speaker.

LBB It's only been during the writing of this book that I've learned to worship the terminal constraint of the poem as a form. I remember a time in 1979 when Richard Howard, who was my teacher at Johns Hopkins, asked us all to submit a poem in order to be admitted to his graduate workshop. I gave him an eighty-something page poem called "Pornography," and he handed it back to me a week later, put his monocle on, and said, "My dear, there's not a line break in the whole eighty pages." At which point I thought I would writhe on the train station platform where we stood. I thought, "What do you mean there's not a line break? Look at the lines, there are thousands of them!" But I had no concept of what a line break—no less a line—was. You spend a lifetime making up your

line. Or . . . in every book, you reinvent the thing itself.

cm I've been writing for fifteen years
and I only now understand how the
parenthesis really works, or a paragraph. It is a devotion of a lifetime.
I love your comments on form in
the poems themselves: frost on the
pane of glass as a form . . .

LBB "The sedative of frost composes its
infinity of dormant melodramas on
the glass." That's about form, yes.

cm And then, "Only the unbruised
slant of a neck broken by fear,
limp now and perfect in the fluidity of damaged form." Your strange
synapsed progressions of images
are very effective. The poems feel
far less flamboyant than in the
past, and much more deeply felt.
The erotic and the dangerous and
the furious seem to be fused, over
and over. There's also, with this
rage, terrible loss, that this work
keeps circling. Is writing for you a
means of retrieval or exorcism?

LBB Neither. It counts as further injury.
Insult to injury.

cm Eliot said that a poem presented
itself to him as a series of
rhythms. How do poems present
themselves to you? How do they
appear to you, and how do you
move through that process?

LBB Rhythm is the last thing for me. I
have my rhythms; they're inalienable;
I can't mess with them. I know what
syllable goes where and it's not nego-
tiable, but it's not an act of cadences

that triggers a poem. It could be a
title, I love the names of things.

cm Clearly. Reading the table of contents reminds me of Stevens'
tables of contents: they're poems
in themselves.

LBB What a high compliment. You know, I
run this 800-number for title services—anyone who wants to call. I love
to name things, poems, vehicles . . .

cm Cats.

LBB Cats, pieces of land, strands of hair . . .
so a title will often come long before a
poem. Then, it could be an image that
has nothing to do with anything, some
little minor wound that is in the body, a
rather unremarkable scratch to the outside world, but felt by the person who's
carrying it, and then the irresistible
impulse to touch that sore, you know,
the tooth that hurts, the tongue . . .
that's what begins this kind of poking,
needling, a tampering, toward that inci-
sion, to peer inside. I've recently learned
a wonderful religious term for this, a
"morose delectation."

cm So it is almost a visceral feeling
that you're trying to get, or get
near?

LBB Yes. I listen to the poem. First I hear
the provocation and the name, and
the trouble, the trouble in mind. But
then what I listen to is not what pro-
voked the poem, not what named the
poem, not what I originally insisted
that the poem was going to be about.
The poem has to have its own circula-
tory system, and I begin again. When
I'm "composing" it, I can say any-

thing, no one's looking. I can be over-wrought, underfed, I can be anything. It's in the editing of it that I allow the poem to tell me what its particular truth will be. Even if that truth is autobiographically incorrect.

And one more thing, as a long-term and unrecovering practitioner of the prose poem—which I disapprove of, and find indulgent, and feel help-lessly drawn toward—the sonnet is the finest and most perfected little cage for a poem.

cm That Dickinsonian legislator com-ing out.

LBB To say what's what and who's who. Henri Cole used the term "violent concision" and the sonnet is that form of violence, and concisely, because there's this metallic cage you can rattle the bars of, but you can't get out of. Just as it should be: a place where you can't go on and on. In prose you must go on and on, and, in a prose poem, you have to account for the leaps and the white spaces and the deletions in a differ-ent legislative world. Sometimes when a student can't write, I suggest writing a blathering, indulgent, bub-bling, frothing, mess of a prose poem. And then you put on the rub-ber gloves, put your hand down into it, and get out a sonnet. Like the time in the middle of the night that I dropped my only set of car keys down the toilet at a rest stop on the Massachusetts Turnpike.

cm How to retrieve that glittering key?

LBB Yes, how to retrieve, and even if you don't have rubber gloves, you've got to get the key, or you're not going home.

cm How do you think that the prose poems and the sonnets coexist in the manuscript?

LBB I had a dire compulsivity of arrange-ment for the book. For the first five years I allowed no arrangement; the poems were just floating around, no page numbers, no nothing. No pageantry whatsoever. I didn't want to commit it to a narrative, or an architecture. On the road to shaping the manuscript into a book, initially, some of the choices were arbitrary ones—I picked the magical number fifty-six for two reasons: one, Dickinson was fifty-six years old when she died. Also, I knew the book was going to be in four sections. I don't think I will ever write a book again in four sections. For me, the magic of a book of poetry usually occurs in threes. But I knew that the book was dense and heavy, and that it needed four corners to go into, maybe because there are four sea-sons, though I would never arrange a book "conceptually"—winter, fall, spring; earth, air, fire, et cetera. I knew it would be four, and there were fourteen sonnets and fourteen prose poems. Four folds into fifty-six four-teen times—a way to control the grazing pasture lands and to put up electric fences. I believe wholly in the slim volume of verse, I believe in the slim everything, I like the trees to be slim in October. As it turned out, there are finally fifty-two poems in the book, largely due to the resistances and druidries of my editor, Harry Ford. I'm quite certain he is the sternest and most brilliant editor of poetry alive in America. There is a quiet cult of worship around him, though of course he would never acknowledge this fact. He's the inventor of many things—including the *Harry Ford Tall Book*, the tall ships of poetry.

cm So many of these poems are literally stunning, literally arresting. Did you think about momentum and what kinds of juxtapositions and dialogues you came up with? You pull it off. It's very difficult when you have poems that just stop you.

LBB Well, the arrangement of the book is not translatable into English. It's not a narrative arrangement, but what Stanley Kunitz calls "that state of knowing becoming gradually luminous." That is as close as I can get to describing how the arrangement works.

cm There are all kinds of motions that I noticed, but in the fourth section I think it is a pronounced motion. Throughout the book there are various forms; surrender, for example, is tried on and tested and flirted with and riffed upon, and sung. But in the last section, surrender seems to come closer to being enacted, or embodied, after a long and extraordinary descent. I'm looking at "The Interrupted Life," "How Can It Be I Am No Longer I," "The Sleeping Hollow

of His Face"—that is such a tender, utterly lovely poem to your father right at the end of the book. And then "Am Moor," which is the homage to Georg Trakl, and is a terrifying poem; his troubled life and his suicide resonate in all of this. Is the book a farewell note?

LBB I think not. The only other person who asked that question outright was Helen Vendler, who read a version of the manuscript years ago and phoned me immediately and wanted to come over and make sure I was okay, because she read the book as a . . . major departure, shall we say. But that was a long time ago, and that was a very different version. I can't say that the poems have gotten any lighter, in fact, I'm sure they've gotten darker. As a reader you don't have access to the order in which the poems were written. But the last thirteen poems written—which are not the last thirteen poems of the book—are the ones I feel most connected with. To me they feel the most earned by life, by the real world. They're pretty grim.

cm Herb Liebowitz, who wrote what you called "a drive-by paragraph" for the book jacket, said that reading these poems was "like watching Phillipe Petit walk a tightrope across the space between the two World Trade Center towers, without a safety net underneath." He talks about how the book is about bliss and blighted hope.

LBB He is the first reader to have seen any

salvation in the book. "The patch of blue the prisoner calls the sky."

cm There are lots of things that are hopeful, just the energy of the language and the integrity of the conception, and the wholeness—even that last poem is still in gorgeous form. Nothing is dissolved about it.

LBB The book is so lanced with irony, that if you get worried about me when you're reading these poems, turn the page to a slight angle, to a different slant of light, and you'll see—it's like those hidden 3D pictures where if you tilt it one way you get the subterranean picture, the equal, secret opposite, like a laser postcard, and you'll see—shimmering beneath it a riotous circus of "other."

cm I did see a black and outrageous humor, and that is part of that hopeful life urge in it.

LBB My sister Julie has a little girl, Elizabeth, who I adore. She's three years old. She's just starting to make up fairy tales and they're little amalgamations of things she's heard. She just made one up that started with this line: "In her wisdom she felt hopeless."

cm This is from a three year old?

LBB Yes. And I thought, that's really smart. And, in fact, wisdom is the end of hope, finally. Jorie Graham says "contained damage makes for beauty." Damage and salvation, dark and light—I have this theory that there are two kinds of poems: the first kind is the Seamus Heaney ilk—the inclusive,

universal, political, religious poem full of humanity, where his finger is curled: come here, come hither: *this is what it was like*. I think that's the line that starts every poem that was ever written: mine, yours, anybody's. When you are quit of that line, the poem begins. And then the other way to enter a poem, or concoct a poem, would be the other kind—a Frank Bidart poem, which is also a come hither: *listen, you have never felt like this*, as opposed to Heaney's *you have felt this way*. When you enter a poem of Frank Bidart's it's so foreign, and formidably and brilliantly just . . . unfathomable. You can enter it, but you have to give in to it in a different way. You listen and acquiesce. When you arrive at a Heaney poem, that door into the dark is surrounded by a spool of light.

cm Where do you see yourself in your theory?

LBB I'm of the go-away, get-out-of-here school. I'm of the come-here, nothing-ever-felt-like-this school. That's just one way of looking at it, just the negative, the black and white, because I am very interested in real life and its benevolences, and a whole kind of moral code that I live by: a tribalness, a loyalty, a connectedness. But in poems I feel much more wicked, more distant, rather cruel in ways that I've never noticed in myself by way of the real world. I put poems, my poems, in a very separate realm.

cm What role does magic play in your work?

LBB Some of the pieces in the lexicon that

inhabits this book, which is, in some ways, an arched and embellished version of what real life is like to me, are certain emblems of sorcery. There's a line in the prose poem "You Can't Always Get What You Want," which states: "There are no sorcerers left, only mechanics to fix things as they break down." But I have long sought to live in a sorcerer's world, his apprentice—my home, my love, my life—the poem as prayer, as a form of incantatory protection.

cm Many of the figures in the poems are mythic and archetypal. The sorcerer, larger than life, and magic actually. Talk to me about "Grimoire," the poem that appears towards the end of the manuscript.

LBB A *Grimoire* is a little book of black magic used to invoke demons or cast spells. This was one of the final poems that I wrote. It's a kind of summation of the whole enterprise of writing *Master Letters*, as a book of black magic, a noctuary. As Dickinson wrote: "The Supernatural is only the Natural, disclosed."

Padgett Powell, © Curt Richter. Courtesy Henry Holt and Company.

PADGETT POWELL victoria hunt

BOMB # 55, Spring 1996

Padgett Powell's ability to capture regional dialect has led critics to compare him to Twain and Faulkner. Simons Manigault,
the protagonist of his award-winning first novel, *Edisto*, and its
sequel, *Edisto Revisited* (just released by Henry Holt), has
been compared to Huck Finn and Holden Caulfield.

This interview was first taken in the winter of 1994, at
Kate's Fish Camp in Gainesville, Florida. Handwritten signs
posted on trees read: Bank Fishing $1.00 + Tax. Inside
there's a pool table, bathrooms marked Inboard and
Outboard, a huge and dirty sheepdog sprawled on the cracked
concrete floor, and a few grizzled regulars nursing beers at the
bar. Powell was waiting in one of the five vinyl booths. We finished the interview one year later on a balmy winter day in my
backyard when *Edisto Revisited* had been completed.

victoria hunt It was Barthelme who
guided you through *Edisto*. Was it
great, or was it terrifying to have
your first novel be so successful?

PADGETT POWELL First, let me say that I
was too cool and cocky and stupid to
realize that its reception was an irreg-
ularity. I said, "Well, of course." It's
been the normal reception of my subsequent two books that has reeled me
back to the world.

vh But *Edisto* brought you a lot of good
things. You won the Whiting
Award, the Rome prize, and it got
you your position at the University
of Florida, right in your hometown.

PP Which I had the wit to conceal during
the job interview. When I came back

here, I was taken on a tour of
Gainesville, past my grandmother's
house, and my great-grandparents'
house, which is yet called the Padgett
House. There's even a plaque to this
effect on the front. I can remember saying, "Oh, look at that nice big house."

vh You were intentionally trying to
mislead them?

PP There's a bias in academia against hir-
ing from within your own program. A
homeboy might fall under that same
bias, so I thought it best not to mention that I'd been born four blocks
from the university.

vh You've mentioned Denis Johnson
and Josephine Humphreys as two

of your favorite writers. The choice of Josephine Humphreys surprises me, she writes such narrative-driven novels.

PP I'm doing what I'm doing now because I met Donald Barthelme and subsequently lost part of my mind—my original literary mind. Barthelme's aesthetic, as I grasped it, got me tired of a certain pedestrian storytelling, whether for good or for ill. When you lose some of your mind, you don't have any trouble with formlessness. It alerted me to an impatience in the absence of surprise. Barthelme was cubism and jazz to my crayons and rock n' roll—he was after something altogether new on paper, I'm not. I should have included under favorite writers Peter Taylor and William Trevor, whom we can call old-fashioned to the discomfort of no one. They have beginnings, middles, and ends—resolutions. And they are intended to satisfy the reader who looks for the customarily dramatic in a story.

vh You attribute a lot to Barthelme, and yet more than a few critics have commented on Faulkner's influence in your work. They talk about your ear for regional dialect. Do you consider yourself a Southern writer?

PP Sure, why not?

vh What about a local colorist?

PP What other kind of colorist can one be? Brett Harte is doomed to local, but if you get good enough, like Faulkner, then you're universal, blah blah blah. Hemingway said, "Some guys paint great big pictures and some guys paint great small pictures." There's Tolstoy on one hand and Turgenev on the other. I'll take Turgenev, too. Call me local.

vh Like a lot of Southerners, you often tackle the subtle, and not so subtle, aspects of race relations in the South. Do you see that as a responsibility of a Southern writer?

PP It's not a responsibility, nor is it, in my case, what I would call a moral compulsion. It's just that when I am writing something, sooner or later blacks show up. And it's arguable that nothing really good is happening until they do. Why that is, I don't know. But given the time and place that we are in, given the proximity of the races to one another, given our attempts to work things out, and the impossibility as I see it of ever successfully doing so, race has to be on the mind of anybody paying any kind of attention here.

When I went to college, I was singled out by the dean of men to be the only white guy living with a black roommate. My family was too far away from the school for me to go home very often, but his wasn't. So we went to his neighborhood a lot for entertainment. He took care of me there, which is the generation of certain scenes and sentiments in *Edisto*. I was a star of sorts, because I was the only white guy, and an innocent one at that, in his black club. And my roommate, Marion Jenkins, was kind of a star, too, because he was in college—his friends at home weren't— and he was living with a white guy. Hanging with Marion was part of the generation of my character Taurus, though Marion appears in unadulterated form in *Edisto* as the minor character Jinx and in *A Woman Named Drown* as the narrator's sometime sparring partner.

I do seem preoccupied with racial things. I make comments that are risky. All "racial" utterance in this country today is deemed racist by certain profiteers of political currency, black and white. If you acknowledge difference alone, you're a racist. Saul Bellow pointed out to me once that I'd be in big trouble if anybody ever read me.

vh Your narrators are often poor, undereducated, hard-drinking, blue-collar males. I assume many of them were the people you met when you were a roofer. But now you're a tenured professor, working in what some call the ivory tower. Do you ever feel isolated by your academic position?

PP I suppose it's a bit like going insane. You don't really have the equipment to register the damage. Outsiders will monitor and measure that for you. I'm not sure that environment—unless it's cruel and unusual—changes anyone much after you're five. My character was set by five, six, at the outside. People can live full, productive writing lives in spite of their positions within the university. Take my colleague down the hall, Harry Crews. I don't think many would regard him an ivory-tower writer. But Harry's been teaching almost thirty years. Peter Taylor, Robert Stone, Joy Williams—there are a lot of good writers, writers

of the world, who get paid regularly by some university. It can be done. It has to be done.

vh All three of your previous books have gotten good reviews. But I was struck by something I read. One critic said that in all your work there seems to be a "mistrust of life." Do you think that's true?

PP Life is scary as shit. I see absolutely nothing *not* scary about life. Nothing.

vh Concerning your outlook on life, in the essay you wrote for *A World Unsuspected*, at age thirty-five, you called yourself "arbitrary, foolish, with a streak of petulance and defiance, and finally, confident." Is that still true at forty?

PP Except for the confidence. I've entered doubt. Actually, I could change every one of those adjectives: arbitrary to scattered, foolish to loutish, with a streak of trash-talking and belligerence, and finally, doubtful. How's that?

vh It's good to know you're moving on.
PP *Laissez les bon temps roulez.*

vh In that same essay, you say that you are an assembler of "strange truths into less strange lies." Do you consider that your job description?

PP That's what fiction does, I think. There are all kinds of little homilies about what fiction is, does, ought to do. I like the idea that fiction is a license to lie. It takes the mundane and constructs something interesting out of it. Fiction is usually a perversion of what happened into what could happen. Fiction converts ordinary life into hard gossip.

vh In a lot of your writing there seems to be a dis-ease with women.

PP I've heard that before.

vh How do you respond to it?

PP My dis-ease probably comes from my attraction. Writers write about the things that make them uncomfortable—hence the eluctable presence of "a problem" in fiction. And the problem is not just anyone's, in the best of all possible worlds, it's one the writer knows something about. That may be the first rule of writing.

vh But it sometimes seems that women are peripheral in your work. Sometimes they're just not there.

PP Not there? They're always there!

vh But in somewhat of a problematic way. I can't help thinking about your story "Flood." The woman is floating down the river while the narrator maintains a fairly banal conversation.

PP But she's there.

vh Yeah, but she's dead.

PP He's in love with her, goddamnit. And the poet mooning along about his wives, alive and dead—it's a flood of women, that story. World-stoppers, I submit. And you can't dismiss the two novels before that. Women are the center of interest, the power source. Does that reflect my dis-ease? I don't

know. But I don't think you can say they're not there.

vh Maybe I made a poor word choice, maybe dis-ease implies too much.

PP Well, what am I going to say? That I don't have any dis-ease with women? If I were totally comfortable with women, I'd be gay. I am still exploring the limits of my discomfort.

Saturday, December 16, 1995, Tallahassee: Even for Florida, it's an exceptionally warm December day. Padgett arrives in a mud-splattered, four-wheel drive Toyota truck. I throw a flowered tablecloth over a metal table in the backyard— "Almost like Paris," Padgett says— and we begin.

vh Not to bring up a sore subject, but after reading *Edisto Revisited* I figured out your dis-ease with women. There's something downright Oedipal about Simons' relationship with his mother. Does it reflect your feelings about your mother?

PP I don't want to raise any eyebrows by protesting too much, so let me just say, good God, no!

vh You have to give more than that.

PP Okay, let me tell you what happened. When I was twenty years old, the woman who was teaching me sophomore literature discovered (in her living room) that I had not read Faulkner. In horror, she left the room and returned with a copy of

Absalom, Absalom, inscribed with her maiden name, and gave it to me. That moment was the birth of the literary mother taking care of the unlettered, untutored son, who I was. There were what you might call Oedipal longings for that woman. Her husband was in the way! To that extent, the portrait of this mother is a maternal and also sexual portrait. But untenable in terms of author and own mother.

vh Has your mother read your books?

PP Yes.

vh And she doesn't say, "Everyone's going to think this is me."

PP There's a curious thing that operates in this respect. To the extent that a portrait is negative, no one will identify with it: That is someone else, always. To the extent that one little wrinkle is positive, they identify. Now the woman in question has read these books, and knows that it's her.

vh You told her?

PP I didn't have to tell her. I'm still in touch with her. I'm still longing for her. Her old man is still in the way!

vh What were you doing in her living room? Sophomores aren't allowed in their teacher's living rooms!

PP Well, I was a protégé. I was a brilliant student. In fact it was her telling me this that helped flood my head with the presumptions that I could write. She was mothering me from the very beginning. She said one night, "Padgett, I've had intelligent students,

but I've never had a brilliant one." And I said, "Aw, thanks, Ma'am." But it had its effect, it worked. She was a good mother. A very good mother.

vh And so the family here is a fictitious family?

PP I did spend a summer in bed with my cousin. Although the character in the book is not modeled on my cousin at all. I rather like the woman in the book.

vh You have written hard-tailed, very butch books. This is more soft, more romantic, almost gushing about women. Are you getting soft in your old age?

PP Just lonelier. It's funny to discover, at age forty-three, that you can still write, or would write, about being in love.

vh Your character, Simons, takes this Odyssean journey, and certainly the language plays to that: he's with Taurus going down the River Styx. But later he has an epiphany and says, "The world is anybody's if you will square off and hit it. This is something I have learned, and I think I have learned it in time. I have learned it, I think, and continue to learn it, I think, from women." Do you feel like you have learned as much as he has from women? Is that you speaking?

PP There are moments in which you have someone say something that isn't your sentiment at all, and then there are moments when the sentiments are congruent. And that's a congruent moment. One of the reasons the quali-fier "I think" is in that latter sentence twice is because I was trying to get that to be a responsible utterance. So if someone said, "Now, Powell, is that the way you feel about it?" I wanted it cast so that I could say, "Yeah, that's about the way I feel about it."

vh So what else have you learned from women?

PP The women that I run with, or want to run with, have a kind of can-do attitude that a lot of men don't have. Maybe had, sought, petered away as they petered out of adolescence and saw that things weren't going to work out. Women seem to be putting their purses on their shoulders and wading into the fray and looking for an acceptable win-loss record. And men seem to be ready to sit down and say, "Next season. We lost this one."

vh Do you have a daughter?

PP I have two.

vh And how old are they?

PP Ten and four.

vh Isn't it partly being the daddy of girls that makes you feel that way about women?

PP Maybe. Because these little girls do that, square off and hit the world, they're born doing that. And it's my personal thesis that boys aren't born doing that, that's why you have to take them out to Little League and warp them and school them and steel them with all these ideas about being a man. You don't need to do that with girls. Girls will naturally do it, if you stay out of their way and don't impede them and don't spray perfume on them. Leave them alone. They shake hands, they look people in the eye, they catch a body coming through the rye and they know its intent. Boys, to my mind, comparatively speaking, are totally fucked up.

vh You know Simons seems awfully savvy for a college graduate from Clemson University. He knows so much about love and war and les-bians. How does Simons know so much about that, being from Clemson?

PP Well, you know Simons' age has always been a lie. Simons wasn't twelve in the first book and he's not twenty-something in this book; what I try to do in the book, as fuzzily as possible, is make him appear to be near thirty which is one way of excus-ing some of his alleged savviness. He's always been impossibly smart, that's the energy of both of the books, that absurd proposition.

vh If I were to describe you, I would say that you're a book away from a Good Old Boy. And yet there's a real hostility about the South in *Edisto Revisited*. Why is that?

PP It's not the South that I have any-thing against. It's a gratuitous pride in place or in history. I don't know that it's gratuitous, I just know that the popular kinds of passion for place have never been obtained in me, or they've been dashed somehow by other disappointments.

vh And yet, every one of your books shows a certain yearning for a geography.

PP If I'm not mistaken, in *Absalom, Absalom*, Quentin Compson keeps saying, "I don't hate it, I don't hate it, I don't hate it . . ." All of this negative business about the South on Simons' part is a refracted latter-day comment on that not-hating/hating. How conscious I am of all this, I don't know. In my own life it boils down to something rather simple. I find, at my age, that buying a plantation of the sort I've just driven through to get here is not going to do it.

vh Are you thinking about . . . buying a plantation?

PP No longer, no. But as a young man, I thought that would do it. A nice, commodious place with beautiful land around, which would somehow put you at ease . . . fulfill you. And now I think, you're going to be no more ill at ease in a penthouse. No more ill at ease in south Italy as in south Georgia. That's all that's being talked about, I hope.

vh [*laughter*] The South. Well, you know, Yankees love to hear us talk about the South.

PP And they deserve to hear us talk about it in a confused and mindless way.

vh Why did you decide to write a sequel to *Edisto*? I mean, certainly one wonders if it was because it was your biggest success?

PP Why does a dog lick himself?

vh Because he can?

PP Because he can. And this was the book that was there. And I wrote it. Uneasy, if not unhappy, with the whole idea of attempting a sequel to anything, let alone to something that has been as successful as *Edisto* was to a small but very good audience of readers.

vh Did you go back and reread the first book?

PP No. No.

vh It was just the same voice.

PP If it is the same voice. Obviously, we don't have the flippancy of the carefree chattering, the funmaking and the excused excesses because now Simons is older, and he's of a frame of mind that he's a grown man, and a real man can't talk that way. But I didn't go back and look at the book because I had no interest in doing that. That book makes me uncomfortable. The absurdity of its tenets are now *too* absurd. I was young too and had my way, which I don't feel I have today. When I began working on that book in that room in which I was given *Absalom, Absalom*, I couldn't recognize it as such a bad idea. And maybe it wasn't. If we went around deeming the preposterous bad, books like *Huckleberry Finn* would not be penned. They'd be thrown down hard.

vh Talking about the kind of internal critic, how do you get past the first ten pages?

PP I've never been comfortable, immediately, with writing that's any good.

The better writing I've done has always been the most suspicious. You put it away and you pull it back out whenever, and when and if the emotion then is, "Hmm! This isn't so bad . . . actually, where did this shit come from?" If you get that emotion, then, it's a wrap.

vh Given that this is a sequel, and Simons is still so young, might this become a series of Simons books? I see Simons as this cynical and sexual Hardy Boy.

PP Yeah, let's put him somewhere between the Hardy Boys and John Updike's Rabbit Angstrom.

vh What else do you want to tell the sophisticated readers of New York?

PP I was once set to go interview a man of whom I'd written who turned out to be a homosexual dogfighter.

vh What? He fights dogs?

PP No. He actually turned out not to be a dogfighter, but a dog breeder, and he also revealed that he was homosexual. And there were more contradictions in this guy's character. He was not a white man, as I took him to be, but an Indian. So he was not a dogfighter as he had led me to believe, but a dog breeder; he was homosexual, he was an Indian— which is a lot different from a white macho dogfighter.

vh Indeed.

PP And I was headed off at a preternaturally depressing time of year, right after Christmas, to interview this guy,

and he was going to show me, among other things, how to pick up soldiers. I was not looking forward to the grisliness of this scene, which was somewhat reminiscent of the dark half of *Blue Velvet*. And I told my wife, "I don't know if I'm up to this." And she said, "Take your scrotum in hand and go do it." [*laughter*] So I went and did it.

vh So you went and picked up a couple of good-looking guys, did you?

PP Well, when that happened, when the subject knelt down and looked through the doorknob hole of the peepshow booth, I remembered I had a tall and yet still fairly cold Budweiser in the van, and I went out there to drink it. I failed as a journalist.

vh There was the joyhole, and there was you, and all you thought of was a Budweiser. [*laughter*] Now wait a minute. Why are you telling me about this guy who was not a dogfighter, and not a white guy, and not a heterosexual—why are you telling me this?

PP Because that was the situation where my wife said, "Take yourself by the scrotum and go do it. Go get this story. It will not depress you beyond measure. Just square off and hit the road."

vh I see. You seem like you feel lucky to have her.

PP I am.

vh You *are* getting softer and more romantic in your old age. You hit forty and got all gushy. I met you right at thirty-nine, and you still had that hard tail thing going on.

PP You're looking at a white-knuckled abstainer. On the million-dollar plan.

vh What's that?

PP I can't have another drop to drink until I make one million dollars by writing.

vh Wow.

PP The day I assumed this position, which was some two years ago, I made fifteen hundred dollars selling a story to *Harper's*. There wasn't a beer in sight in Atlanta on July 21st, 19-whenever that was, that was worth fifteen hundred dollars.

vh So what happens when you make a million, you start drinking again?

PP I have every right to.

vh It's money-motivated abstention? It's not about your health?

PP No. Health is not enough.

vh It's not enough?

PP No. Nor is vanity, nor is insupportable behavior to those who like you, once loved you—none of that is sufficient. It took something absolutely absurd. Not only will I never make a million dollars by writing, if I were to make a million dollars writing, the writing would be worthless. The whole thing is fraught with holes. Yet, it takes something large to argue you out of a habit that large.

vh Let me ask you something since you brought it up. Usually when people drink, something critical happens to make them stop drinking.

PP One thing?

vh No, of course not one thing. But there's that one climactic event, when they say: I can't keep doing this. Did you have that?

PP No. It was an aggregate moment of some insupportable behavior, strung over time. I reached the point where the logic of drinking said: Be drunk all the time. The work of sobering up looked absurd. Desperate. Just pointless. You've gone to all this trouble to get really drunk, now why dig your way out of it? And deal with the tremors, and fear, and depression, to get back up on the other side, and go around making all the apologies? Why do that if this is where you want to be? I'd reached that point, and I didn't think I could support, among other things, a two year old and an eight year old that way. These women who have taught me to square off and hit it, I wasn't going to be able to provide with the means of squaring off and hitting. And you've got to understand, that within a month or two, a couple of accidents happened, and that beer would have cost fifteen thousand dollars.

vh What do you mean?

PP I sold some papers and some writing, and in several months, the fifteen hundred dollars which was already a pricey beer had increased to fifteen thousand, twenty-five thousand dollars.

vh 'Cause when you drink you don't write?

PP Oh yes, I wrote. I wrote much more. I

wrote better. I didn't write drunk—no one writes drunk who's any good. But you go do a good morning's work, and at eleven thirty—whenever you get that beer out of the refrigerator—you reward yourself, and shake your head at your genius, or go sit in the woods with your whiskey and shoot squirrels, as I understand Faulkner did. That's where the booze comes in, it takes you off duty. It lets you punch off the clock. Otherwise, you're at work all day. Hemingway has disquisitions on this, getting your head running on a different plane after a day of using it writing.

vh So what do you do now? Some sort of aerobics?

PP I don't do anything now. I'm a little bit awash. That reward system has not been replaced by anything. Narcotics are too hard to come by. I just do testosterone now. There's this notion that writers become drunks. That's not the case at all. Drunks become writers. In being a drunk, you've betrayed a predisposition to entertain failure on a daily if not momentary basis, which is what you do when you write. So the specter of all these drunk writers is to be regarded as a yardful of writing drunks.

vh Say you make the million dollars, *Edisto Revisited* hits the stands in the spring, and all of a sudden, it's like how many books can you sign in a minute and the ladies are waving placards, waiting overnight to hear you read, Hollywood's beating at the door, the incestuous cousin surfaces . . . So what happens then?

PP I've got a friend in West Virginia, a boozist shotist who also had to quit. I call him, and I tell him to expect a delivery to his basement from the local distiller. I tell him to throw all the car keys in the pond, and rip the phone off the wall, and I will be there.

vh What about the wife and kids, can you leave 'em a note?

PP Leave 'em a trust fund.

RUSSELL BANKS pinckney benedict

Russell Banks and I arrived at Princeton University at roughly the same time, in the early eighties; he as an accomplished novelist and faculty member, I as an undergraduate with an interest in fiction writing. In the narrow confines of the Creative Writing Program, we crossed each other's paths frequently. Russell was known among the student denizens of the program for his perspicacity, his wit, and particularly for his honesty. Stinging honesty. Occasionally brutal honesty. He brooked no laziness in his disciples, suffered no fools.

He's like that in his own writing as well. Honest about what pitiful creatures we humans are, honest to the point of bleakness sometimes. And he's hardworking. He's produced half a score of solid volumes, *Continental Drift*, *Affliction* . . . in addition to his other writing and teaching duties, and he's still a young man. Relatively young. He turned fifty-five a few weeks ago. He's a big, vigorous, hardy guy, and he's got quite a few years of writing left in him. If we're lucky.

His most recent novel is *Rule of the Bone*, the story of a kid criminal on the loose in the wide world. It's a likably brash book, funnier than much of his earlier work, though by no means light reading.

"I don't know why people write books that normal people can't read," says the eponymous Bone in this new book. Me neither. Russell Banks has for years now been writing books that normal people can, and do, read. I only wish more folks did likewise. We spoke at his home in Princeton.

BOMB # 52, Summer / 1995

pinckney benedict You spend a lot of time in Keene, New York, a rural community where you write, and at Princeton where you have an endowed chair. How do you make that double life work?

RUSSELL BANKS Well, they're like different halves of being and they don't really work together. I have always lived a bifurcated life, and this is just another manifestation of that. I'm very fond of my life at Princeton but it has little, perhaps nothing, to do with my magical life as a writer. My life in upstate New York, even though it's a rural community on the edge of the rest of America, is much more a part of the country and has everything to do with my imaginative life. I do like dealing with people who are serious about ideas, either students or colleagues. Nevertheless, I know that's

Russell Banks, © Marion Ettlinger. Courtesy HarperCollins.

got almost nothing to do with the real world. And I live in the real world for most of the year.

pb   What we're describing is acting out in life your own psychological dividedness; most writers are profoundly divided. Some years ago we were out drinking and you said, if only your personal life were as ordered as your professional life.

RB   If my personal life were as ordered and consistent as my professional life has been, I would probably be a miserable, suicidal, withdrawn man. That's not something I wish for. I said that only in a frivolous, drunken way.

pb   Why did you choose to teach at Princeton, which is exclusively an undergraduate program, rather than a school with an MFA program?

RB   When I was young, there was much about me that was despicable. But there were a few things about me which were admirable and which I would like to maintain and retain into old age. And one of them was that a book or a conversation could change my life. I was still open to enormous changes at the last minute: the kids that I end up working with here are at that point in their lives. I'm an agent in the formation of their views on death, sex, marriage . . . . So there's that opportunity. And then there's this incredible burden of responsibility because you can, in fact, do exactly that. But the tension between the two keeps teaching alive for me. I was never happy teaching graduate students because they're beyond that point.

pb   So what's your take on MFA programs? What's the value there?

RB   It keeps young writers off the streets.

pb   [*laughter*] And some old writers, too.

RB   As teachers, yeah.

pb   Do you talk to your students in a realistic way about what their professional prospects are?

RB   I talk to them in a realistic way about life, but not at all about the professional aspects of their life. I'm much more interested in dealing with sex, death, and class issues. One of the most important things that I learned early as a writer was to separate my work from my career and realize that they are two entirely different enterprises. I could deal with my career the same way I could deal with balancing a checking account. The work was something else. If I couldn't make that distinction, I was either going to be a very confused man or a very harmful man. Finally, what I can say about a writer's career is relatively little and relatively useless anyhow. So much depends upon luck and superficial social characteristics, the accidents of marketing and how they interface with the accidents of the surface of your work. That's nothing you can control: all you can control is manners—the tiniest part of a career. One thing that relates in this life to the larger writing life is that the danger for a writer who teaches is the same as for a writer who preaches, like John Donne or Jonathan Swift. You come to identify with the institution which is supporting you and its interests and ambitions, and that is absolutely essential to avoid. It's fine to be established and connected to a university as long as you continue to view it as an outsider and as long as you continue to feel that you are there under false pretenses. I could not have gone to Princeton as a student, and my colleagues, Toni Morrison and Joyce Carol Oates, could not have gone to Princeton either, for gender, race, or class reasons.

Universities have become the main agent of patronage for writers in this country in the last twenty-five years. Real writers who are social critics, outlying figures and loners are suddenly playing a corporate role. How can one do that and still maintain one's integrity and function adequately as a teacher of the arts? I believe you can only do it if you regard it as temporary and tentative, and mutually exploit the situation. The university is exploiting me and I'm exploiting the university, and I make no bones about it. That's the only way I think I can function.

pb   But you're tenured!

RB   Yeah, which means they've already started thinking about my death. [*laughter*] 'Til death do us part.

pb   **That's right, it is kind of a marriage. You and I have been keeping in touch over the past couple of months through the Internet. Do you use computers to compose?**

RB   I do about ninety percent of the time.

pb   **And what's the other ten?**

RB   Every now and then I get stuck and I'm frozen by it. It's so clean and it's so detached. I have become increasingly sophisticated and have internalized the process so that it's not really that different, no greater an extension from my body than my hand is. Yet every now and then I find myself locking up, and I have to return to the body in a more literal way and start writing out in long hand. My whole life I've had this tendency to close down and withdraw from my writing for various reasons, some of which I understand, some of which I don't wish to examine.

pb   **Your books are sizeable books and they're not infrequent. I would have assumed that you were a five-thousand-word-a-day man.**

RB   No way. That would be a day of great suspicion. And that's part of it, I grew up suspicious of language, suspicious of storytelling. I was raised in New England, in a Protestant, restrained, and reticent family that had a good many taboos, not in terms of their behavior but in terms of their linguistic expression—the description of that behavior. There was a master-story about the family, a cliché, and any attempt to vary the story or to tell different stories of the family was shot down. So telling stories and talking a lot were both a blessing and a curse for which I was marked. "Oh, Russell is telling stories again. Isn't he cute, but isn't he a pain in the ass." And that kind of ambivalence about storytelling I've maintained into my adult life.

So I've devised various means of

overcoming this psychological disability, given my desires and my needs, this compulsion to go silent and simply observe from the outside and not comment, not describe, and not articulate in any way what I'm feeling or what I'm seeing, and that occurs in this most mechanistic way. I change the technical means by which I speak and shift back down to writing by hand with a fountain pen on lined paper. And when that doesn't work, I'll shift the medium and move to a regular typewriter. The computer is the most liberating because it is the fastest: I can sneak up on myself and write things that I would never dare to say or write if I had to write it out longhand or if I had to say it publicly.

pb Not too long ago, you were joshing Joyce Carol Oates about how in her latest novel, *What I Lived For*, she knows so much.

RB Male underwear.

pb Exactly. How does she know so much about men and men's sexual attitudes? [*laughter*] Her comment was that there's this cultural knowledge that we all have . . .

RB She's one of my dearest pals, but she was avoiding the question. What I think happens is that fiction writers' main gift is to extrapolate. It's not just the ability to tell a story. Seeing her father's shorts in the laundry at thirteen or fourteen—from that she could extrapolate the whole history of male sexuality. [*laughter*] The best fiction writers are the ones who can do that. Not the ones who spend their

lives researching meat packing in Cairo, Illinois, but the ones who have the ability to take the tiniest clue, the tiniest piece of evidence, and from that read its history backwards and forwards in time. It's like taking a tiny bit of DNA and creating a dinosaur; it's like *Jurassic Park*.

pb Here you are, in *Rule of the Bone*, writing about this homeless kid, a criminal who hangs out with bikers. You're extrapolating his life. Is it right for you to be writing about this kid?

RB Well, if I didn't I wouldn't be using the gift that I have. Mark Twain was a middle-aged bourgeois gentleman living in Hartford, Connecticut when he wrote *Huck Finn*; and he wasn't telling the story of himself as a boy.

pb Do you know kids like your character?

RB Oh, sure. My life was marginally like his in some ways, but that was in the 1950s. I've known kids like him too, but only briefly and superficially. It doesn't take much to find the common bonds and strands that tie us together, a middle-aged white guy and a homeless teenage mallrat. We have much more in common than we don't have in common, when it gets right down to it. Part of it is in the genius of the American language. It's a democratic language. The language that we have available to us as American writers is a chorus of voices; it's not officially classified as upper and lower or middle, it moves in and out, it invades itself. It converts and alters itself on an ongoing basis. It's this big, crabby, wonder-ful, loving family of voices—the English American language: southern, and northern, upper class and lower class, black and white, Hispanic . . . That's the beauty of the American language for writers—access to speak-ers comes through language, comes through voice. If you can hear the voice, you can speak in that voice, and then you can imagine the speaker. And for me, the access to *Rule of the Bone* was not through some sociological experience, but really through lan-guage. Once I had that voice in my ear, then I had the character in my heart. Journalists can deal with sociol-ogy; that's simple. The hard part is getting the heart of the matter or the heart of the character down.

pb   I remember hearing you say that a first-person narrator was like an interview with just the answers. That posits an interlocutor, some-body who's asking the questions. Is it you who's asking Bone questions?

RB   As I've gotten older I've imagined myself less and less as a ventriloquist, as somebody speaking through a char-acter, and more and more as someone listening to a character. And I did think: I've got to listen to Bone and I've got to move around and rearrange myself, I've got to invent myself as the intimate, trusted listener, who is, in a sense, the ideal reader. It's an ego reversal. Only when I could do that, could I then begin to transcribe what Bone seemed to say. It's very concrete, and it began in a prison workshop that I was teaching in upstate New York,

one of these boot camps where most of the inmates were eighteen to twen-ty-two-year-old drug dealers. They were white and black from inner cities and suburban Schenectady and were bright, as bright as my Princeton stu-dents. They were really good at math, because to be a drug dealer you have to be good at math. And they had incredibly developed social skills, because to be a drug dealer, you've got to be a superbly gifted and practiced salesman. If you gave the SAT to those guys, they would be off the graph. So these were really brilliant guys—and so alive. Access to those voices was the opening for this book.

pb   This voice is really different from your other work. It's wildly funny in places, but it is a stark book in its circumstances. It would have been easy to make it a maudlin horror story, a freak show of con-temporary America. But Bone's commentary is very wise and dry. He's not ironic, but in the distance between his perception and ours there is a comic tension, a comic energy. The tone of it—light's not the word. But there is a subtextual humor that I haven't seen in your writing before this.

RB   It's a violent humor. It's cold humor, survival humor. Bone knows the world. I was talking to some high school kids in Miami a couple of weeks ago and one of them said, "This is the first book that tells the truth about adults." And that's right, it's not about kids, it's about adults, about the world these kids are inheriting, about the people who have power in their lives. If the book has any lasting value and power, it's because it's the kid's point of view. Bone sees the lack of power he has, but with a gallows humor. It's a redemptive book, however, Bone is triumphant in the end, spiritually and morally.

pb Yeah, the final passage creates a morality that will last him the rest of his life, regardless of whether he is powerless or powerful.

RB He is finally able to see the adult world realistically and with humor and not identify with it. He's still seeing: I am different, and I will remain different forever. He doesn't think he is excused of the responsibility to have morality. But he will never, never say, "I am they."

pb That outsider stance has unravelled and undone so many people in your early work. They don't find redemption, there is no knitting back together of the various skeins of their lives. They just come apart. But Bone comes back together.

RB There are several factors involved here. The other protagonists are adults, for whom in a sense the battle is lost. When their story begins the battle is over; they are who they are. Their destiny is closed.

pb Is it predestination?

RB No, but options are closed off very early in this country. Now options are being closed off at age eight, nine, and ten. When I was growing up they were

closed off at nineteen, twenty, twenty-one. You become commodified, you become a part of the economy and a part of the system at that age. Bone is the first protagonist that I've had who was a kid, who still wasn't bought. And he has a chance to create a morality for himself freely and independently. He has an existential life still available to him that in two years you can't imagine him having. Bone is free because he is so young. And so he's not as trapped and not as tragically doomed as Bob Dubois in *Continental Drift* or Wade Whitehouse in *Affliction*. He's a free agent, and he recognizes that, which most fourteen year olds don't. So, if there is a redemptive element to the book, and I do believe he's triumphant in the end and is morally empowered, it's because he's young enough at the start to still have that option available to him. I would hate to have to write a book about Bone two or four years later, as a sixteen or eighteen year old kid. It would be a different story completely. But at that moment, when he's on the cusp of adult life, he's saying, "If I do it this way, I'm dead. If I do it that way, I'm free. I might be lost, but I'm free."

pb Bone's best buddy, a guy who is sixteen, he's already lost . . .

RB He's an asshole. [*laughter*]

pb He's not admirable. You named him after yourself?

RB It's good to name a minor character after yourself. It puts you in the position of being a spear-carrier in the story and it takes you away from the foreground and into the background.

pb **So then it was conscious.**

RB Oh, yeah, quite conscious. I named a minor character after myself to get myself out of Bone and move out any temptations I might have to overidentify with Bone, or to make his story my story. All that was neutralized by making his asshole pal named Russ have some of my worst characteristics. Russ is a garrulous, fast-talking guy who's always got a plan, a way to deal, and he's also, of course, a Tom Sawyer. He's the slightly idiotic, conventionally smart guy. He knows how to deal with adults in a way that makes adults happy. Bone doesn't quite get how to do that, but he doesn't want to get it. But as a strategy for a writer it was useful for me to get myself out of the story.

pb **I had that thrill of recognition when I came across in *Bone* the schoolbus that in your novel, *The Sweet Hereafter*, was in a wreck that killed many of the children of the community.**

RB And in *Bone* it becomes a squat for homeless kids. A school bus is a very important image in American social life: it's emblematic. It's the first means by which we hand over our children to the corporate state, it's where they first lose the protection of their parents. It turned out to be central to the story. It seemed silly not to appropriate and use the same schoolbus that I had wrecked in *The Sweet Hereafter*, because in some ways the

two novels are very related. *The Sweet Hereafter* is, in parable form, the dramatization of what I view as the loss of our children. That is to say, there has been an abandonment of children in our culture, so that we no longer feel any compunction about not protecting them. And it has occurred most dramatically in the last quarter century and manifested itself in thousands of ways which we're only now beginning to recognize. By turning children into a consumer group we colonized them and made them into little adults. We sexualized them, because that's the easiest way to colonize people, to sexualize them and then sell them the goods that will reinforce their sexualization. And we did this primarily through the means of television, which is the first time corporate America invaded the home. Up to then you could always turn a salesman away from the door. Now you can't. Now you turn on the television and the salesman sits down with you in your living room. A hundred and fifty-seven billion dollars' worth of consumer goods were sold to children last year. We're talking only legal consumer goods, we're not talking tobacco products, or alcohol, or guns, or drugs. Just legal goods: sneakers, hoodies, clothing, makeup, video games, and whatever, sold to children.

pb **They make up a big part of Bone's world. He has this Homeric catalog, but it's video games—how can he resist?**

RB And in order to maintain a moral reality in the world he has got to resist that. The only way he can resist that is to become a homeless person, a marginalized person. If he's a regular kid, he is completely colonized.

In the past, we refused to sexualize children because we know that makes them vulnerable, we refused to allow them a role in the economy because that made them vulnerable, but somewhere in the fifties all those familial taboos were violated and broken, primarily by TV, and we ended up as a culture entering into the practice of auto-colonization.

We have devoured ourselves. We have eaten our future. Parents control—to such an extraordinary degree that it's shameful—and relate to their children overall on the basis of their being consumers and parents being providers.

pb **I don't mean it as a contradiction, but by making them into small adults we also infantilize them, it seems to me, well into their twenties.**

RB But that's always true of colonization. They're not cracked up to be adults, to be autonomous, free and existential human beings. And really, from the point of view of economics, it's a self-renewing colony. The other colonies dry up or they get independence or have revolutions.

pb **I was going to say they get angry.**

RB Well, what do we have in front of us now? We've got a whole colony which is rebelling, which is refusing to play the game by our rules anymore. And so to go back to the early question of

the school bus, *The Sweet Hereafter* begins with the school bus accident and the children's death, and then the story is about how a community lives without its children. I view that book as a parable: what is it like to live without your children? And then *Bone* is what it's like to be the child in a society that is trying to live without its children. To be an abandoned child, a homeless child, a child no longer protected, who has no sacred space in which to become a mature human being. The two books are meant to fit together. I think of *The Sweet Hereafter* as a German folktale, an allegorical novel, and *Bone* is a more realistic and first-person narrative. I'm retelling the same story but from the point of view of the kids who have been commodified and exploited. So much of what we see happening in Washington today with the "Contract with America" bullshit is the reaction to this delayed discovery that we don't have many kids who look or act like us. Why is that? The first response is to punish them for it. We're punishing our children for not being like us, because that's a way of not admitting that we have done something to our children that previous parents never did. Previous parents protected their children, gave them a sacred space, gave them time and room to become adults. Now we have "Toys R Us." I love that name, it's just diabolical. [*laughter*]

But we don't need to understand kids better, we need to understand ourselves better, our own nefarious methods and motives. We have to understand our weaknesses and fears and the degree to which we're manipulated by the culture of corporate America that we live in. We have to build an ideology in order to become moral and caring, custodial, protective human beings. To me, that's the great secret in American life, this betrayal and abandonment of the children.

pb   The American character is convoluted, complex, and multilayered, and you've been taking it on book after book. The project you're into now concerns somebody who it seems to me is the ultimate adult. How does he fit into your exploration of the American tapestry?

RB   He's an archetypal figure, John Brown the abolitionist.

pb   Harpers Ferry, West Virginia—my home state.

RB   He's like the leader of every cult we've seen in America, going back for hundreds of years. Someone who with his force and single-mindedness stands in our childlike imagination for what an adult is supposed to be: clear. So the attraction to him is irresistible in a culture like ours. The fact that John Brown is the only white figure who is included in the pantheon of black heroes by black people but almost across the board amongst white people is regarded as a madman, is to me very clarifying about race in America.

pb   Hero and madman aren't mutually exclusive, are they? George Patton, Custer had a little bit of each . . .

RB   Yeah, but they don't articulate in their lives what Brown does in racial terms. W. E. B. DuBois said the problem of the twentieth century is going to be the race line. And the problem of the twenty-first century is clearly also going to be the race line. We're still there. A defining event that Brown led up to, the Civil War, was that same race line, and the fact that he's viewed in diametrically opposite perspectives, depending upon whether you're white or black, is very clarifying—not about Brown necessarily—but about America.

pb   And the book you're working on now is a novel?

RB   It's an intimate, private, personal novel about John Brown, the man. It's not about John Brown, the historical image, although I'm very attracted to that.

pb   I've been hearing Brown's name a good deal recently, but in connection with Paul Hill, the guy who shot the abortion doctor.

RB   Well, the antiabortionists are invoking his name in order to sanctify violence. It's a parallel between Brown in the 1850's as a radical abolitionist using violence against slavery, and the antiabortionists in the late twentieth century who embrace violence on the same grounds—it's a clear, easy parallel to draw. Outside of Israel, there is no other nation created out of a moral necessity. Unlike say France, or England, or Russia, we have this moral destiny, which is biblical, and we seem forever doomed to play out our history in moral terms.

pb We're a nation of Shakers and Branch Davidians.

RB It's true. We still have this biblical mission to build the New Jerusalem. And not just simply to survive, the way France wants to, or survive and dominate the way England wants to. We want to survive as the City on the Hill. This is our basic religion, and in some ways it's how we entitle ourselves as citizens. We're not just patriotic, we're saved. That kind of patriotism is supranationalism. This creates a deep and profound conflict with our idea of ourselves as a nation that is a secular welcome wagon for every goddamned religion in the world. We have this deeply neurotic conflict which is bound to explode in violence every now and then.

pb Tell me about Potawatomie.

RB Potawatomie is historical material. But what I view it as, and what I think John Brown viewed it as, was the first example of terrorism committed in this country, perhaps the world. I believe John Brown went to Harpers Ferry with a certain amount of strategy: to begin from that point a guerrilla war which would be maintained in the Appalachians, running from northern Tennessee all the way up to the Adirondacks adjacent to the Underground Railroad. That was in some sense a fairly rational plan, and it might have worked had it been conducted in a certain way. It failed for various reasons, primarily because Frederick Douglass, at the last minute, decided not to join him. It's the next chapter in his life which is the most puzzling and wonderful chapter about him from the point of view of a novelist. The great puzzle for me is why John Brown, having lost very important elements which would have made Harpers Ferry the successful beginning of a guerilla war, nonetheless continued. He jumped from being a radical planner of a guerilla war to a martyr, consciously and deliberately. He knew he would not get out of Harpers Ferry alive. Puzzle one: why did he choose to become a martyr at that point? And puzzle two: why did he choose to martyr his children? He brought three sons with him, two died there, one escaped. And a son-in-law, and close devoted friends, people who followed him for years. What threw that switch is what intrigues me. What kind of hopelessness, what kind of idealism makes that possible? I can catch him up to that point. But then he steps off into space for me and I don't catch him. I don't know what he's talking about, what he's feeling, and that's the great moment for a novelist. That's where my novel focuses finally.

pb I thought this was a really interesting sentence very early on in *Rule of the Bone*—it hearkens back to the opening of *Huckleberry Finn*—"This is nothing but the truth." It's very provocative to find that line in the beginning of a novel. What did you feel like, using that sentence as a prologue to a fiction?

RB Of course, it's stated with a certain amount of self-deprecating irony. And it is a deliberate allusion to *Huck Finn*. And to *Catcher in the Rye*, which is in itself a deliberate allusion to *Huck Finn*.

I was trying to get down and let this kid have his story in an intimate, private, secret way, as you tell a story about your life. I imagine Bone as being where I have been in certain moments of my life, lying in a bed looking at the ceiling in the dark, with the person whom I loved next to me, either in the same bed or the next bed. It could have been when I was a boy or when I was a man, and the person in the next bed could have been a woman or a man or a boy, but a person who was also in bed looking up at the ceiling. And you start to talk at that late night hour, and you could lie, or you could tell the truth. And I just imagined Bone at that moment, lying there looking up at the ceiling deciding to tell the truth, even though it might be boring. He was willing to risk that. I wanted to clarify the relationship between the narrator and the reader, clear the decks and say, this is where I expect you, the reader, to be: it's dark and I trust you, and you're lying next to me and we're near sleep and I'm going to risk telling the truth.

WALTER MOSLEY thulani davis

Novelist Walter Mosley, already a cult favorite among mystery readers, suddenly appeared on television and in the papers in January when newly-inaugurated President Clinton named him as his favorite writer. Mosley is the author of three novels: *Devil in a Blue Dress*, the tale of troubles caused by an illusory woman who forces people to cross dangerous taboos; *A Red Death*, which brings the fifties McCarthy witchhunts into the churches and Africanist meetings of black L.A.; and *White Butterfly*, the chase for a serial killer who does not interest police until a white woman turns up among his female victims in a black neighborhood. The books incidentally chart the lives of the unseen "blues people" in L.A. in the fifties and early sixties.

Mosley has of late become a hot lunch ticket for movie stars happy to meet a guy who could fill a shopping bag with adventures of a freewheeling black detective named Easy Rawlins who lives in South Central Los Angeles, with memories roaming from Depression-era Texas to wartime Europe, and all the space between. Easy also has a seductively dangerous guardian angel, his childhood friend Raymond Alexander, better known and feared by most as "Mouse." Mouse is a clean dresser who smiles when he kills.

Mosley was born and raised in L.A., leaving at eighteen to go to Goddard College in Vermont. He dropped out and stayed in Vermont for five years, finishing his BA at Johnson State College. Mosley now lives in New York's West Village with his wife, a choreographer.

BOMB # 44, Summer 1993

thulani davis In your essay in *Critical Fictions* you say that you got into writing mysteries because editors didn't respond to your other works. What other writing did you do?

WALTER MOSLEY Oh, everything. I was writing short stories, and I was studying poetry. I don't think you can write fiction without knowing poetry, metaphor, simile, the music of the language. I wrote a novel called *Gone*

Walter Mosley, © Jill Krementz. Courtesy W.W. Norton and Company.

Fishin' about my two main characters, Easy and Mouse, when they were very young in the deep south of Texas. You could call it a psychological novel. Mouse was looking to steal from and kill his stepfather, and Easy was looking to remember his own father, who had abandoned him when he was eight. I sent it out to a lot of agents. They all liked it enough to send back intelligent letters. But none of them thought that a book of that sort would make it in the market. This was like '88, '89.

td So, Easy and Mouse have been around a long time?

WM Mmm-humm.

td Why Texas?

WM Well, the books map a movement of black people from Southern Texas and Louisiana to Los Angeles. So, that's why Texas. A lot of my family and a lot of people that I know come from there.

td When you wrote *Gone Fishin'*, was your intention to write a series of books that mapped that movement?

WM Yeah. I just didn't think they were going to be mysteries. Have you ever seen the movie *The Third Man*? Great movie. I loved Orson Welles' character. I read the novel, and in the beginning Graham Greene says that he was hired to write the screenplay, and he wrote the novel first, to work out the kinks. I thought that was such a great idea I decided to do it myself. Of course, I got about three chapters into *Devil in a Blue Dress* and forgot any-

thing about a movie. I was going to City College Graduate Program in writing, and the head of the program, Frederic Tuten, asked me if he could see the book. To abbreviate the story, I came back from a trip and he came to me and said, "Walt, my agent's going to represent you."

td That was great!

WM Yep. Wonderful.

td And now the novel, *Devil in a Blue Dress* is being made into a film. What about writing the screenplay?

WM I didn't do very well at it the first time. I mean, I want to try it again sometime. Carl Franklin, who directed *One False Move*, is directing *Devil in a Blue Dress*. He called me the other day, and he's asking all this stuff, which is nice. He certainly doesn't have to. His first three pages are like my first three pages. But what Easy was *saying*, he made *real*. For instance, Joppy's bar is on the second floor of a butcher's warehouse. So in the script, Carl has a guy with an apron, blood all over it, sitting next to Easy, saying, "I gotta get back to work." The thing is, to change everything into images. I have an idea of that now. I certainly am going to write screenplays again. It takes a long time to learn. Also there's a different emotional relationship. I think of it as larger than possible.

td What does that mean?

WM Most directors I've met, have incredibly large, irrational hearts. They believe in things passionately—did you see the movie, *Hearts of Darkness*, the movie about Coppola making *Apocalypse Now*? He explains what he did by saying, "In order to make this movie about Vietnam, we did what America did. We took too much money and too much equipment and went out into the middle of the jungle and got lost out there." That's what he did. That's where that movie came from. That's what you have to do if you're going to do something that means something.

td That's what he does anyway.

WM Yeah, but a lot of good directors do that.

td So, you're going to have a film noir?

WM I don't think so. The one thing I love about Carl [Franklin] is that he understands what I am saying. My novel is about a man facing his fear and his ambition in a new world after passing through two very strange worlds. The first, you know, is the deep South. Easy was completely convinced that that was reality. And then World War II, which totally blew everything asunder, and then didn't put anything back together. Now, here Easy is in California with a chance, with all that baggage. He's trying to face those fears. The novel is about that. The language is the noir language, part of it anyway, and certainly the time and the place—the fact that Easy is a reluctant detective. But, it's not really *that*. Carl's talent is character development— *One False Move* is a movie about characters.

td I thought that film was brilliant. I had never seen a black director deal with race from any number of points of view, and yet not make race the subject. Everyone had a way of dealing with it. So, with very few characters, he covered the spectrum of what a lot of us do: from using race, to being flexible about it, to responding to it. For me, as a writer, it felt liberating.

WM One of the problems with talking about racism, the relation between whites and blacks, is that it eclipses what real life is for black people, which is just life among each other. But so much of our intellectual heritage, which is good on one hand, but baggage on the other, is the discussion being in racial/political terms.

td And whites frequently have the feeling that is what black people do all the time—relate to the world through race, if not actively protesting and complaining about it.

WM And with very severe lines drawn. The thing that I really like about the genre of mysteries is that they're exotic, and you can write about things which are unknown. One of the things I adore writing about is the black community. This guy's a carpenter, this guy's the head chef at this restaurant, and they all get together in this park or on that corner because it's sunny. They all have a drink together and they like each other. They're all middle-class working men, as opposed to whatever other image people, black or white, may have of them.

td The people who are in the periphery in a lot of movies—it is as though we are looking at *those* people. It's as if, in your stories, there was a Chandler or a Hammett or a James M. Cain story and suddenly we see what was going on on the other side of town, in the same space of time. Easy does work for this police station with one black cop in it. Is that one of the reasons you picked the fifties? Because it was a time when the police really would have needed an outsider to go into this black world where they had only a superficial interaction?

WM That's interesting. It happens to work out like that.

td It wasn't intentional?

WM No. I mean, you still have the same problem. Black people are not going to talk to a police detective even if he's black. He's still a policeman, which means he's an enemy.

td It seems like an exotic world, 1952, 1953. The assumptions that the white characters make about blacks go unchallenged. And by having Easy do the detective work, the white authorities don't have to find out anything about that community. They're not concerned with the particulars, they just want the results. So it remains his turf.

WM The way police treat black people in the community is not like, "I need your help." They're like, "C'mere nigger, I want to know something." We instantly don't want to respond to

that. And as Easy says, the people the police want to talk to are "the element." They don't want to know about the churchgoers, they want to know about the people who are out there in the street, who know what's going on, who might be doing something. These people don't talk to the police. But they do talk to Easy, because Easy's okay.

td Easy doesn't apprise the police of the black nationalist's Garveyite activities. He's a fairly moral character in unconventional terms. His principle is to leave black people alone who aren't interfering with the FBI or the police or whoever is important in the power structure. He doesn't expose his people to a certain extent.

WM Many people think the noir genre is simply a mood. But there's a lot of elements to it. The noir genre is like the white hope in a world that has lost its hold on the string that ties it to morality and goodness. It's a man in his forties who knows the ropes and is ethically defined. He has no mother, no father, no wife, no children, no property. He doesn't owe anything to anybody. If the police say, "We're going to put you in jail until you talk," he can go to jail. He doesn't have any kid out there he needs to feed. He doesn't have any wife that's going to find a new boyfriend because he's a damn fool. You know, he can do anything.

td This is emblematic of Western culture as well; the rootless man on a quest for truth . . .

WM . . . And for justice in an unjust world. Which Easy does do. But Easy is so practical, and he's so pragmatic. He's always changing. My essay in *Critical Fictions* starts off talking about what you learn from poverty. My father told me this: you learn how to cook, how to sew, how to build things out of wood, how to wire things, how to plumb things. He only had a sixth grade education, but he could do anything he needed to do in this world. If his car broke down he could fix it, because that's the only way it got fixed. That's much more what my Easy Rawlins books are about.

td You say also that people knew what everything cost.

WM Yeah. In both senses. They know how much beans cost, how much pants cost; they also know how much their own dignity costs, and at what point they will give up that dignity, their sense of right and wrong. And then they're always aware of things: when somebody's door is unlocked, or when it's quiet next door, or who's on the corner. These are manifestations, awarenesses of someone who lives in poverty.

td All of your characters have that— they don't miss anything. And they never volunteer what they know about anything.

WM What they think.

td Because frequently, when we tell what we know, we learn nothing.

WM Right, you can't give away anything.

td It's a blues sensibility. The charac- ters in the book come out of a construction that is a blues world. Their codes of conduct are like the wisdom that is dished out in a blues song—the vision that you might not be alive tomorrow.

WM The relationship in a black world, or a nonwhite world, to the whole world is so complex. I've heard Taj Mahal sing this lyric, "I woke up this morning/With the blues three different ways/One said go/And the other two said stay." That's the problem; you don't know what to say, you don't know what to do. You know what you're going to do, but it's going to break your heart to do it.

td Most of your characters are very rooted in the now. Easy stands out for continually attempting to make long range plans. By the second book, he is protecting his stash; his land, his house, and everything that it has produced. He'll say in relationship to Mofass, "Oh he doesn't have the big picture that I have." Yet he's prepared, in the samurai sense, to go down at any time.

WM He has to be, because that's his life. That's what he's learned. He's seen people die all around him. The one constant in every manifestation of life is that people keep dying. He can never be confident of having what he wants, but he wants it anyway. It's like that blues concept you were talking about, "I know I'm not going to get it but I'm still going to try." One of the ways he does it is by incorporating different kinds of people into his life.

One of the beauties about fiction is that its world is filled with so many different kinds of people, and we can talk about those people. So you have someone like Jackson Blue, who is the smartest person Easy has ever met in his life, but he's also small-minded, a coward, emotionally very unstable and irresponsible. Once you have a character like that, or you have a character like Mofass, or Odell, or Dupree, who ends up taking Easy's wife at the end of the third book, then you have an interesting world. My novels are really about these people. Each one of my novels has some subject other than the subject of the mystery. *Devil in a Blue Dress* is a man coming to know himself, and in *Red Death* it was the relationship between the oppression of white people throughout the McCarthy period, and what the oppression of black people is about. The discussion at the end between Easy and Jackson Blue, when Jackson explains, "Easy, you don't understand. You'd be better off on the black list, because if you were on the black list then you could get off the black list." Then you have *White Butterfly*, which is the conflict between men and women. Of course I realized early on that I couldn't write about the conflict between black men and black women because it's too complex an issue for a small novel to take on. But to write about a whole bunch of black women, therefore, all kinds of women, like Etta Mae, who are so rooted to the earth that they can lift boulders and trees grow out of their ears and stuff. Or the Caribbean woman, mother of

the murderer, Saunders. She's a very strong and powerful woman who scares the shit out of Mouse, but doesn't have the strength to deal with her son, and is somehow afraid of him. It's so easy to choose sides in fiction, but I don't want to, I'm writing about these characters that I love to death.

td A couple of people have told me they find Mouse fascinating. They love Mouse. In *Red Death* he seems to be coming apart at the seams, he's completely scary, because you already know he'll do anything. But then you see Etta so glad to have him back. Why did you make him attractive?

WM Because I love my father so much. My father just died on January 1st, which is the worst thing that happened to me. My father gave me the feeling, when I was a kid, that nothing bad would ever happen to me. I knew that if the police came to get me that he would protect me. I knew that if somebody was trying to kill me, he would be out there with a gun, because that's just the way it is. In Easy's world this is really necessary, because Mouse says, "Listen man, them white guys got people on their side, man, you'd be a fool not to have me."

td And you have that feeling about Mouse?

WM Yeah. When the guy is about to kill Easy, and Mouse enters with a, "Good evenin' Frank." Frank says, "Oh shit, Mouse is here!" and then everything changes. When you live that kind of life, everybody's sad and depressed, and all of a sudden that one person is there and everybody's happy.

td Is that really why so many readers like Mouse?

WM One, he loves himself. One of the most constant problems in the black community is that there are so many names for black people: colored, negro, Afro-American, black, African American—now those are the official ones. There's also brother, blood, soul, soul brother. Then there are the slurs, the slang: nigger, coon, jigaboo, but all names used by black people, all of them. "Yeah, I saw that nigger came up here, I saw him." That means something. The Eskimos have thirty-seven names for snow. The names are always changing, and control over what we are named is important, which is why you can have a political leader who wants to change the name.

td But Mouse?

WM Mouse is Mouse. He's not looking for a new identity, he's not wondering, he doesn't want to read about slave history or African history. He doesn't feel bad about white people. He doesn't feel inferior to them; he doesn't feel afraid of them. Easy says, "This white man got trouble." Mouse will say, "Where does he live?" But if it was a black man it would be the same thing. "I don't care. It's either him or me, and you know it ain't gonna be me." And that "you know it ain't gonna be me" is a rock-solid certainty that most black people don't have. Poverty brings up all those

moral questions. "I know just how far you have to push me before I will go into that drawer and pull out my gun. I know just how far." Most people in the middle class, black or white, don't think about that. But ask a young black man in a working-class-on-down community, "What would it take for you to kill somebody?" He says, "I'll tell you. You mess with my sister, you mess with my mother, you offer me a thousand dollars." There's a whole list of things where "I will go get the gun."

td If you asked me that, I would say you would have to try to kill me.

WM And that proves that you've thought about it.

td I have thought about it. I've had somebody try to kill me, that's why I've thought about it.

WM That's too bad.

td Yeah, it is. I think if you've had the experience of coming in contact with your feeling or desire to kill somebody, then you don't have to think about it. It's an experience you've had.

WM And if you face it everyday . . .

td Chester Himes, did you ever read him?

WM Umm-hmm. That's so funny— there're people I like, black male writers, mostly they're poets, it turns out. Somebody like Etheridge Knight makes me so happy I can't stand it. But it's more than just that. I try to think of what lineage is. It seems that so many black writers are always creating who they are in the world, because there isn't the kind of lineage that you have in Eurocentric white male literature, where people actually do come out of each other. You have a great poet and he has a great poet who studies under him.

td But the critics who write about us are not familiar enough with the tradition to pick the people we came out of.

WM People say Chester Himes about me.

td Do they?

WM They do. But, you see, I don't feel like I come out of Himes. He comes from a very angry, a very disenfranchised place. Life was very hard for him and he needed to get away from it. People didn't pay any attention to him. I don't live under the kind of racism that he lived under. And even though I think it made decisions much clearer for him, which in some ways makes things easier, I wouldn't want to trade it. I learned more from Chandler.

td Who was the first mystery writer you read?

WM Ross McDonald. I loved him. I still love him, as flawed as he is.

td How do you see yourself fitting in with your contemporaries among black writers?

WM I was in Philadelphia a couple of years ago. Quincy Troupe was teaching a poetry workshop. I was just sitting in the back listening. It was a crowd of black people. Quincy was saying, "I want everybody to write poetry. I want all black people to be writing poetry and making poetry and living poetry and . . ." You know how Quincy is, he said that again. He said, "In order to write poetry, you gotta write good poetry, you gotta write real poetry. You can't just be writing something and say it's poetry. Just because you have the right politics, doesn't mean that you're writing poetry." He said, "I hate Bush." He said, "That's right, but it isn't poetry." And it was wonderful. 'Cause, you know, Quincy is such a powerful guy. Everybody was looking up at him and they were very serious and he was saying the truth. And very often in black art and literature, the mistake is made that the correct political stance makes good art, when indeed the correct political stance has nothing to do with good art. Nothing. The only issue for me is good writing. The job of writing is to hold, somehow, in a crystalline form, the language of the time. When, a hundred years from now, someone reads this, they will know what life was like at the time. They won't need to look at a history book to understand what life was like. They can see it and feel it through the language and description of life in that book. The contract of telling a story is that the reader has to wonder, what's happening next? And then there has to be a subtext, there always has to be a subtext. I think I'm writing good fiction. I mean, I'm not saying I'm the *greatest* writer in the world.

td OK, let me ask you in a different way: Writing mysteries has given you a wide and widely mixed audience. But has the genre restricted you at all? I'm interested in you, but I'm not interested in studying the genre. So, do you feel that there's some other audience out there who has yet to find you?

WM I'm being slowly, though not so slowly anymore, discovered by a black audience. The mystery audience is almost exclusively a white audience. I pressured my publisher for two years to get me into the various black distributors. They wanted to do it, but it was very hard for them. There was reticence, on behalf of the black distributors, to deal with Norton. They said, "Who else do you publish who's black? He's the only one and you want us to do all this work?" But I think black people are happy that I'm writing.

td Yeah, I think so. A funny thing happened. I was watching the news after the inauguration and they said that the new things that are *in* now that Bill Clinton is president are saxophone pins, what I would call white soul food, and Walter Mosley. Were you surprised to hear that?

WM The people who own a bookstore where I give readings in Arkansas had given him my books, so I knew he had them. Clinton, not at all a stupid man, wants to reach out to the black community and the Latino community and the gay community and say, "Hey listen, I'm interested." Now, you could look at this with a questioning eye, which, of course, makes sense to do. But at the same time, I figure this: if he read my books, that means that black language and black life, at least from one point of view, entered his life. Even if it hasn't entered his life, it entered other people's lives who have said, "Let me take a look at this book" and "Wow, this is what he's reading?" So I like it, I'm happy with it, and not idealistically or unrealistically.

td Well, it brought you some kind of notoriety. I read an interview with you in *Vanity Fair*, where you were asked a lot about being a biracial person. Is it a constant subject that people ask you about and therefore annoying?

WM No, actually. I enjoyed the *Vanity Fair* piece for a variety of reasons. My mother is Jewish, and I was raised among Jews and blacks; my father, obviously, was black. And I'm in a world today where there's all this conflict between Jews and blacks. So, the fact that Christopher Hitchins wanted to concentrate on that I liked, because it's a dialogue that I don't mind getting at. I was on the Staten Island Ferry once with a guy who I liked a lot, a Muslim who turned to me and said, "Hitler didn't really kill as many Jews as they said he did, and he really shoulda oughtn't a done it, but the Jews had all the *guilder* and them Germans just wanted to be free." This is like ten years ago, but I just can't forget it. I don't like anti-black Jews and I don't like anti-Jewish blacks. It's not that I don't like them, I just don't like the stance.

td But frequently publications treat an interview with a black writer as a situation to talk about race politics, and they'll forget to ask you about your books. There's a point at which any writer would be annoyed at being interviewed at such length without anybody saying, "By the way, you write books, don't you?" Do you get much of that?

WM Yeah, that happens, but I want to deal with it. I'm kind of easygoing. My books came out in England. Yours did too, in fact ours came out at the same time last year.

td They interviewed me about the L.A. riot.

WM But they needed to know, they were asking, "What's wrong with these people?" I didn't feel badly about answering them because I really wanted to give this other point of view.

td But, see, no one ever asked me about craft, no one ever asked me questions about how the novel was made. They really were asking about narrative content and how it compares to reality.

WM I often change the subject, even when I'm talking to you I do that.

td Let me ask you two more things. I take it Easy Rawlins is going to be around?

WM He's going to live a long time. I think I'll keep him alive until maybe 1990, 1991.

td There's a lot of stuff about World War II in your books. It seems to have made a particular impression on you. And you were certainly interested in the black liberators of Nazi concentration camps before most people ever heard about them. Were images from the war, stories about it, vivid to you in your childhood?

WM Yeah. Everybody, every black man was in the war.

td You knew that growing up?

WM Yeah. And they're proud of it. They loved it 'cause this was the first time they got to do a lot of things. And it was worthwhile.

td And did you hear about the liberation of Dachau firsthand before you read about it?

WM You know, I don't know. I don't really knock myself out over historical accuracy. I knew it but I don't know why I knew it.

td What I'm really asking, Walter, is what kind of information makes a larger impact on you, the oral, or something you've read, or are they equal?

WM It's the oral, definitely the oral. Black history is oral history. The reason black literature is the most alive in America, which I do believe, is that it comes from oral history, and oral history always has this weight. For instance, I'm telling you stories, and I want you to remember them, so I have to tell them *really* well. I have to tell a story that you'll be saying when you're talking to somebody else. And that story wants to go on and live on. You want to breathe life into your fiction, and people who read that fiction are supposed to experience that life. There's a kind of terror or elan or whatever. Much more than political rightness or wrongness, because that's secondary really. So certainly, it's oral history. Even now, my favorite thing is to have people tell me stories.

td I met a guy who had liberated a camp, and it was a story he had not told, not in twenty years, for some reason.

WM The concentration camps themselves, for black Americans, are so poignant, because, for black Americans in the 1940s, it was worse than America. This was a serious thing.

td And it was a sign that things could get worse.

WM "You mean you're killing them 'cause they Jews? And you do this to us?" It's incomprehensible, even for a black American from Mississippi. Did you see that liberator's film? When the guy says, "What am I doing here, when people are dying all around me at home?" And then when he gets to the camps—he didn't say it, but it's like, "Once I saw that, I realized that no matter what my problems are, I have to be here, I have to be doing this." And again, that's like a blues mentality. You have to do certain kinds of things. And of course, when I'd write about Chiam Wenzler, who can say, "Well listen, I know what it's like to be burned and shot at and beat and killed and put in ghettoes. We named ghettoes."

td You told me you wrote another novel that's not a mystery. What's this other novel?

WM There've been a few, but the book I've finished is called *RL's Dream*. Those are the initials they used to call the musician, Robert Johnson. He was Robert LeRoy until he found out his real name. And that book is a blues novel, not so much about RL, but about a fictional character who once played with RL and is now dying in New York and trying to come to grips with his life and his history.

td You said to me something about wanting to write about the music.

WM Ah. Now I remember that discussion. The most revolutionary moment of the twentieth century is black American music. I believe that it knocked down the walls of Russia. I believe that it touches and transforms everybody. It certainly starts with the blues. I'm not a musician, but I want to write about what music means, the only way I can write about it. I want to write about a black musical life. Robert Johnson's life. A life that is so hard and painfully and specifically itself that my main character, Soupspoon Wise is his name, says that by leaving the Mississippi Delta, he abandoned the blues, because you can't play the blues without a blues audience. You just can't take the blues out of the South. That music belongs there. It belongs on the streets and the roads and the paths. It belongs to the people. He thinks that he abandoned the blues, but this is a much later realization. It's a realization that haunts him. He didn't realize it at the beginning, but he felt it. He felt it from the beginning. His life has disintegrated. Now, in his old age, when he's dying—one of the other aspects of the blues is trying to come to grips with it—death and loss.

td Did you do anything in this book that you haven't done before?

WM It's written in third person, so there's that. That was very nice because I could deal with my female characters a lot more easily. I'm limited by Easy. Easy, I think, is a very broad, big character, maybe bigger than me, in life, but not necessarily in language. In language I have to be careful how Easy talks and what he knows, whereas in third person, it depends on whose shoulder I'm on in that moment. My narrator is closely involved with the other characters, so he takes on the characteristics of whomever we're looking at from that point of view at that moment. So the language can be much more lyrical. The language can reflect the mood. I can get really wild, and I do. I get really wild.

td That's good. And what next?

WM About the near future, I have a four-book contract at Norton and that's three mysteries and this book, *RL's Dream*. We'll see what happens from there. So, my next four years are spoken for.

Jeanette Winterson, © Jillian Edelstein. Courtesy Knopf.

JEANETTE WINTERSON   catherine bush

BOMB # 43, Spring 1993

When you read a page of Jeanette Winterson, you instantly know who's writing. Her voice is like no one else's: passionate, punchy, lucid, lyrical. She's a contemporary fabulist who spins strange, brief tales, and believes adamantly in reinventing the novel. Born in northern England, she lives in London, a self-declared outsider on the London literary scene. Still only 33, she is the author of *Oranges Are Not the Only Fruit*, (which was made into a BBC TV movie) *Boating for Beginners*, *The Passion*, and *Sexing the Cherry*. She is currently working on a feature screenplay. As a writer, she sure isn't marginalized and her books have been hugely successful on both sides of the Atlantic.

In previous novels, Winterson has switched androgynously between male and female narrators, delving into both gay and straight affairs of the heart. She's capable of being coy (think of a title like *Sexing the Cherry*). In her new novel, *Written on the Body*, Winterson has, she insists, created a narrator who isn't gender-bound at all—who is never specifically defined as male or female. But the narrator's sensibility seems, in fact, decidedly gay and female (as I and plenty of others assumed while reading it). One of the risks in creating a genderless narrator is that this person must of necessity remain oddly bodiless. Instead the narrator's attention fixes on the body of "her" red-haired lover, Louise.

I met Winterson at her London rowhouse on the outskirts of Hampstead Heath, a couple of months before the English release of *Written on the Body*. She is a small woman, still with a trace of the North in her accent, feisty and unflaggingly spirited in defense of her vision.

catherine bush Can you talk about the origins of your new novel, *Written on the Body*? Where do you begin when you start a new work?

JEANETTE WINTERSON I'm most interested in what you can do with structure and with style. I think the concerns of a writer are how to make things new, how to shock, how to revive the commonplace, how to take the banal, everyday experience and make it into something specific which has resonance—so that people see their lives not simply offered before them as a photograph might be in a flat, two-dimensional way but offered with proper resonance, magnified so that they see the dignity in the little life. Their concerns and love affairs are the stuff of tragedy and drama. It's not some squalid little bypassed under-world. It's not as though only the few people who end up in *Dynasty* or *Dallas* are worth looking at. Often writers make the mistake of portraying such lives as very urban and depressed, the dirty realism way. For me, the point has always been to take people who are exiled or come at life at an angle, who are slightly askew to the mainstream vision of the world—which, let's face it, most of us are (the majority is so small I can never find it)—and then to use the glorious power of art, the power of language, to really elevate these lives.

cb A kind of transformative power?

JW That's what people deserve. It's one of the reasons why opera isn't elitist at all, because in opera even ordinary people in ordinary situations are given this sense of huge, lavish spectacle. You cannot fail to go and feel you're part of something important and your life matters. I wish to give people that huge and lavish spectacle in my work.

cb Is opera an art form you feel a strong allegiance to?

JW Very much so. I like strong visual explosions. I like things to be said loud and clear. Not in a crude way but shouted from the rooftops to be heard. Art's not a shrinking violet. Certainly in *Written on the Body* I wanted to try and move my own style along further, make it tighter and more precise. I also wanted to deal with the problem of gender as I see it. I don't think that viewing sex from an androgynous model is necessarily a good idea but I do think there's too much emphasis put on gender. If you could take away all the obvious clues, all the structures and scaffolding around which gender is normally constructed and have a narrative voice which is really powerful and moving but nonetheless is not identified as either male or female, that would be a very liberating thing. So I decided to do it. I wanted to have somebody who is passionate, who is sexy, but who is also vulnerable, subject to the whims and misrules of the world. A narrator that men and women could identify with.

cb Have you found that happening?

JW It's very interesting—people of course read from their own assumptions. So even at Cape, my publishing house in England, a lot of the middle-aged, male sales reps said, "She understands men so well, men really think like that, I can't believe a young woman has written it." Then my editor said, "Well, how do you know it's a man?" They were absolutely horrified. They said, "It must be a man, of course it's a man." I'm sure a number of women will read it as a woman and I'm glad about that. The point is that it doesn't actually matter. What my private view is doesn't matter. What matters is that there's a space created in a text into which a male or female consciousness can enter and be redefined.

cb You don't think people will read it in an obvious, autobiographical way, knowing that you're a woman.

JW No, I don't. Well, if they do—you can never guard yourself against absolute stupidity. People are so desperate for certainties that they would rather art were not art. They would rather it were history or autobiography because art's really scary. If you're saying this comes from nowhere, then they have to contemplate that. They have to contemplate not only the act of creation but the fact that things do come from nowhere, they're not always propped up with experience and with precedent. That's quite hard to deal with. It's also very liberating.

cb There's been a lot of debate within the literary world about whether things can just come from nowhere—what gives fiction a validity of experience, a kind of authenticity. It's liberating to hear someone validating the power of imagination.

JW Experience and experiential writing is given far too high a value in our culture. It doesn't actually matter what has happened to you if you're a writer. It doesn't matter who you are. Your own character, your own preoccupations are of no interest. What matters is what you can do with the raw material that is your life. And that is why a writer must be very humble as well as very imaginative because you must be prepared to do the Indian rope trick and disappear at the top. It's not about you, it's about the work. Over and over again, I say to people, particularly in

connection with *Oranges Are Not the Only Fruit*, forget about me and look at the work. Certainly, when I read or look at pictures or go to the cinema, the shaping spirit of the artist is important to me, but most of all I want to be affected by the experience, quite apart from who did it or why they did it or what mood they were in when they did it. After all, I hope that my work will outlive me. In fact, when people write to me, as they often do, saying, "Can you give us some more information, or, what did you mean?" I just say to them, "Look, consider me dead."

cb You're talking about creating a narrator who is androgynous, who is trying to disappear behind the text. On the other hand, do you feel that describing female sexuality is a particularly pressing issue for women writers today?

JW I'm not interested in writing about women who are not in control and who are not strong. I'm quite prepared to display their vulnerabilities and their questionings and conflicts, but I don't believe women are weak. The overall portrayal in much fiction of women as essentially weak is very disturbing. As a woman writer you would want to redress the balance on that because it is not true.

cb Especially in terms of how women are portrayed sexually?

JW The stereotypes abound. Either they're vampires or femmes fatales or madonnas or mothers. In fact what's fascinating about women is their complexity and their wholeness. I have always tried to create women who have to be in control of their lives and in control of their environment. They make things happen. Whether it's the Dog-Woman in *Sexing the Cherry*, who has this exuberant hugeness and this refusal to take anybody's rules as her own, or Villanelle in *The Passion* who says throughout, "No, I won't do it your way, I must to do it my way"— although she's very sympathetic—or now Louise, the object of desire in *Written on the Body*. All these women share this particular thrust. It's very important that the women in my books should make things happen. The men—Henri or Jordan or even should we choose to say the narrator in *Written on the Body* is a man—belong within the sphere of their women's happenings. They are buffeted about by them and directed by them. If they're the little ships, it's the women who are the sea and the wind and the moon. And so it should be.

cb In *Written on the Body* the narrator tries to seize control of the situation, often in this totally misguided way.

JW It's really trying to seize control of love, which you cannot do, because it's much stronger than you are. It's Louise's particular passion and very pure certainty which really push the novel along. She is absolute in her vision whereas the narrator is always wavering. I wanted to have a woman with that nineteenth-century heroine's certainty and absoluteness about what she was doing. As you know, Louise is sometimes described as looking like a pre-Raphaelite heroine.

She walks out on her former life without even a single bag. You can keep that pleasure of having a heroine who knows her own mind and still make her complex and multidimensional. For me, the problem of nineteenth-century fiction has always been that the pleasure of the narrative drive and its structure often inhibit the characters it would release—particularly women. The women are very circumscribed and yet they have many advantages which I wanted to bring through to my fiction.

cb Do you feel a tie then to nineteenth-century fiction?

JW Only in so much as you have to destroy it. I'm totally uninterested in the traditional narrative novel. The terrible thing is that, in this country since Virginia Woolf died, nobody has really bothered about experimenting with the shape and the form of the novel in a way that keeps it readable and pleasurable. That experiment must be continued. It's shoddy just to go back to traditional narrative structures inherited from the nineteenth-century, which I'm sorry to say is what started to happen here after the war.

cb There's a tension between breaking down the form and sustaining the pleasure of reading. Losing that pleasure usually means losing readers.

JW I think it is possible to bring the two together, to go on pushing forward the boundaries of the novel and still make it something that people really want to read. I want to reinterpret this art form. Other people developed the nineteenth-century novel and for me to use it is just theft of the worst kind. To use the experiments of modernism without doing any work myself would be theft. It's important to push the form further. So with all the preoccupations of modernism, which are my preoccupations, and the glorious realities of the nineteenth-century, I hope to bring together a different kind of fiction, certainly a fiction that makes space within it for the female voice in all its complexity.

cb **Your book is narrated by an androgynous figure. You describe Louise as a heroine and yet you also talk about her as an object of desire. Of course, what traditionally happened to women in romances is that they were turned into an object of desire, objectified by being endlessly described. Are you running the same risk here?**

JW I think Louise is an object of desire. She is also the subject of desire, and really it is she who decides that her marriage will end and she will have the narrator at any cost, although not at the cost of herself. By the end of the novel, the narrator's heroics have caused Louise to rethink her position. She is present throughout that last section, if invisible. It's her choice both to go away and to come back on her own terms. The moral lesson the narrator is taught is very Shakespearean—what you lose cannot return to you until you know why you've lost it. I feel all the time that Louise is in the background

orchestrating this transformation for the narrator. I wanted to see whether I could bring about that sense of absent power in the second half of the book with someone that we've met and to some extent fallen for in the way the narrator has. It's one of the problems, isn't it, with feminism and the women's movement. You have to be very careful that you don't take away things simply because in a particular form they have always imprisoned you. Romantic love, for instance. It's been a very bad thing for women, it's stereotyped them, it's put them in a very particular role, forced them to act in certain ways. That is, however, a very male interpretation of romantic love. It doesn't have to be like that. Passion can be wonderful and it should be that women can be adored and pursued and looked up to. Why *can't* they have all that and have it on their own terms? It's the same reasoning that makes me look at clichés and think, well, nothing can be a cliché unless it's had a particular effect. Things become clichés because they mean something to us, just as conventions of stereotyped love are clearly very deep within the individual psyche as well as the social construct. I don't think you can say, "Let's get rid of it all because it's bad." I think you have to say, "Let's reinterpret it and take the best for ourselves." That's what I want to do.

cb **So it's possible to be a late twentieth-century romantic?**

JW Of course it is.

cb The latter part of the novel, where Louise is not present but is at the same time a presence, has an almost elegiac tone. The narrator tries to deal with loss, and tries to capture someone who physically isn't present. When you're writing about sexuality or desire in the late twentieth-century, does this mean dealing with loss, with illness, with absence? The conflation of sex and death has become very powerful in our culture.

JW The first sentence of the book, "Why is the measure of love loss," is a sentence that I carried around with me for quite some time before I began the book. I'd been thinking both specifically and generally about the failure of the human heart to truly value what is present. Only in absence is true value revealed. I've dealt with this in *The Passion*. I'm not sure I'll ever finish with this question because for me it's a rather serious and big question and you can come at it from so many angles. Again, it was bothering me before I started *Written on the Body*. Also I was wondering how it would affect me: What would I feel if someone I loved very dearly was gone? I'd been talking to friends of mine who have lost lovers or people who were close. One of the things that both frightened and interested me is the fossilization, the atrophy of the beloved once gone. There's a reference to it in the novel: the person can no longer go on developing— rather like a photograph. I wanted to look at two views—both the finality of "it's over, it's gone, this person is dead and lost to me," and the sense that

this person is not gone but you are having some strange, quasi-spiritual relationship, which I've also heard people talk about.

cb In the book there's a sense of intense physical loss experienced not in terms of sex but in the attempt to recreate someone's physical presence. There's no way to overestimate the intensity of that loss. Is part of the dilemma for you as a writer how to capture the physical presence of someone on the page, using nothing but ephemeral words?

JW I'm a very physical writer. The hallmark of my books is their strong visual images and their texture. I like to think that people can put their hands into them like thick clay and find that these words are not ephemeral, they're strong and sinewy. Certainly, for me, words are strong and sinewy. And I think that language is the best way to describe those feelings which verge on being entirely incoherent. When your throat's so clogged with words that you can't speak, you must get those words out, find out what they are so that they no longer have any power over you but you can have power over them. Writing *Written on the Body* was very difficult because it's so easy in dealing with an emotional situation to let the emotion itself carry the thing for you, to run away with it. So, for instance, I was very careful not to exploit Louise's illness because I thought that would be cheap. I didn't want her to have a more commonplace cancer like breast cancer or throat cancer. I just did not want all those associations to start overwhelming either my work or the reader's response. The more you go into boggy terrain where emotions are flying about and you have very little control over them, the more you have to be disciplined with what you're doing with language. You have to keep restraining it, pulling it back. Oddly, the more you pull back, the tighter and more powerful the effect will be. But it is a matter of great discipline. It would be far too easy to go down the Dickens route and have everyone weeping and wailing and end up in bathos. Rather I want to use language in a very raw and tough way so the reader can't pull back from the experience, from how shocking the experience of loss is.

cb What does the title of the book conjure up for you?

JW A book deserves the best title that the writer can imagine and it has to be a title that will stick in people's minds. For me, the image of *Written on the Body* is about being tattooed with love and with loss. The middle section, the poetic section, is the best explanation of that. I want people to look at the title and be intrigued and curious and want to read on.

cb There's been a lot of talk, certainly a lot of trendy theoretical writing about how to talk or write about the body, especially in terms of articulating a female language of desire or sexuality. Do you think it's a good thing or even possible to create a particularly female language of desire?

JW I think that you must simply tell the truth as you believe it to be, not the truth looking over your shoulder wondering what people will think, not the truth as you have absorbed it through corrupt mediums. Women find it very hard to be in touch with their real expressions of desire because they're told so often what those feelings ought to be. The business of a writer, in every area but particularly in the area of the heart and of sexuality, is to dust away the layers of prejudice and presumption and get down to that raw, vulnerable level where you might be able to tell the truth about yourself through the agencies of the characters or the story or the structure. I do not feel trapped in any way by language. I don't feel it's a male language that I have to deal with, although it's been largely wrought by men. I feel enormous freedom in the face of language. This gives me certain advantages because I know a lot of women don't feel this. I believe I can bend it to my purpose, and because I am a woman those purposes will be womanly ones. In *Written on the Body*, it wasn't so much that I wanted to create an androgynous character. I didn't. I wanted to create a character who could act in ways that were stereotypically male or predictably female and have those clues continually undercut one another, so you have a narrator who is soft and will cry or will punch the shit out of somebody on the front doorstep. I don't believe these things are contradictions, I believe they run together. For most women fantasies of violence are very strong. It may be that they act them out, or if they don't, perhaps they will. It should not be shocking to think of a woman slugging somebody on the steps. It should not be shocking to think of a man crumpling in a corner and weeping. And yet those images are shocking. Particularly if you are a woman you must simply write those things out and not attribute particular gender characteristics to them but say, "This is within the human complexity, this is within the human psyche, male or female." And wait for people to identify themselves with those emotions, with those events. I think *Written on the Body* is quite a sexy book, not because it's a particularly female or male book—but because I'm interested in how human beings express their sexuality and I like writing stuff that's tough and moving, that's palpable. That's my job. I didn't sit down thinking I must create a language of sexuality or of physicality, I simply wrote what I believe to be the case. And if that works for people, good. I don't think it's a matter of politics or a matter of theory, I think it's a matter of words. If the words on the page say what you really want them to say, if you believe that you have been true and honest, then that's going to work for other people. Probably they'll think that there was a theory behind it but there isn't, there's nothing behind it but the language.

cb If, as a fiction writer, you start off with an agenda and are simply trying to transfer it to the page, you're going to run into problems.

At the same time it seems to me that as a writer working within a cultural milieu there are things you may be thinking about even if, when you sit down to write, you're using another part of your brain entirely.

JW In fiction there is a much wider agenda for the writer to contemplate, which is the area of love and passion and human emotion. I do think that love is the most significant achievement and most people never realize that achievement whatever else they manage. It is my purpose to dignify love and rescue it from all those pasty-faced misnomers and lies that are so often used against it—both in the conventions of romantic fiction and in the conventions of pornography and in all those spaces where sexuality is addressed in a way which minimizes its terror and danger and also its liberating pleasure. We were talking earlier about how people were afraid to look art in the face. It's the same with sex, with love—human beings run away from anything big because they're scared. I'm really trying to drag people back to these big questions and say, "Look at them, and yes, it's frightening, and yes, you may be turned to stone, and yes, it may ruin your life, but what life is there unless you do face up to these things?" People who are lost to art and lost to love tend to lead very comfortable lives, watching the television and having a cup of tea with their partner but that's not living. If we're only here for seventy years, let's do it to the uttermost.

cb Your books draw on the qualities of archetypal tales, like folk tales or fairy stories, stories in which big, elemental emotions certainly play an important role. Could you talk about this presence in your work? Has your language also been influenced by the language of biblical stories?

JW One's cultural heritage is something that no serious writer should turn their back on. It's there for us to use. And if you don't use it—there are American writers like Easton Ellis or McInerney, to name but two callow examples, who don't wish to use it and want to start at year zero, I think that's facile. Embedded in all of us, whether we recognize where they're coming from or not, are stories and archetypes and shapes from which we cannot escape except by confronting them. I really believe in confrontation in life, not in an aggressive way but simply by facing up to what is going on. If you've got inside yourself endless amounts of stories and shapes and myths that you've never brought to light, you are not free—not unless you know what kinds of things affect you and why.

cb What do you feel are the particular challenges for a novelist today?

JW The challenge for anybody working with words is entirely the challenge of language. It's a problem that language for us is the speech of the everyday. It's our shopping list, our laundry list as well as our poetic expression. No other art form suffers from this so particularly. When you give people a

book, or when they think about writing a book—which is one reason why so many people write and do it so badly—they don't know how to make the distinction between the language of the everyday and a poetic language. This is absolutely necessary for the stuff of fiction. Unless you are prepared to heighten your language, to intensify it to such an extent that it absolutely leaves behind the commonplace vernacular that we all use in order to get by, then you cannot really say you're a writer. All you're doing is using what's available, and using what's available with no work isn't art. It pains me very much that people are not trying to redeem, transform, heighten, and intensify language, that they're still prepared to use it as though they were just speaking to a friend on the telephone about a meeting for coffee. This is what's so bad about a lot of women's movement confessional novels. There's simply no art there, no artistry, no craft.

cb Do you continue to identify yourself and write from the position of an outsider, from some kind of psychological exile?

JW It is a place I write from and I doubt that will ever change, because there are not any women writers who have come from the working class and are lesbian who are anywhere near as successful as me. And this is a funny place to be. At the end of Virginia Woolf's *A Room Of One's Own*, she says that sometime women are going to come along and start writing about themselves and about their experiences and it will be art, it won't be polemic. It's taken a long time. We had to get through the seventies confessional and now women are doing just what she said they would. But this really is early days for women to be entirely independent economically and artistically, to be free from the shackles of male thought and—crucially—not necessarily to be middle class. Certainly the novel in Britain has been entirely taken over and colonized by middle-class writers. That isn't a position of exile, it's a position of absolute insiderness. Literary London is a very nasty place, a very bitchy, particular place where people just like to rub each other up. It doesn't matter now that I've got a great deal of money and a huge house and all the trappings of success. The point is that I came here from nowhere, from a two up, two down with no bathroom, and fought both for education and for the kinds of openings into the writing world that would have come as a matter of course if I'd been white, male and middle class. There's a point where you have to have something to push against, you have to have something that drives you on, the flinty edge, the spark. If you're always on the inside, which is a nice, comfortable place to be, how can you really grapple with anything artistic or political within your work?

cb **What do you read, for inspiration, or nurture, or curiosity? Do you read much contemporary work?**

JW I don't get very far. I get everything sent to me and I look at it and I think, "OK, where's the style?" And if I can't find any I take it down to the Oxfam shop in disgust. I want to be chal-

lenged. I don't care about the content particularly—or I don't care about it first and foremost. I want to open a book and have somebody, another voice in this room that will speak to me in accents that are unmistakable. If I can't find that, forget it, because it's just going to drain you off, it's going to take rather than give and that's very dangerous. I tend to stick to poetry for reading pleasure and I always have. I still read the Bible a lot because it's such wonderful prose and I read Shakespeare a lot. I like things that use a really wide vocabulary, that aren't afraid to use words in strange places and take risks. I'm sorry to say that ninety-five percent of the stuff I get now doesn't go very far. Martin Amis, for instance, is a great stylist but he has no heart; however I can bear to read him, even though his level of self-disgust is very worrying—I can put that aside, because he really cares about the way words hang together.

cb **I notice you don't use a computer, just a typewriter.**

JW I like the physicality of the paper. I like to hold it in my hands, I like to see the words coming out and I like, of course, to throw it away. I'm an extremely fast typist. I change things a lot. I cut masses and masses. You often find that it's all been said anyway. You have to be a conductor, a lightning conductor of experience and imagination. It has to pass through you very powerfully in order to reach other people equally powerfully. All your own weakness and your worst fears will be highlighted in the written work, therefore you really have to be your own surgeon and cut out all the bad parts, all the feeble, scared parts. I always burn drafts. I never leave work extant. I burn everything. It's not good enough, so why should I have it anywhere? If it's crap, throw it away. I burn it on the fire. If it's not good enough for me, it's certainly not good enough for somebody else.

cb All your novels are lyrical and very compact. Are you making a deliberate choice about length?

JW The question of length is a real one, it's not arbitrary. Life's too short. This is not the nineteenth century. People's lives are far busier than they ever have been before, particularly among the reading classes. I think you have to recognize that. So you have to get them as quickly as you can. It's a choice that Bergman made while he was preparing to cut two hours off Fanny and Alexander for commercial release, even though the original film was five and a half hours long. Yes, you can have your dream vision and your triumph of imagination—of course you can and you must, but it's still got to go out there. I don't think these decisions are compromises. There's a fine line between compromising yourself and simply being bullheaded about the realities of life and being rude to other people. I think it's rude to write long books. I prefer to make a talisman for people to carry in their hands rather than create a huge suitcase that they have to drag around with them and open now and again to get at the contents.

cb When you look at your own work, from *Oranges* onward, what trajectory or development do you see between them?

JW There's an obvious development in style and language. One of the things I'm glad about is that at least if you read a page of Jeanette Winterson you know who it is because it's a distinctive voice. You've got to have a voice. If I didn't have a voice, I'd give up. It's so rude to write and offer yourself to the public and just be like some ventriloquist or some gramophone with nothing new. I will go on working until the time comes when I feel that my own experiment is complete. It isn't complete yet. I don't know when it will be but I think I'll know when it is and when I really can't go any further—God help me if I go back and start writing the same book. I hope that I'd have enough self-knowledge never to do that. If, for instance, my personal experiment had been complete now with *Written on the Body*, I wouldn't write again. However it isn't and I know that there's further to go, but there will be a point—you know when you look back chronologically at a writer's work, when the work's extant and the writer's dead, their last works are very rarely their best. You can see with hindsight the point where they achieved the apotheosis of their vision and after that things trail away or become repetitive, or dilute. I don't want to do that. I'd rather be able to stop. I think I will know because I keep such a close eye on it, and then someone else can take over.

SHEILA BOSWORTH guy gallo

BOMB # 39, Spring 1992

Sheila Bosworth, like her novels, surprises. Her work possesses a narrative grace, an unabashed affection for the normally afflicted (that is to say, for us all), and a palpable reveling in the wicked pleasures of word working. She finds the grotesque within the most ordinary, the ordinary in the most unforgivable, and forgives them all. Her portraits frighten in their familiarity.

The transcript that follows needs a setting. A musical setting. And the music most pervading as I recall the summer afternoon of its occurrence is a soft Southern voice continually shifting, always generous, attenuating normally curt single syllables into luxurious lulls. Fill most pauses with the hum of unvoiced pleasure. The laughter is never loud, never cruel. The wit pierces, yet manages a gentility.

guy gallo What are we doing here? [*fumbling with the recorder*] Two New Orleanians in Manhattan. It's a mystery. How did we get here?

SHEILA BOSWORTH It's a mystery.

gg Do interviewers always ask you about being a Southerner?

SB Only a Southerner would ask about being a Southerner. A Yankee would ask about "being from the South."

I think being from the South is a blessing, it gives you an edge, a special shading in the way you see things, as a storyteller, as a stylist. It's a different culture, a completely different culture. The danger of homogenization is everywhere in America and the South is still resisting that.

gg They have ways of phrasing things that are a little bit bent.

SB Yeah, a little demented. [*laughter*]

gg What's always struck me as interesting about the South is that everybody's a storyteller. The majority of people may not read but they're all writers. The ones that come north get paid.

SB It's a matter of having a somewhat skewed perception of things. The opposite of blandness, the opposite of evenness. You can be really unhappy in the South but I don't think you'd ever be bored there. Maybe that's the difference. You die of something else but you aren't going to die of boredom.

gg How did you meet Walker Percy?

SB I had heard of Walker Percy many years before I met him. I went to The Sacred Heart Convent in New Orleans, and Walker's daughter, Mary Pratt, was in my class. And she would stand up during history class and say, "My daddy says this and my daddy says that." Finally after several weeks of this—she was new that year at school, we were both new, it was 5th grade—somebody asked Mary Pratt, "What does your father do? He has all these ideas. What does he do?" And she said, without hesitating, "My father is a philosopher." [*laughter*] None of us had ever heard of this before. Philosopher! So I'd heard about this philosopher years before he had his first novel published. And the next thing we knew he had written *The Moviegoer* and won the National Book Award. Years went by. I didn't actually meet him until after I got the contract for my first book from Simon and Schuster in 1983. I wrote him a letter and told him about it and he invited me to come over and have lunch with him at a restaurant in Mandeville, across Lake Pontchartrain from New Orleans. When I got there, he drove up—he had an old blue pick-up truck—and his arm was out the window. He was wearing a black sweater with big holes in the sleeves. We sat down, had lunch, and were friends from that day on. He was kind enough to read my first book and to give me a jacket blurb or whatever you call the endorsement. And we stayed in touch. He wrote me some very lovely letters. It's hard for me to acknowledge that he is gone. The last time I saw him was in a restaurant parking lot in Covington. It was on Thanksgiving day, the November before he died. And he bawled me out because I hadn't finished my second novel. I'd been wasting time.

gg Wasting time?

SB Yeah, I'd been wasting time, as he saw it, working with a theater group in Covington. I was doing some directing, writing. And he got me out in the parking lot and said, "Well Sheila, make up your mind. What are you going to do?" I could tell that he had lost faith that I would ever finish *Slow Poison*. Then, within the same week that he died, I finished the manuscript. I can never go to him and say, "Here it is; it's done." But maybe that's a blessing. Maybe he wouldn't have liked this book. There's no leap of faith at the end, no truly positive take on God as he had in his books. So maybe he wouldn't have liked it.

gg But there is a very poignant opening, a sense of possibility at the end, isn't there?

SB Yes.

gg Tell me about *Slow Poison*, how does it differ from your first novel, *Almost Innocent*?

SB Well, it's very different from my first novel. One critic described *Almost Innocent* as lyrical. I've come to hate that word. So this book is not lyrical. Kurt Vonnegut once said that he wanted to write a book that was funny but you couldn't laugh at it, and that

was sad but you couldn't cry about it.
So that's what I hope *Slow Poison* is—
a sad comedy.

gg What did you mean when you said
they describe *Almost Innocent* as
lyrical? Why do you hate that
word?

SB Because I think I was in love with the
sound of the language to an excessive
degree, the beat of it, the poetry of it.
I have a horror of sentimentality. The
flip side of lyricism is sentimentality.
You don't want to get into that, the
maudlin. Better to understate it.

gg Let's talk about the first novel.
How did you come to write
Almost Innocent?

SB I've never done a whole lot of writing
just to write. Truman Capote said he
began writing when he was four or five
and he kept writing 'til he was seventeen. At seventeen he realized he was
ready for the world. Shortly after that
he published *Other Voices, Other
Rooms*. That's not the case with me.
The written word was my first love,
my strongest love and the love that
has lasted throughout my whole life.
But it was other people's words. I did-
n't feel a compulsion as a child to tell
a story; I wanted to read other people's stories. I read to the extent that I
don't know how I didn't go blind. I
can't even enjoy eating unless I'm
reading at the same time. And I think
that by reading so extensively, I served
a writer's apprenticeship, as some people would by keeping a journal.

gg That's not so far from a novel. Was
this association of food and reading from early youth? Where did it
come from, do you think?

SB Probably they both bespeak a hunger
of some kind. The reading feeds your
soul, the food your body. That's a
double pleasure. There's an emptiness
there that I was trying to fill up and
probably still am. It's a basic hunger.
If I go into a bookstore, for instance,
I get very excited and I almost feel
sick at the smell of the print, the way
the books smell.

gg So you get nervous.
SB Yeah, yeah, real nervous.

gg Perhaps it's more than nerves.
Perhaps it's the slightest touch of
Catholic guilt . . . pleasures of the
body and all that. As a New
Orleanian you can't escape
Catholicism. It's almost beyond the-
ology; it's just part of the culture.

SB It's one of the few cities in the United
States run by Catholics. It's infused
with the Catholic spirit; it's cultural
as well as religious.

gg One of the interesting things to
me about your characters is their
skepticism. They are very infused
with the rituals of Catholicism,
with the calendar of Catholicism,
yet none of them seems pious, in a
catechistic way. They are pious in
a personal way, there's always a
tension between the catechism and
how it functions in their lives.

SB Right, because the Catholicism of
these characters was not a choice.
Catholicism was bestowed upon them.

The Catholic church will tell you it is a matter of divine grace that you are chosen to receive the True Faith. Where, in effect, it was a matter of your parents taking you to a certain church, having you anointed with water and oil and that was your religion from then on. That circumstance of no choice doesn't lend itself to piousness or piety. There's a lot of anger in *Slow Poison* that wasn't in *Almost Innocent* and one of the sources of the anger is the idea of the Catholic church teaching us that God is going to be our protector. Southern women in particular are taught that they're always going to be protected by someone—Daddy's going to protect you, or big brother is going to protect you or your husband's going to protect you—and God of course is the greatest protector of all. And it just isn't true. You're not protected by any of these people. The grand silence reigns.

gg And yet all of these women, who you draw as Southern belles, who are inculcated in the fashions and rituals of the society, who have this preconception that they are going to be protected, turn out to be exceptionally strong, individual women. In both novels, what on the surface seems to be a very delicate woman turns out to be an extraordinarily powerful woman, I think precisely because of the tension and anger that they finally express about betrayal.

SB Right, betrayal is the central theme of both of these books. Betrayal on several different levels. The betrayal of a child's trust in her father; the betrayal of the woman's trust in the lover as protector; the betrayal of the child's trust in God as protector. Anger comes in the wake of betrayal.

gg In both books there is an extraordinary father that the main female character never leaves, never gets beyond. Or let's put it this way, who's always influencing how they love the rest of the world.

SB Of course.

gg Talk about those characters, the male father characters, in opposition to the male love characters, the love interests.

SB Well, *Slow Poison* is divided into two main sections. In the first one, we see three young daughters, children, with the central figure, the father, in the house. In the second half of the book, we see the choices these women make. Why does this woman choose this man? You see the pattern. The man may use the same nickname that the father did; he may call her "kid" as her father had. The answer to many of the choices women make is to be found in the father-daughter relationship. I can't think of any relationship that is more far-reaching, not even mother and son. It affects her all her life. She's compelled to repeat that first male-female relationship and get it right this time around. In *Almost Innocent*, Constance's husband, Rand, was charming but weak. He didn't even try to come across as strong. He was an artist, he was a shoulder shrugger. He had a golden smile, but no gold in his pocket.

gg Yet Constance's father, the Judge, was this cultured, powerful man. That's the father that I think of as influencing the course of *Almost Innocent*.

SB Right, but that father convinced Constance that she could make a choice based solely on her emotions because he, Big Daddy, would always be there with the money, so she didn't have to be practical in her choice. Rand was older than Constance, he would carry her up the stairs when she had an asthma attack, but when the Judge's house of cards collapsed in on itself and there was no money, that left Rand without any backup.

gg What you just described is interesting. Rand with his strong arms and Constance with her asthma, and yet the whole central reversal of the book is that Constance is doing everything that changes their lives. She is the one who is making the decisions and being strong, if misguided, to keep them afloat.

SB Eamon, the father of the three daughters in *Slow Poison*, is very different. He appears to be strong. Domineering, willful, and yet he too is weak. He takes care of nothing, in the end. He's an addict. He has his own secret passions that don't include his daughters, that don't allow for his daughters' well-being.

gg Eamon is perhaps very typical of the Southern gentleman in that he takes care of other people much more effectively than he takes care

of his own family.

SB He goes through the motions. One touching thing about Eamon, the father in *Slow Poison,* is that after his first wife dies, his mother-in-law and his sister-in-law move into his house with him and his three young daughters. Then he marries again, but he never abandons his late wife's mother and sister. Even through his second marriage, they are with him. Even after that marriage ends in divorce. But he's not there for any of the women in his household in any real sense.

There's one part of the book where Rory goes to her father, who's having a rare moment of sobriety, and says, "What are we going to do about this situation with my sister?" He says, "Well, there's nothing we can do. Just tell her we're here for her. Don't worry about anything." Rory is sitting there thinking, "How long are you going to be here, be here in your right mind? I miss you and you aren't even gone yet." Daddy was home, but he wasn't home.

gg What did you do in the theater company? Did you write plays, direct?

SB A short story I wrote, a little memoir really, was made into a one-act play in New Orleans, *Didn't Mean Good-bye.*

gg Did you do the adaptation? [*yes*] What was that like, writing for the theater as opposed to writing for an editor and audience of novel readers?

SB It was the most exciting, most addictive thing . . . to see characters that I created brought to life by really talented actors and to see these words come alive on stage. On the other hand, I've never been more terrified in my life than when the lights went down. These people who'd bought tickets were coming in good faith to see this thing that I'd made up, and the lights were going down, and they were sitting there, coughing, programs were rustling, and I was backstage clutching one of the actors until he couldn't breathe, driving everyone crazy. I'm not well enough to be a playwright. [*laughter*] That's the end of that.

gg You aren't going to do it again?

SB For one thing, I'm not sure I have what Lillian Hellman referred to as that "special light" that a playwright has. There are some very fine novelists who simply don't have that light in their heads. It's a special gift. I'd rather write novels. It was a thrilling experience, though. I used to think if I could have one wish, a magic genie wish, it would be to be the most successful, prolific playwright in New York, to have this thrill over and over again. But it's so difficult, emotionally, to sit there and watch people react to your work. And then you realize the heart, and the soul, that all these other people have put into it—the director, the actors, the lighting crew. It's so collaborative and yet the writer, while taking no credit for the whole production, must take the blame. Truly I feel I would have to take the blame if it went under. If it wasn't successful, well, I started this. These are my words.

gg When you say the "special light" that the playwright is required to have. . . . One of the noteworthy things I find in your work is how you can draw a character with a simple response. The way they answer a question tells you precisely who they are. Your dialogue is exceptional. I suppose the "special light" you are speaking of has more to do with dramatic form?

SB It's a very strict, strict form and you don't have the safety net of the verb. You don't have the narrative stretch.

gg Do you have an imaginary audience when you write?

SB Lillian Hellman said that every writer writes for only one person, the person who stands behind her chair, a person whose face changes through the years. And I think that's true. I bet you couldn't get most writers to say who the person is.

gg Because they don't know or because they won't tell you?

SB Because they won't tell you. [*laughter*]

gg And with that, I've absolutely got to ask you, who is it?

SB I won't tell you. [*fruitless badgering deleted*]

gg Both *Almost Innocent* and *Slow Poison* are about characters learning to live with their particular terrifying secrets.

SB There's a danger of melodrama in writing about the South, of sinking into melodrama. But it's not an exaggeration. People think we're exaggerating. These are the sort of things that go on. I'll call my sister, Constance, in New York once a week and say, "Guess what happened now?" And she'll say, "Please don't tell me any more." Someone jumped off the bridge, somebody else hanged themselves, somebody else went spinning over a cliff. You know, an amazing variety of black things happen in the South. I've heard that the suicides are always higher in tropical countries. Have you heard that? I'm sure the heat has something to do with it because the heat will drive you mad. It will. The human body is not geared to breathe underwater and so . . . something happens in all that humidity.

gg Do you miss living in New Orleans' hell?

SB No, I don't, because I grew up there, and there's something sad to me about going along the same streets that I did when I was a child, whether because the childhood was unhappy or because I'm a prisoner of nostalgia. Nostalgia is a tremendous force in my life. I can feel overwhelmingly sad just at the sight of something that reminds me of another time, whether that former time was extremely happy or extremely sad doesn't matter.

gg You're sad at the memory of it?
SB Yeah.

gg I understand . . .
SB Just at the passage of time . . .

gg Your main female characters are tradition bound. Is that a fair

statement?
SB I would say, yes, but I'm not sure in the second novel that's particularly treated. The first one, set in the fifties, is more tradition bound.

gg There are ways in which Constance in the first novel, *Almost Innocent*, is trying to make sense of her marriage to Rand and her background as a privileged child, a privileged woman, a Southern woman who submits to the expectations of society. That could very easily be misread as not proper feminist politics, as not politically correct.
SB Right . . .

gg She seems to accept the idea that a woman requires external support, requires a strong male presence . . . and yet, underneath it, she is the controlling force, so there's this very subtle reversal. My question, I guess, is: Have you experienced criticism from more "edgy" critics or writers who have objected to the way your women are portrayed?
SB No. As a matter of fact, Emily Toth commented on the fact that when Constance dies in *Almost Innocent*, she doesn't call for her father, or her husband; she doesn't pray to Jesus Christ, she cries out for her best friend, another woman. And this critic was quite taken with that, that the thread running through the story was that women do depend on other women. And they recognize their strength at crucial moments, in themselves and in other women.

gg I think that, in some sense, is what I'm trying to get at. They seem to be measuring their progress by how they've been accepted by father, by the success of their relationship with a man, when in fact it's almost as if there's a secret society, a witchcraft coven that the men know nothing about.

SB No, that's exactly right. They have absolutely no clue. The men are taken by surprise by the women in both of my novels. By the women of all ages.

gg In *Slow Poison*, Rory's father is talking to a potential beau of Rory's, the saxophone player:

"I was born in New York State," [the sax player] sobbed. "You know what it's like, a guy like me falling in love with a Southern girl? It's like, you're inside this beautiful house with no lights on, and it's night all the time, and you keep falling and banging your head on the walls because you can't see where you're going! Hey, where've they got the goddamn rules of the house posted?"

The interesting thing is, in both these books, even the Southern guys are in over their heads. I hate to use the phrase "steel magnolia" because it trivializes what we're talking about, but all of these women are extraordinarily brittle in one sense, while lacy in others.

SB People are complex. They change from one moment to the next. I do think that there's a certain amount of culpability in the women in my nov-

els. One of the characters, Johnny, at the end of *Slow Poison* says, "You gave me so much rope." But in this case, she drew it in and tied a little noose around his neck and he can swing, hang by the neck until dead. "And is that what gets you off?" he asks her. The women are not totally innocent. There are women who will choose a man, give him a whole lot of rope, convince him that they're a doormat, and just when he's convinced he can do whatever he wants, pull the doormat out from under him. He says, "Well, wait a minute. Why didn't you warn me?" She says, "I didn't feel like it."

I have a friend from Nashville, a great beauty who lives in New York. And I once said to her, "What ever happened to that man you were going out with?" And she said, "Oh, I broke off with him." And I said, "Well how in the world did you do it? You were so crazy about him." She said, "I got him at lunch one day and said to him, 'You know, I love you the most, but I think we've missed our moment.' And if he was too sleepy to see it coming, then he'll just have to live with it."

gg But there's something so absolute in that, isn't there?

SB Yes, there is.

gg Very unforgiving. And I think that's what I'm trying to explore. Precisely that crystalline conviction. That the characters may be completely confused in the process of their relationship, or, on the way to love, and in the allowances they give one another, and then there'll be this moment of pure logic.

SB That moment of pure logic often comes at the cost of love. Rory, in *Slow Poison*, admits she never warned Johnny he was in trouble because she was too much of a coward. She didn't want to risk playing games with him, and telling him "if you don't shape up, I'm going to leave you," because what if he said, "Okay, bye?" She wasn't ready for that. She can't even threaten to leave, because she loves him so much. The price she pays for that sort of cowardice, that unwillingness to take the risk, is that eventually love is killed by anger. There's no getting it back. Beyond anger is nothing, you know. Indifference. Then it's really painless. You're unconscious again. Oh boy! [*laughter*] Blessed unconsciousness.

gg Have you started on the third novel?

SB I have started on the third. I have it all mapped out, and things written down. That means that nothing that I have written down will ever appear. [*laughter*] I know enough about the process that I go through now to know that. But it gives me a false sense of security. I have the title. And, you know, the basic theme. I always get the title first, for some reason.

gg It gives you something to aim for.

SB I know I want to write a book about people who are trapped, and other people who want to rescue the trapped. What happens between the would-be rescuer, and the would-be rescued.

gg I see a pattern here. Time has passed. Anger has accumulated. And in the book you're now talking about, there may be an attempt to save.

SB Right. You know, the title of this book, this third book, I found in Thomas Aquinas' spiritual and corporal works of mercy. Some of the corporal works are to feed the hungry, to clothe the naked, to give drink to the thirsty, to visit the imprisoned, to bury the dead, and to ransom the captive. I thought, "to ransom the captive," there's the title. But what if the captive doesn't want to be ransomed? What then? You know, Walker said, "Put a man in a given situation, and see what he does." So, what about a person who appears to be trapped, but doesn't really want to be rescued, and all of these rescuers keep coming out of the woodwork?

gg We shouldn't talk about this. Isn't it bad luck to talk about?

SB Yeah, it is bad luck.

gg Your work has a very specific sense of place.

SB The things that are wrong with the South can infuse a work of fiction with a depth that perhaps a work about a more homogenized place would not have. I think of Milan Kundera's novel, *The Unbearable Lightness of Being*, which is set in Czechoslovakia under the Communist regime, and then I think of his latest novel, *Immortality*, set in Paris. There's a tremendous lightening of the work. The darkness is not there, the oppression.

gg Do you think the reading public in America wants to be challenged to look at that kind of complex shading in fiction these days?

SB I don't think it matters a bit whether they want to be challenged or not. I think if you feel it, and you have it in you to write it, then you have to write it. You write it.

gg See, my fear is that people are forgetting how to read altogether.

sb It's such a bad fear. So bad I can't even let myself think about it. I know what you mean, though. I'm heavily into denial when I think about that problem.

gg The biggest example to me was during the last election, where political discourse has been reduced to these forty second lies. Very depressing.

SB Sound bites. It gives you the feeling, "Drat! Born into the wrong century again." You know?

gg For the people who haven't read *Almost Innocent*, why don't you synopsize it?

SB *Almost Innocent* is about the betrayal of trust between a father and a daughter, between a wife and her husband and daughter, between children and their parents. That's the main thing. Betrayal. It's about wrong choices . . . how people can go through life perfectly content, unless they happen to make a crucial wrong choice. Such as Rand Calvert made in Constance. It's about people fighting their natures to try to get what they want. For instance, Rand fights his nature as an artist in order to win the prize he assumes Constance is. He's not true to himself in that sense. At one point he makes the horrible mistake of actually getting a nine-to-five job to try to please Constance. He betrays his own nature for her, and it ends up a disaster.

gg The book that's coming out now, *Slow Poison*, how would you characterize it?

SB Ummm . . . that's hard. [*pause*] It's about love and death. [*laughter*]

gg Is that all? Several generations of love and death?

SB Several generations of love and death. Again, there are betrayals. Betrayals of trust.

gg Do you ever wonder how you did it? Wrote a novel? Ever wonder how you'll do it again?

SB Absolutely. As the character in *Slow Poison* says, "Where've they got the rules of the house posted?" Where have they got the rules of the house posted for writers? Well, the beauty of it is, there are no rules. It's very hard, at times, not to feel that you are wandering through a beautiful house without any lights on. And you might happen to bump into the right word and the right moment for your characters, and you might not. You might just end up tumbling down the stairs backwards in the dark, taking your reader right along with you.

JAMES MERRILL   thomas bolt

James Merrill, who has just turned sixty-five is one of America's most distinguished poets. Critic Stephen Yenser has called Merrill's epic poem *The Changing Light at Sandover* "a landmark in American literature." Certainly it's the only epic poem mostly dictated on a Ouija board to its two mediums, JM and DJ (Merrill and his coadventurer David Jackson). In a career including—so far—two novels, two plays, a book of essays, and thirteen books of poems, he has been awarded the Pulitzer Prize, the Bollingen Prize, the National Book Award (twice), and, most recently, was inaugural winner of the Rebekah Johnson Bobbitt National Prize for Poetry, awarded by the Library of Congress.

He has lived in interesting times. The house he lived in until he was five ("18 West 11th Street," also the title of a poem on the subject) was blown up by the Weathermen in 1970. His poems of the sixties, sometimes berated then for a lack of surface topicality, are alive and well today. Merrill's work has never lost its uncanny capacity to surprise, change direction, or even (as in "Syrinx") change all directions:

> Nought
> Waste   Eased
> Sought

A poet who works fluently in traditional forms, Merrill has been called, by Harold Bloom, "the Mozart of American poetry," and he has admirers, by now, across a wider political spectrum than most poets living at this fractured moment in the history of poetry. Traditional does not mean conservative, and Merrill has accomplished, at both the highest and the most easygoing moments of his art, "Things unattempted yet in Prose or Rhyme."

James Merrill, © William Ball. Courtesy Knopf.

James Merrill started using a Ouija board in 1953, promptly encountering an engineer "who'd met Goethe"; but the board lit up in the summer of 1955 when JM and DJ contacted a spirit called Ephraim, "A Greek Jew/Born A.D. 8 at XANTHOS" who was killed on Capri, "throttled/By the imperial guard," for having been a lover of Caligula. Ensuing adventures in the other world led to "The Book of Ephraim" in 1976, now the first section of *Sandover*, where one meets Auden and Jane Austen as well as Plato, Alice B. Toklas, God Biology, the angel Michael, and the Architect of Ephesus, to name only a few. Merrill has said of his oracular method, "if it's still yourself you're drawing upon, then that self is much stranger and freer and more farseeing than the one you thought you knew. Of course there are disciplines with grander pedigrees and similar goals. The board happens to be ours." And ours: whether Merrill's other world is beyond or within is left up to the reader, who may find the Ouija board, which consists of no more than twenty-six capital letters, zero, nine digits, and the words YES or NO, to be the perfect metaphor for language. In any case, the poem is a singular success: in *A History of Modern Poetry*, David Perkins calls Merrill "one of the most moving, imaginative, and ambitious of living poets," and says of *Sandover* (excepting works by Hart Crane, T.S. Eliot, and Ezra Pound), "no other long poem written by any American since Whitman can be ranked above Merrill's."

The subject was pursued cross-country for this written interview, by mail, fax machine, and telephone; but since Merrill's manners in his conversational verse and versatile conversation are wonderfully alike, I had no trouble imagining we were sitting down to chat before a quietly uncoiling tape.

thomas bolt The traditional question: what are you working on at the moment?

JAMES MERRILL It's hard to say. My *computer* is working on a memoir of the early 1950s, and I'm simply hanging onto its coattails. Prose was becoming increasingly laborious to write—I could spend a week simply working up my courage to start a three page piece.

The computer changed all that. I am
Kundry to its Klingsor. I rise from
sleep with a shriek to do its bidding

tb Why the early 1950s?

JM It was a turning point. I went to
Europe and stayed for two and a half
years. Not a particularly happy time,
but I must have needed to break with
what I knew.

tb Was something of this period in
your life evoked by the mood of
Francis Tanning at the start of
your novel, *The Seraglio*? What,
precisely, were you breaking with,
and how? Was it a time of experi-
mentation, sort of an internal
Wanderjahre? Were you writing at
the time?

JM I wasn't writing, no. Francis Tanning
wasn't writing either; that's one reason we were both so unhappy. He
seems to represent the person I
might have become if I'd had no talent. Not that I was at all sure of *having* talent, back then. The point, in
any case, was to break with con-
straining ideas of how I should live.
My parents' ideas and my friends',
but also my own.

tb There's more than one way to
break: in the middle of *Water
Street,* in the middle of the poem
"To a Butterfly," the poem's tone,
after a "sincere" beginning, is
shattered by the word *ENOUGH.*
The sentiment, the metaphors so
far developed (and the reader's
yes, isn't that so) are called abruptly to account and rejected.

Goodness, how tired one grows
Just looking through a prism:
Allegory, symbolism.
I've tried, Lord knows,

To keep from seeing double,
Blushed for whenever I did,
Prayed like a boy my cheek be hid
By manly stubble.

The poem proceeds by
encompassing and developing in
its own critical contradiction.
This kind of deflationary reinvig-
oration, the midstream thought-
correction so central to *Water
Street* and nearly everything
you've written since [1962],
seems to have become, in your
work, a consistent basis for
investigation, a way to reconcile
hope and fear, a Romantic's reality and a realist's disgust with the
Romantic. When and how did
you first develop your technique
of abrupt dislocation of tone?

JM The technique probably came to me
from writing dialogue. After my *First
Poems* I wrote a novel and a couple of
plays. They loosened me up some.
Especially the plays. Writing for the
stage, you didn't feel obliged to carry
an idea to its conclusion, to make the
kind of "argument" you try for in the
single unbroken flow of a lyric. If
things got sticky you called in another
voice to interrupt. In a poem the voice
would usually be your own, but from
another part of your self.

tb How important is this tactic (this
way of thinking) to your work?

JM The danger is that the tack becomes a tic, an automatic escape route to the exclusion of all others. At worst it keeps me from facing my true subject or its implications. I try to save it for moments of genuine impatience with my "material"—if that word covers both form and content.

tb A related question: your poems are continually surprising, in part because of a propensity for self-correction, but that only accounts for part of the inventive unpredictability. How important are surprise, astonishment, an awkward brush with the unknown, to your art?

JM All that's part of the silver lining. Life's advantage over art is its genius for the unexpected. Just as new wrinkles in the tradition imply something unforeseeable in the life of a particular artist, so dislocations in a text or a painting can take on the look of shorthand for life itself.

tb Are you *yourself* in poems, a version of your real self, or the famous "I-character" of the old New Criticism? If your lyric "I" is James Merrill (apart from JM of *Sandover*) how does the literary James Merrill differ from the one met outside the books?

JM We shot a film of *Sandover* last summer. I've just spent a couple of weeks in lush Hollywood editing rooms, watching the special effects be added. It's amazing what can be done. Our demonic "bats" now appear in black-and-white negative with a gilt mirror-

frame—so simple and so weird; in close-up their teeth look black and the dark inside of the mouth reads as a kind of terrible snow-white saliva. But that's not what you asked, is it? I'm one of the actors. I play myself; "JM" rather. When it's over Helen Vendler interviews a me who isn't at all like the character in the film.

tb How do you account for the difference?

jm Well . . . Perhaps it's that JM was at no loss for words. The script had been written and he's memorized his lines. *My* lines, if you like. But the person being interviewed has no idea what he's going to say next, so that his face and gestures and tone of voice are all noticeably more ingratiating, more placating—as if begging pardon for all the dumb things he's going to end up saying in a "live" situation where he can't collect himself and work up his answers in solitude.

tb Like *these* answers.

JM Exactly. Well, that's just one instance among dozens, or thousands. It doesn't surprise me, does it you?—that we should be different people in our work. Or should I say the same person at different stages of composure? I mean, after all, if art has any advantage over daily life it's that it allows us to get things *right* for a change.

tb You have a poem, "Santo," in *Late Settings* [1985]; and a one act play in verse, "The Image Maker," in *The Inner Room* [1988], features a Santero. How did you come to be interested in Santería, a major religion in my Lower East Side neighborhood?

JM It wasn't Santería itself that interested me so much as the idea of repainting and renaming the statuette. This seemed so much like what the artist does—recycling his material, trying it another way if it no longer does the trick. That little poem ["Santo"] struck me, after writing it as expressing in miniature the whole self-revising nature of the *Sandover* books where no truth is allowed to rot under a single, final aspect. I mean, in *Sandover* God himself is given a new name [God B, or God Biology] and new attributes; you can't get much more antifundamentalist than that.

tb A remark by Vladimir Nabokov ranking Bely's *Petersburg* with Proust's *Lost Time* and Joyce's *Ulysses* resulted in an immediate English translation and a new readership, as it was probably calculated to do. Assuming poems are allowed, anymore, to be great (no capital G, but also without quotation marks), what great poems of the twentieth century are we missing out on?

JM Auden's "The Sea and the Mirror" and/or "For the Time Being." These two long poems were the first Auden that I read with full appreciation. Along with everything else, they're wonderful showcases for forms and tones. "Artorius" by John Heath-Stubbs. Everything he does has distinction. This is an especially rich and nutty affair based on Arthurian leg-

end. One section is a little Noh play in which a wandering scholar meets Guinevere's ghost. John Hollander's *Visions from the Ramble* and *Aspects of Espionage*—these are marvels of vision and wit. The former's rich, nostalgic frescoes depict the shaping years of a New York poet. The latter shows him irrevocably committed to his codes and fellow agents, working in secret for the mother tongue. "In and Out" and "Academic Festival Overtures" by Daryl Hine. Both autobiographical, both dealing poignantly and hilariously with early sexual stirrings, both triumphant vindications of meter. I should probably mention "The Return" by Frederick Turner; Irving Feldman's "All of Us Here," Alfred Corn's "Notes from a Child of Paradise"; Gjertrud Schnackenberg's "The Lamplit Answer"; Richard Kenney's "The Hours of the Day" and "Orrery"—where to stop? Shall I embarrass you by including "The Way Out of the Wood" by Thomas Bolt?

tb I'm beyond embarrassment, but off to the bookstore. What poem of *yours* deserves closer attention, or seems to have fallen through the cracks?

JM I can tell you one poem I wish *would* fall through the cracks. It's called "Kite Poem," and no anthology for young readers would seem complete without it. So many anthologists do their work by culling from previous anthologies rather than the poet's actual books. When I was a young firebrand of forty I implied as much in a note to a professor somewhere, who'd asked for permission to use "Kite Poem" in his forthcoming textbook. It really touched a nerve. He wrote back a letter beginning, in effect, "Why you little shit . . ." Elizabeth Bishop had the same problem with "The Fish." It was made to seem at times like the only poem she'd ever written. Of course it's a hundred times better than "Kite Poem." One Christmas I received a book all about the zoology of fish. It was inscribed to me from Elizabeth Fishop.

tb   Very nice. Was Elizabeth Bishop an influence as well as a friend and a colleague?

JM   Oh goodness yes. I should have added her to my list of instructors in the art of breaking. Her way of interrupting herself—but much more. Her natural, completely unaffected intelligence. Her love of the trivial: birdcages, paper flowers. The human scale of her work, so refreshing next to the modernist "giants" like Pound, or her friend Robert Lowell. The lucid, intimate tone of voice. She set standards for me as no other contemporary did. I don't always follow them but I can never lose sight of them.

tb   Who, Proust or Cavafy, is the slightly larger inspiration? Why?

JM   Proust more than Cavafy. I love Cavafy. I've learned a lot from him as a poet: his desert-dry tone, his mirage-like technical effects—something one would never guess from his translators. But he hasn't shaped my way of seeing to the degree that Proust has. For one thing, Cavafy is a miniaturist; for

another, he writes without metaphor. I mean it! Virtually nowhere in his work will you find metaphor or simile. He's John the Baptist eating locusts in the desert, far from any "Jordan" of metaphor. Whereas in Proust that water table is all but flush with the surface of the page.

tb   Do *you* ever write entirely without metaphor? How important is metaphor to poetry; and what do you think of the flat, photorealist ametaphoric verse that's been popular the past decade or so?

JM   A lot of metaphor must be in the beholder's eye. My kind of mind is so used to "seeing double" that it finds unwelcome subtexts in an instruction manual. To put it too bluntly, I think metaphor *is* poetry; and if I open to a poem without any, I can't help trying to see what's there in a faintly metaphorical or symbolic light. It's the way I'd look at a photograph, if it comes to that. How else could a picture be worth a thousand words? A psychiatrist friend calls the creative temperament Janusian—after Janus, whose nature is to look both ways. I thought everybody was like that but he said no, that for him, the implications of phrases like a "dark white" or a "burning cold"—which are mother's milk to me—left him feeling, you know, seasick.

tb   Speaking of metaphor, my candidate for the greatest American poet of the nineteenth century is Emily Dickinson—what do you think?

JM   Hear, hear! I mean that. She brings off

so much of it through puns, rhyme, cadence—things only the ear discovers.

tb Who is A. H. Clarendon, the authority you cite in the midst of "The Thousand and Second Night"?

JM A saintly human being and a superb hand at bridge.

tb Duplicate?

JM You got it.

tb Do you feel any kinship with William Blake? Are you on the side of wild prophecy, or careful consideration, or do you moderate between the two?

JM I'm on the side of careful consideration. I'm suspicious of the wild, the grandiose, the larger-than-life. Taking up all that emotional space. I love the side of Blake that saw eternity in a grain of sand. What an inspired metaphor! So much better than "fear in a handful of red dust." (Wait, though, do you hear, in the Eliot? "Dead rust . . .?") Even in the prophetic books—not that I've read them—there'll be ravishing details that show Blake's early love of Pope. Of course *Sandover* simply swarms with "wild prophecy," ideas, everything I've tried to avoid in my work, or think myself incapable of. It's the unconscious—personal or collective—taking its revenge.

tb The word *red* is not in the original. But a poet's mismemory is often revealing . . . Now, one of your biggest fans I know is a sewer worker who has a band in which he plays electric guitar.

JM Hmm. . . . Clean him up and bring him to tea?

tb He's quite clean; he'd be delighted. But transitionally speaking, one wonderful thing about good poetry is the surprising broadness of its appeal. Yet some people appear to want to communicate only in shorthand with a cozy group of folks with shared political or aesthetic assumptions. Is there a kind of discipline that reaches over the obvious problems or disaffection, miscommunication, plain disagreement? What's good and bad about "the tendency toward progressive decentralization in contemporary poetry?" There used to be two or three camps, and now there are, seemingly, hundreds.

JM To me, what unifies or centralizes all those different camps—and might conceivably discipline them, too, if they gave it a chance—would be the past. The past they derive from whether they know it or not, as well as the past they'll have become in five or ten years. That's all it takes nowadays. Am I wrong?

One gets the sense of tribe after tribe of poets who eat—*read*, rather, only their still-living kinsmen. Even the cannibal who devours his enemy has sounder instincts. I don't mean that you have to have the Grand Tradition of World Poetry at your fingertips; just that there's more to learn from an ancestor like Byron or Herbert than from your buddy in the workshop who reads Neruda in English.

What's good about this situation? It siphons off into harmless backwaters hundreds, perhaps thousands, of young people whom poetry will fulfill and civilize without their really amounting to much. The few of them who do will have had a great deal of provincialism to overcome, a diet of Wonder Bread and Coke. A new regime will make them stronger, more original, more resolute. Like a fat child (I was one) who knows better than ever to let *that* happen again.

tb Are you saying that awareness of past literature is enough to make what we write more worth reading?

JM Oh God, no, is that what I—strike it from the record! I just mean I wish people read more widely and wrote less narrowly.

tb I think everyone could agree with that—why miss out on anything? You've given us batwinged angels with glowing eyes, and transmutations to the peacock form; please describe your muse.

JM You've seen her described at some length in *Sandover*.

tb Right, wow, yes, all nine muses appear.

JM No, no, not a bit, that's just vaudeville. The poem's real muse is Maria—"Muse of my off-days," I called her in real life. Mild, self-mocking, worldly; a slow gardener; dressed in black to match her humor; private, attentive, polylingual. Then we get a more unnerving muse in Nature, who turns out to be a version of Graves' Triple Goddess; her other names are Psyche and Chaos. *She* can appear in

any guise she fancies. Her characteristics—the benign ones—are boundless autocratic energy, lack of humor, and uncommon charm. In part to defuse or domesticate her, I pictured her to myself as the actress Ina Claire: bobbed blonde hair, big blue eyes, dressed in white with black ribbons, for a Chekhovian house-party.

tb Speaking of "The Book of a Thousand and One Evenings Spent/ With David Jackson at the Ouija Board/ In Touch with Ephraim Our Familiar Spirit" . . . in some incidental and some intrinsic ways, *The Changing Light at Sandover* is an apotheosis of homosexuality.

Refreshingly, certainly, compared to the traditional aposiopesis of homosexuality.

JM My all these Greek words! Perhaps one or two of our readers are wondering what that second one means.

tb Aposiopesis means—but I blush to tell. It means leaving an expression of any thought suddenly and resoundingly incomplete, having become flustered, or tripped over the social obstacle of unmentionability. A last minute self-repression, ending in embarrassed silence.

JM Very nice.

tb In a well-known passage of the "Mirabell" section, a bat still named (numbered?) 741 proclaims, as he is ("*FILLD/ WITH IS IT MANNERS?*") changing into the peacock Mirabell:

LOVE OF ONE MAN FOR ANOTHER OR LOVE BETWEEN WOMEN
IS A NEW DEVELOPMENT OF THE PAST 4000 YEARS
ENCOURAGING SUCH MIND VALUES AS PRODUCE THE BLOSSOMS
OF POETRY & MUSIC, THOSE 2 PRINCIPAL LIGHTS OF
GOD BIOLOGY.
            [. . . .]
FOR EVER SINCE THEIR SHAPING OF THE ORIGINAL CLAY
& THE PLUCKING OF THE APE (OR THE APPLE) FROM ITS TREE
WE HAVE HAD AN IRRESISTIBLE FORCE TO DEAL WITH: MIND.
UNTIL THEN ALL HAD BEEN INSTINCTIVE NATURE A CHAOS
LIKE FALLEN TREES IN THE EMPTY FOREST NO ONE TO HEAR,
OR AUTUMN'S UNHATCHED EGG NO ONE TO REMEMBER & MOURN.
NOW MIND IN ITS PURE FORM IS A NONSEXUAL PASSION
OR A UNISEXUAL ONE PRODUCING ONLY LIGHT.
FEW PAINTERS OR SCULPTORS CAN ENTER THIS LIFE OF THE MIND.
THEY (LIKE ALL SO-CALLD NORMAL LOVERS) MUST PRODUCE AT LAST
BODIES THEY DO NOT EXIST FOR ANY OTHER PURPOSE

This passage is followed instantly by the disclaimer "Come now, admit that certain very great / Poets and musicians have been straight." but one must feel your double mind is at work. The breeder/reader is perhaps uneasy, but the twentieth century hasn't been particularly easy on readers of any stripe. And of course the real slur here is on painters, though you have written admiringly of Corot. Comments?

JM I always winced at that put-down of painting. We get a defense of painting in a later volume, but it doesn't amount to much. A kind word for Chardin and Sesshu . . .

There's a vast amount of questionable dogma in *Sandover*. Remember that the speaker of this passage is demonic. Still, childlessness gets praised by just about all the characters in the poem; yet its high point,

for me, is when that baby—Robert Morse's new incarnation—gets born in the "Coda." Nature herself coos and simpers over it. Of course that particular baby has been programmed to become a great musician, which sugars the pill—sorry, wrong metaphor. I wonder, by the way, where they get the idea that homosexuals aren't breeders. I know quite a few who are.

As for any apotheosis of homosexuality, in a cosmos as perpetually self-revising as *Sandover*'s, this or that idea can easily be raised to the highest power, then demoted when it's no longer of use. I'm guardedly grateful for this emphasis within the poem. We have so few texts of really high quality—Shakespeare's Sonnets, some Platonic dialogues, some of Gertrude Stein, Oscar Wilde's criticism—for gay readers to find themselves in. Without, I mean, the obligatory pity and terror of say, *Death in Venice.*

tb Your poems are included in various anthologies, everything from *The Contemporary American Poets: American Poetry Since 1940* to the more recent *Gay and Lesbian Poetry in Our Time.* Besides satisfying curiosity as to which poets are what and come from where—I never knew that poet was American!—how useful are such categorical breakdowns? In combining the two, I don't mean to infer (though some have) that one's sexuality is a nation-state. But in a time when we who might prefer to read (without hunting in a hundred crannies?) all the good poetry we can, feel absurdly cut off from Australian, Jamaican, Israeli, English, Irish, Scottish, and even Canadian poetry written in this language—not to mention all the many American groups a little or a lot off the meandering mainstream—have anthologies become overspecific?

JM This goes back to what we were saying about all the different camps. I hate this taxonomic bias. So did Elizabeth Bishop. She wouldn't even allow her work to appear in a women's anthology. Until recently men and women could read and admire each other's work. Now I know a woman poet who doesn't allow men's and women's books in the same room. It's the Salem witchhunt with the genders reversed!

tb If books rubbing up against each other spawn Literary Criticism,

keeping them apart might not be such a bad idea. But back to categories: what special strengths come to your work as a result of your being an American, or being gay?

JM The forms I use came originally from Europe. Being American allows me to question them, to adapt them freely and without guilt to my own needs. The attitudes I live by were no doubt first instilled by my parents, but being gay I can turn them inside out, if I like, and having grown up and seen how humanly fallible my parents were I can—well, you see what I'm saying. At sixty-five I'm no longer a national or a sexual being so much as whoever I've become over the years. When I go abroad, or join a dinner party of husbands and wives, I feel like a well-disposed ambassador from the other side; we make one another feel worldly and tolerant. Most of the time, that is. Get me caught in a demonstration and who starts shouting "I'm Canadian!" In six languages.

tb What kind of anthology would you find most meaningful?

JM Aside from the multi-regional ones you propose, I'd go for the old-fashioned kind, like Untermeyer's or Oscar Williams's. Kimon Friar and John Brinnin did a marvelous one in 1951, full of new criticism explications, and including passages from *Finnegans Wake* and *Nightwood.* Those were the good old days when literary politics were literary rather than political or sexual. For example, Oscar Williams in person was shall we say rather a creep. Be that as it may,

Kimon and John decided to include a couple of his poems; you can be a creep and still write well. But do you know what poor insecure Mr. Williams did? He had his publisher ask for a letter from the anthologists, saying that they weren't including his poems in order to hold them up to ridicule. It breaks the heart.

tb What's the importance of music to your work? Whose and how?

JM When I was fourteen or fifteen opera was my *éducation sentimentale*. It gave form to the wildest emotions; I tried them on, one after another, posturing in front of the phonograph. As I grew older I'd find some of my technical problems solved by reference to a Beethoven piano sonata, a Berlioz song. I wrote "variations" on the model of Mozart's *A Major Sonata* or Beethoven's *Opus 34*. The very distancing helps, letting your concerns ricochet off another medium. You learn about tempo and tone, the uses of dissonance, modulation into a new key. I'm not sure how this works but it often does.

tb What's most fun about poetry?

JM To engage as much of the self as possible . . . and then to forget the self— is that fun? I think so. Innocent fun. I'd like to stress the innocence. Hours go by and nobody's been harmed. The neighbors don't even know you're at home.

bell hooks   lawrence chua

BOMB #48, Summer 1994

Love takes us to places we might not ordinarily go. Ask anyone who's engaged the work of bell hooks. Her fearless inquiries and passionate provocations have left us questioning the once familiar terrain of cultural identity while simultaneously affirming the complexity of our own lived experiences. In her many books of critical writing, including *Black Looks*, *Yearning*, *Breaking Bread: Insurgent Black Intellectual Life* (with Cornel West) and the forthcoming *Outlaw Culture*; her self-help book, *Sisters of the Yam*; her recent collection of poetry, *A Woman's Mourning Song*, her artistic collaborations and her many public presentations, hooks has hit raw nerves, delving into the possibilities of culture as a place of resistance to white supremacy, capitalism and patriarchy. While most critical theorists speak about popular culture from the lofty perches of the academy, hooks has always insinuated herself in the fray. She is one of America's most indispensable and independent thinkers.

lawrence chua   Recently, you were at a conference on black cinema where Stanley Crouch suggested that artists like Snoop Doggy Dogg should be exterminated. How did you respond?

bell hooks   While it's crucial to critique the sexism and the misogyny of rappers like Snoop Doggy Dogg, it is essential for everyone to remember that they are not only more complex than the way they represent themselves, they're more complex than the way white society represents them as

well. This notion that Snoop Doggy Dogg defines himself "as he really is" is something I reject. He clearly defines himself with a persona that works in cultural production in this society. The most discouraging aspect of that conference for me was this insistence on liberal individualism, as though people's acts are disconnected from larger structures and larger forces of representation. Even Stanley Crouch wasn't responding to my points. He was actually playing to those larger, mainstream cultural

bell hooks, © Donna Dietrich. Courtesy Henry Holt and Company.

forces that reward him for saying really negative things about rap. I don't believe it when people like Stanley Crouch say they are really concerned about misogyny. One can certainly read his essay on Toni Morrison and see incredible examples of virulent sexism and misogyny. I saw a continuum between the violence of a Snoop Doggy Dogg and the violence of a Stanley Crouch, and I didn't really see them as being separate and distinct entities. At the conference, I confessed that I have really violent impulses, that sometimes listening to some panels I had wanted to come out and shoot people. The audience laughed, but I wasn't being funny, and I wasn't saying it to be cute or exhibitionist. I was acknowledging that the violent impulses don't just exist out there in black youth or in the underclass, but that they reside in people like myself as well—people who have our Ph.D.'s and our good jobs. But that doesn't mean that my life is not tormented by rageful or irrational, violent impulses. It does mean that instead of shooting people, I go home and write a critique. My irrational impulse to want to kill people who bore me or whose ideas are not very complex clearly has to do with an exaggerated response to situations where I feel powerless. I think black people, across class, have many moments in our lives when we feel utterly powerless to change the direction of situations. And we don't deal with this collectively, because we're so in denial about it. It is significant that the urge to exterminate was aroused

by a moral standpoint wherein vulgarity must be dissed. This has a lot to do with censorship. I'm not talking about mainstream censorship. I'm talking about groups that claim to have progressive agendas, but also have practices of censorship, that involve their wanting to check people around crossing boundaries that "don't make our movements look good." There is a whole way of structuring conferences so that they end up being these celebratory events where a certain censorship takes place in the interest of maintaining unity. I see that as part of the colonizing mentality that says, "In case white people are looking, we need to present ourselves as this unified nation so we can't have these all-out dialectical exchanges where we show our differences." We need multiple voices that mirror our multiple subjectivities. There's a cognitive dissonance between what is really being said by cultural critics—we're into border crossing, and cultural hybridity—and yet, when we come together, we still mirror the model of a unitary voice.

lc How is your own work challenging those boundaries? When we had lunch a few months ago, you were about to go on a TV talk show. You said you were doing this because you weren't reaching the audience you needed to start reaching.

bh I went on the Ricky Lake show and it was a disaster. But it was a great experience. There are academics who do work on popular culture, but who really just do a lot of theoretical talking about popular culture and don't actually enter those spaces that are much more full of contradictions, hostilities, and tensions. I heard those black folks in the audience at the Ricky Lake show saying, "We don't agree with Doctor hooks. We're not even going to call her Doctor. She doesn't even know what she's talking about." I felt seriously assaulted, but at the same time, this was a different rage experience than sitting at home writing my cool article on the discourse of talk shows. To actually go there, and to participate, and see, and walk off the TV set because the politics of what was happening there were very disturbing to me. They had told us that there would be a "special guest" but they hadn't said that it would be this Nazi woman. But I wanted to go on that show because Ricky Lake has an incredible number of black viewers between the ages of sixteen and twenty-five, and those are exactly the people who are not in women's studies classes, or in cool cultural studies classes where they're learning about a Cornel West or a bell hooks. I used a quote by Snoop Doggy Dogg at the NYU conference on black cinema, that really meant a lot to me. He said, "I don't rap. I just talk. I want to be able to relax and conversate with my people." Are we, cultural workers situated in the academy, developing a jargon about cultural production that does not allow us to "conversate and cross" these very borders that we're talking about how cool it would be to cross? If we don't find a way to "con-

versate," all we're ever talking about is that those of us who have certain forms of class privilege can enter the low-down and dirty spaces and take what we want to get out of those spaces, and take our asses right back home. That is really crucial for the future of cultural criticism in the United States, for the future of magazines like *BOMB*, and the other kinds of magazines that many of us enjoy: *Vibe, Details*. How much are we "conversating"?

lc How does your own work accommodate that kind of "conversating"?

bh I am willing to debase myself in whichever way possible, and be treated like shit as I was on the Ricky Lake Show. We can't minimize that because it's a very different experience from lecturing at places like Yale and Harvard where crowds of people are bowing down and saying, "We're not worthy, we're not worthy," than to be among a whole crowd of young people waiting to get in to this show and talk, who could give a fuck about bell hooks. Or to be in Flint, Michigan, talking to a hundred fifth graders, who have no idea what I'm about, and to have to come up with a language that can cross those borders effectively. The point is not just to be some sort of sterile role model who stands up and gives a canned talk. One of the things that I've been critiqued a lot about is the level of confession in my work and my public "performances." If you read my early work, there's very little attention to the details of my life, very little personal stuff. One of the things that I found, as I tried to cross boundaries, was that I had to give people something that allowed them to identify with what I was saying, and not just offer some abstract idea that might not have any relevance to their lives. That is all about the function of story. When those little fifth graders had question-and-answer, the first thing they wanted to know was, "How much money do you make?" Now, these fifth graders are coming out of one of the most economically depressed states in this country. Most of their parents work in the auto industry. How much money you make is more crucial to them than the relationship between feminism and Marxism. But to answer that question honestly and openly can be a way to then talk about feminism and the structure of capitalism. In fact, we went from how much money I made to, "Did you guys know how much on the average women make?" People were really shocked, because they so believe in the myth of democracy, they all thought women receive equal pay for equal work. Crossing borders means that at times I share things that I don't want to share. But if you really see yourself as a worker for freedom, then the challenge is also on you to sacrifice whatever notions of privacy that many of us would want to hold onto, especially if we are clinging to bourgeois models of self and identity. These fifth graders wanted to understand book production, because I know that they have parents who are saying, "You

don't want to be a writer, writers don't make anything. If you work in the plant this is what is available to you." Class is the most uncool topic in cultural studies in the United States. It's easier to look at the black identity of the Hughes brothers who made *Menace II Society*, than to acknowledge the class positionality of these young men and to talk about how it may have shaped their opinion. Maybe they find a gangsta in the 'hood really glamorous because it's not the world that they emerged from. That's a class critique that gets submerged under an evocation of racial solidarity, or racial intervention. These young black men are intervening in the Hollywood apparatus in some ways by their very presence, by the racial images they create. Whereas, if we look at class, we don't see intervention in Hollywood. We actually see a reproduction of a certain relation to the working class and the poor. Hollywood has always had visions of the working class and poor, cross-race, created by people who often are mired in contempt and fantasy, and/or voyeuristic fantasy about what those class realities are really like.

lc Your last book, *Sisters of the Yam*, speaks to and across many of those class borders. It was conceived of as a self-help book. How difficult was it to write a book that was not going to be sold as an academic text?

bh It was exciting for me to write *Sisters of the Yam* and try to find a more vernacular way to talk about certain things. It's also exciting to get a response from that. People would be shocked by the number of everyday people who take the time to write me a letter about a book. It wouldn't matter what kind of books I was writing, if I didn't get the feedback from communities of readers who let me know that the books are actually working. That fills me with a certain joy. To think of certain ways of writing as activism is crucial. What does it matter if we write eloquently about decolonization if it's just white privileged kids reading our eloquent theory about it? Masses of black people suffer from internalized racism, our intellectual work will never impact on their lives if we do not move it out of the academy. That's why I think mass media is so important. Popular magazines and television have to be seen as central vehicles for the dissemination of intellectual thought. We are looking at a culture where millions of people don't read or write. If I want to get the message out there I have to use some other format. I do a lot more radio than I would like to do because it still has a place in the lives of many working-class people in our society. It amazes me.

lc There are some obvious limitations to personalizing theoretical writing. How do you debate the theoretical element of a sentence that begins with "As a twenty-seven-year-old Malaysian house queen" without taking on the identity of the person who is saying it?

bh Since we live in a cultural climate,

especially in the academy where the realm of the personal is devalued, when you use that standpoint it may lead listeners to mishear. That voice may be very complex but people actually may not hear the complexity. I gave this talk framed around the idea of "love takes me to places I would ordinarily not go." I raised the whole question of love in a very psychoanalytical way, framing the discussion around notions of recognition and mirroring. I was really sad when so many people came up to me to say, "We love you," because they'd missed the point. When you are a woman and you use a confessional narrative, people tend to think there is not some more complex structure of thinking or philosophy behind that narrative. I needed to bring some of that background thinking more to the fore, otherwise, it failed. But even if it failed to do as much as I wanted it to, it does not devalue the courage of trying to bring the voice of lived experience and confessional witnessing into our intellectual processing in a way that does not reduplicate that whole pattern of estrangement from self and ideas. I am passionate about ideas. They're not just the stuff of spectatorship and entertainment to me. They're a lifeblood, and that's what makes the intellectual process so radically different from the academic process. Part of the challenge for insurgent intellectuals, particularly those of us who are artists in this society, is to pull back from academe, actually, and academic settings, precisely to break this notion that has become so popular in the culture, that the two experiences are one.

lc I was curious how your own critical language is developing, with that strategy in mind.

bh I've been trying to use different languages for different settings, and it's hard. One of the things I'm trying to do is break with the traditional essay format, which has been an exhilarating and exciting format for me. But it also takes time. I'd like to do work that is more mixed media and pastiche. But when you want to make a shift, then you come up against an industry that doesn't want you to because they've already got a proven product. This has been very harmful to African American writers in general. I am constantly working to shift my voice and to try to use it differently. In my poetry writing, for example, I use a voice that tends to be much more abstract than the voice of my writing. A lot of people, when I first tried to get my poems published, said, "There's nothing black about these poems." Damn, how often do you have to prove that you're black? It's not enough that I'm a black woman writing these poems, but there has to be something in the language that tips off the reader, that you are reading something by a black woman writer. There's this constant struggle to actually have a lived practice that really mirrors this theoretical bullshit about hybridity and polyphonic voices. I've always cursed like a sailor. I learned how to curse from my grandmother. I've always had a certain kind of street

language that has been essential to how I've defined myself. But, it's a language that I keep under wraps. In certain settings, you can let that language out, but if you let it out in this other setting, you'll get checked immediately. I'm putting a lot of pressure on myself to "come out of the closet," that great metaphor for everything these days, in the sense of trying to speak certain languages in locations where I didn't speak them because I tried to conform to the dictates of those locations. What is border crossing, if in every setting you simply scan the place and figure out the appropriate rules and abide by them? That ends up sounding much more like social fascism than any rigorous transgression.

lc In *Yearning*, that "street language" is often set apart from your theorizing by quotation marks, while in *Black Looks* and *Sisters of the Yam* it's a more organic component of the syntax. Have editors become more receptive to that linguistic transgression?

bh I went through this period where I would try to use more street language and it would all come back to me, completely edited back to standard English. These few months that I've been living in New York, I've really been overwhelmed by the degree to which there is no racial integration in publishing in our society. I'm awed by the lack, not just of the concrete visible presence of people of color, but also the failure to have progressive white people. We should be able to have spaces in this society where people of color are not present, but where antiracist perspectives will inform how things are organized and what takes place. No wonder the wheel has to be invented again, and again, and again. We're being told by the publishing world that our major buying audience is a white audience. The presumption is of an unenlightened white audience, and when everything you write should be pitched to that audience, it becomes a really troubling question of what voice you use, and what space you can occupy. We're not just talking about the straight publishing world, we're talking about those vehicles in our culture that claim to represent some kind of alternative. That says that we have a lot of work to do to truly create a culture of resistance, that's not just occupied by people of color individually knocking on the door for change, but that's really occupied by lots of people who see the necessity for having a more complex intellectual artistic life in this culture.

lc **Debates around representation have focused almost exclusively on who is in the frame, as if it were separate from how the narrative unfolds. That's made it difficult for black writers whose work refuses that separation between truth and beauty to publish.**

bh If your perspective isn't "I'm negating blackness, in the interest of writing more experimentally," but, "I'm affirming blackness and I still want to write experimentally," that's when you have trouble selling your product. The

question I'm asked most often about my writing is: Who is the perceived audience? There's this sense that if you really want to have that crossover audience, you've got to simplify, you've got to translate, you've got to make everything clear. But we know that there are a lot of interesting books by white writers that don't simplify, that don't make everything clear, and people presume that they will have an audience. There's a myth about artistic freedom, that it resides with the individual writer, and not that artistic freedom has to be mirrored in the publishing practices of a culture, or when you're talking about art, the practices of galleries and museums. It cannot be something that becomes a cultural norm simply by individual artists insisting that their work is an expression of artistic freedom. Even though so many of us can name white supremacy, we go on to express shock and naive surprise that things are done the way they are or that our views aren't represented. To some extent, one's views do have an opportunity of being represented if you dare to put forth some of the labor. I feel like I labor for things. A lot of times it is a sacrifice. I have this deep feeling that the meaning of sacrifice has been really lost in this culture. When I look back at the civil rights struggle, I am awed by people's willingness to sacrifice personal comfort and well-being to make some changes. What's sad is that the significance of sacrifice seems to be solely embedded in religion in our society, because religion has not had the force for young people that it had twenty years ago. Look at Malcolm X. Everyone who is pimping him for their own opportunistic gains doesn't talk about the fact that this man lived in relative poverty as he tried to spread his mission. How many of us are committed to living on the edge in that way? I'm certainly not. I'm working hard not to have to live that way, even as I want to hold to the principle of sacrifice and be ready when the moment comes to do what needs to be done to end domination.

lc As you said, the idea of sacrifice is so caught up in religious belief, there is a tendency to oversimplify it. How do you strategize something like sacrifice?

bh Part of why so many of us came out of radical sixties politics and jumped into Eastern religion was because, more than Christianity, it evoked a balance. How do you balance that commitment to social change where you don't just burn out and give yourself over to an almost negative ethic of sacrifice? How do you create inner harmony and balance that allows you to sacrifice when necessary and to withhold when necessary? I can remember how deeply affected I was by the Buddhist nun in Vietnam who set herself on fire in the interest of protesting the war. How far do we go and what do we give? I still find religion to be the place that tempers my spirit. A friend and I have battled around the whole question, "Are there other locations where these values of moral discipline, integrity and sacri-

fice can be taught?" We can teach those ethics to young children without teaching them religion, but it's hard to know how to bring an ethical dimension into political work and artistic practice in a culture that is so obscenely hedonistic. That's why people like me might not fall back on organized religion but fall back on the construction of more private spiritual practice that enables us to think about issues like sacrifice and service. Growing up, we were taught to believe we existed to service the cause of racial upliftment and ending white supremacy. The young blacks that I teach today are into that kind of liberalism that says, "I'm mainly here to service myself first and if I want to join some radical cause I can." For many years I wouldn't have been able to even think of improving without heightening the freedom and wellbeing of my community. It really was entering white institutions of higher learning that disrupted that vision of living to serve the community and the cause of racial upliftment. Where is liberal individualism most taught, but in academic institutions? They exist to produce the privileged classes. To make them come into being it's very important to have people repudiate any ethic of communalism in favor of privatized thinking.

lc I wonder how much of that ethic of communalism comes from being part of a rural, or even a suburban, community. Do you think your rural background has informed a lot of your critical practice?

bh Kentucky is very feudal in a lot of ways. Coming from there carries some of the negative aspects of a feudal culture, but it was a world that really did believe in certain values. The poor are consistently represented in this culture's mass media as having no values or ethics, yet where I grew up there was no correlation between poverty and lack of integrity. Poor, backwoods Kentucky folk, my people had a relationship to loyalty and honor, a whole ethical dimension that was completely divorced from materiality. I find it amazing that across race and class, we live in a country that's very determined by geographic location. We have very few voices that come to us from rural experience in America. The educated people from those regions actually learn to translate away from our vernacular cultures in the interest of getting some play and consideration in the larger public world. I was talking to my dad, who's in his mid-seventies and is doing poorly. He was going on about how he worked for thirty some years and was never absent from his job. One of the things that I tell my dad all the time is that the discipline I have as a writer is not anything that I learned at Stanford University. I got it from this working-class background where disciplined work was really valued. My dad kept using the phrase, "marvelously blessed." To think that a black man working in the South at a "menial job" would reflect back on that experience and declare that he feels marvelously blessed that he was not absent from his job in thirty some years . . . I was touched. He was speaking in the vernacular of our region and I thought about how much I'd lost that capacity because I'm not there enough. There is a beauty to vernacular speech and culture in America. Mass media is one of the forces that aggressively works to wipe out that cultural and regional specificity.

lc When I came in this afternoon, we were talking about the differences between black British thought and black American thought. How do you think these issues are played out across the Atlantic? Why has black Britain been able to produce the kind of radical cultural work and theory that we here in America haven't?

bh Because the material rewards are not there in British culture, there's less of a temptation to sell out in the same way. I'm not acting like I think black British people have some kind of integrity that is different. But the integrity is challenged here by the existence of a structure of reward. I feel more linked to black British thinkers right now, because a lot of the choices that I make in what I write and how I write actually prevent me from reaping those rewards. I'm still struggling . . . politically, morally, and ethically to be an independent thinker. There is this fear of radical openness that's making black social and critical thought infinitely more homogeneous than we should ever want it to be. Why do we have to be threatened by the notion of a different voice or a dissenting voice? I feel this a lot lately around issues of censorship and what I want to be able to talk about in the future. I really want to write in a complex way about black sexuality and I feel that there's tremendous resistance to a discussion of black sexuality that does not reproduce certain norms. In terms of representation, we are perhaps portrayed as the most oversexed group in this society. How has that affected our actual sex lives? Do we exist in a culture where nothing that we can do sexually is equal to the hype? We have uncovered work that suggests Martin Luther King fucked all the time, but we can't find one article that would talk about what the place of sexuality was in his life. To what extent did the enormous sacrifices that he made as a public persona influence his compulsive sexual behavior? Did we see any public discourse about whether Malcolm X had or did not have homosexual relations? If this is our shining black prince, our manhood, does this open up the possibility for a revolution in how we think about black masculinity? Nor do we have a lot of complex writing about black resistance to racism and our simultaneous embrace of American national identity, which we clearly saw exposed during the Gulf War. I think the issues of nationhood are much more central to black folk in Europe because they are such minorities in the countries that they live in and they haven't had the legacies of resistance struggle that we have here. When people evoke Martin Luther King's "I have a dream," they completely erase that radical critique that is present in sermons and speeches

like "A Testament of Hope," wherein he suggests we must move beyond a national identity to a profound critique of imperialism and global militarism. That's the Martin Luther King that will not be taught to every little school kid.

lc You've often juxtaposed the trope of nation and family with the more fluid notion of community.

bh It suggests something that can be made and remade wherever you might be. Communities of resistance suggest something that has to be explained, while nation and family already conjure up specific kinds of images and forms of bonding for people. There's a tremendous mounting fascism in this culture and it's very scary to see it finding such presence in expression of African American life. Basically the educated body of black people who are cultural workers, writers, artists, musicians, et cetera, tend to be deeply invested in bourgeois values on all levels. People evoke jazz as expressive of these far reaching radical oppositions to norms, but they really haven't been carried over in habits of daily life. Those very jazz musicians, particularly the men who were so groundbreaking in their musical crossing of boundaries, tended to be very narrow in their thinking about gender and patriarchy. Miles Davis is such a good example of that because he vocalized his reactionary perspectives on gender. No one talks about the fact that in all these cases of sexual aggression with black public figures, like Tupac Shakur, the woman has been black.

The cultural response would be very different to these events if the women were white. Black men do victimize black women but that victimization is coded as a response to racism, and not as: Let's talk about racism and what black men get from patriarchy. What do black men get through this rhetoric of nation, in terms of their power in domestic space? That's not a discourse that white culture is fascinated with, because they don't give a fuck about what happens in black domestic space.

lc You've talked about how figures like Tupac Shakur and Ice Cube disrupt essential notions of black masculinity. Your understanding of gangsta rap is very different from the dominant feminist line.

bh People presume that because I'm a feminist thinker they know I'm gonna trash rap, especially gangsta rap. I can challenge the sexism and misogyny of it, but I can embrace the rage that is implicit in it and the sense of powerlessness that undergirds it. It is such a challenge to be able to see that you cannot identify with something about individuals and still have parts of them that you might embrace and engage. When I interviewed Ice Cube, he was insisting on the power of the black father in the home. I was yelling, "Are you really trying to tell me that if you have unloving black fathers in the home, we're going to have a generation of healthy kids?" Finally he acknowledged that just having a father present who's not caring is really not going to produce some

healthy children. That's the kind of exchange that we should be trying to bring to the floor and not these simplistic representations of sexism and misogyny. It's so hard because these men both disrupt and reinscribe at the same time. One has to be vigilant in your response but that means you have to be engaged and I think that so much cultural criticism is nonparticipatory. The cultural critic stands so much at a distance from what he or she writes about. That distance is always dangerous in that it has the possibility of reinscribing the status quo, co-opting and appropriating in the interest of making the status quo appear more chic, more open than it finally ever really is.

lc I wonder also how you see the function of groups like The Disposable Heroes of Hiphoprisy, whose work on very obvious levels challenges that kind of status quo, and yet has been met with so much resistance in terms of the marketplace.

bh I follow their work and like it and other groups like Arrested Development. I interviewed Speech from Arrested Development and I talked to a lot of young black women about him. They said, "Yeah, but after awhile their music is just boring." Then I think we do get into the tension around notions of funkiness and getting down and being down. A perpetual tension for any of us who engage in any kind of revolutionary political visions of transformation is how do we keep the funk? We never talk about what if people aren't drawn by the sexism and the misogyny, but are instead drawn by a sense of recklessness, a willingness to transcend limits and to call out shit graphically. Yet we in our progressive visions don't account for those yearnings to be on the edge. I felt that lust when I was young and I feel it now. How can we have some models of radicalism that also incorporate what it is to transgress in a manner that is expressive, colorful, exciting, and even dangerous? What allows me to hold to whatever sweetness I may find in a word like "bitch," that doesn't translate into some subjugation of women? One of the things that I believe is that this kind of theory cannot be done in the same old privatized way. It has to emerge from collaborative exchange, from border-crossing of an Ice Cube and a bell hooks trying to jam it out together and jamming one another. Or for me saying to Cornel West, "I'm sorry Cornel, young black men are not going to say, 'Gee, I really want to look like that guy in those three piece suits.'" [*laughter*] That's not saying that we shouldn't be able to embrace those suits as some sign of cool, but the fact is they are no sign of cool to the young and hip who want to be down! They're not even a sign of cool for me. When I broached this on stage with Cornel, he seemed to be put off by the question and so

was the audience. I was not embracing a rhetoric that suggested black kids should be looking at the man in the suit and not the man in the leather coat as cool, as a role model. I was suggesting that the man in the suit might need to change to hold our interest—to capture our imagination. The spirit of transgression that is so central to both my intellectual practice and my political practice is much more tied in with what people like Queen Latifah and Ice T are saying than with what other academics are saying. These are exciting times. I have this deep belief in destiny, so I'm trying to live with what is my destiny here in New York. This is the last place on earth that I would ever have imagined myself living. I feel driven here by forces beyond my control. But I am excited to see whether I can, in conjunction and collaboration with other people, have New York City be more a place where some transgressively radical open critical thought and artistic production can emerge. That kind of truly avant-garde revolutionary cultural production will not happen if we don't begin to theorize it into existence as well, if we can't see that theory can be a catalyst for artistic practice and vice versa. It is that mutual interplay that might bring the element of risk and sacrifice back into our artistic and cultural practice.

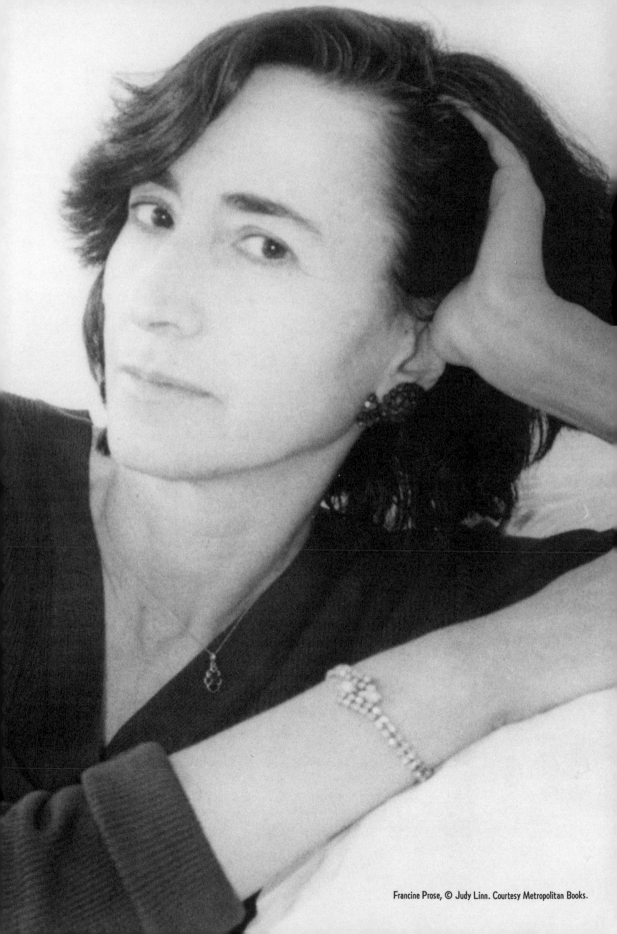

Francine Prose, © Judy Linn. Courtesy Metropolitan Books.

FRANCINE PROSE deborah eisenberg

BOMB #45, Fall 1993

The first time I encountered one of Francine Prose's stories—long before I encountered the author herself—I was agog. The story was like a magic trick that thrillingly employs familiar elements of the world (box, saw, lady) to unfamiliar effect (in half, whole again) and I felt that I'd gotten a glimpse of life from some theoretically impossible vantage point that reveals how it actually works. I could learn to look at things that way myself, I thought, if only. . . . But after reading it repeatedly, I couldn't even see how the *story* worked. And though I've come to know Prose herself and though I read her work with unabating astonishment, I've come no closer, over the years, to understanding how on earth she does it.

Prose lives in Manhattan and upstate New York with her husband, artist Howie Michaels, and their children, Bruno and Leon. The following conversation was occasioned by the publication of her second collection of short stories (and tenth! book) *The Peaceable Kingdom*.

FRANCINE PROSE Did you notice all the places in the collection that I stole from you?

deborah eisenberg No. Great, anything you didn't steal from me, I'll work on stealing from you. You know, I like the title so much—*The Peaceable Kingdom*. It's twisty, just like the stories. Because you assume that it's an embittered or slightly grief-stricken comment about humans. But actually it's much more complicated. I mean, there's lots of human unpeaceableness in the book, and lions lying down with lambs kind-of-thing, but there really are lots of actual animals.

FP Cats and dogs, which is a real surprise to me because I don't particularly like animals and have that cat whom I have no relationship with whatsoever. But, you know, I didn't come up with the title. My editor said,"Your title should reflect what so many of the stories are about." So, I said, "Fine. What a good idea." And then I got off the phone and realized that I had no idea what they were about. But I couldn't call her back and say, could you tell me what the stories are about? There are all these pets causing more trouble than they're worth, and when I read one of the stories, "Talking Dog," at Bread Loaf, my friend Ellen Voigt came up to me afterwards and said, "obviously, *The Peaceable Kingdom*."

de I notice that all the animals have a similar function, which is that they're like angels—they're messengers. Not in quite the way the characters think they are, but an animal often expresses something that one character or another can't express directly or isn't aware of wanting to express. Which is why I often think people have pets. You get an adorable little puppy simply so you don't have to pee on your boyfriend's rug yourself. And that strategy of indirect or oblique communication shows up in all the stories in one way or another. In "Rubber Life," it's a doll. And in "Ghirlandaio," it's a portrait that allows the narrator some very surprising discoveries about her relationships to the other characters. So the stories operate by examining the composition of various moments: the clashing motivations, misunderstandings, the screwy interpretations—everything that compresses into these diamond-like substances that are recognizable moments.

FP The way people project themselves onto objects and use objects—there's a way in which the animals might as well be objects. Animals appear; they disappear; they're there; they're not there; and always as weird projections of the psychic states of the characters. And you're right, it's like something is happening and the characters can't exactly say or do anything about it, and here's the cat or dog standing in for their psychic states.

de Like "Amateur Voodoo"—that

ending I loved so much, which is basically cat ventriloquism.

FP That's the story, I have to say, that's most borrowed from life. Except the husband's affair, I hope. Our cat had gone to the neighbor's, and our neighbor thought it was a stray and took it down the road and did us the favor of dumping it.

de Well, that's thoughtful. I notice that as I'm talking about this it sounds ponderous, or intellectualized. But, actually your stories are very suspenseful, and reading them is a very sensual experience. I spend a lot of time these days wondering what telling a story is. Because what we think of as a good narrative is a very rare thing. I mean specifically the sort of story that's just as recognizable and truthful and illuminating as gossip. And also assumes that life, or the interesting thing about life, is some set of causal relationships between episodes. Your writing is very disguised, because it feels like that kind of narrative, but actually the reader has to supply the relationships. So when I read one of your stories, I get this wonderful feeling that I'm swinging through the trees.

FP Well, I don't understand any of the stories. They all start out as mysteries. I mean, don't yours?

de Sure. But do you start with two things that you know are related and figure out what goes on between them, or what?

FP Yeah, or three things. And those are the stories that are the easiest to write, because they're connect-the-dot stories, but it's the connection—why do these things belong in the same story? I never understand what they are, or what they mean, or why anyone is doing the things that they're doing. But I don't in real life, either. Or so-called real life.

de But how do you know you've got it right? How do you know you've got it right? That that's the thing they're doing? Of course, when I read one of your stories the question never enters my mind as to whether that is what they really did. But how do *you* know? Do you go by your ear?

FP It's instinct, I guess. And it always seems amazing that someone can read the story and even figure out what the plot is.

de In your story, "Cauliflower Heads," a young woman marries an ecologist. They go to an ecology conference where she goes out with a Hungarian ecologist and his wife, and she gets drunk and realizes she shouldn't be married to her husband. That's the plot, but that's not what you'd say the story is about.

FP You know that bored feeling when people are telling you what you shouldn't be eating, or that the planet's dying? You know, you're just so sick of it, you can't stand it. Well, that's where that story started, with that sort of festering. Howie and I were at a poetry conference in the former Yugoslavia. All these people rushing around about some little wrinkle of Slovenian politics. So those two things came together in that story:

the doomsday theories, and watching people having a congress about something and not knowing what it was about. I feel that anyway. Like everyday I'm at this congress about something and I don't know what it is.

de Yeah, that's pretty much life. And I guess letting a story come together is sort of like having a big load of laundry. There are a bunch of socks, and you think, yes, this sock goes with that sock. But, it's interesting that it's one's own brain that is supplying the connections.

FP Or something.

de Yes. Oh, I see—is it one's brain or is it the socks?

FP They used to talk about the muse, which is so disgusting and horrible, but you do get the sense of something else operating, although you couldn't give it a name. Something else. You know that feeling, suddenly the characters are off on some whole conversation that you had no idea would occur? And that's the most fun, those moments when it takes over and you hadn't meant it to go that way, or sound that way, or you hadn't meant for them to be in that room, or having that conversation, but there they are. That's the moment you pray for. When the character reveals that human life you didn't know about. You suddenly think, oh, this goes deeper and is wider than what I imagined. And it's always such a thrill when that happens.

de Do you have actual opinions about the way life is put together or the way people lead their lives, or do you learn what you think by reading what you write?

FP I don't find out about my opinions, but I certainly find out about my obsessions. Who would have thought I'd have this obsession with household pets, and why? But, no, I have no opinion at all about the way life is put together or the way people lead their lives. On the one hand, I think of myself as just the most judgmental person in the universe, on the other hand, I think of myself as someone who is striving to have no judgement at all. And I always feel like those two tensions are working in the stories. Especially in *Primitive People*, my last novel. There, every day I was dealing with people I thought were scum, in some way, and in another way the most sympathetic people in the universe.

de It would be perfectly fair to describe the story, "Hansel and Gretel," in part, as a satirical portrait of the husband and how badly he treats his young wife. But all the same, the reader's sympathy keeps being drawn to the husband as well as the wife. You're simultaneously thinking, oh that shit, and, oh, that poor little child lost in the woods.

FP Well, that's what I mean. Those moments when you do start to think, oh that poor little child, do come from the moments when the characters take over. That's what gives you faith in something outside. For me, it started to happen when I was rushing through the first draft, and I got to the part where they're about to go to bed, and he's been dumping on her all the way

through, and he says, I love you. After not having touched the woman since getting married. And my heart just flopped. I thought, oh God, this poor guy. After going back and writing this over and over and over, I suddenly had a sense about this guy that I didn't have the first time.

de It really is like having imaginary friends. Of course, I never had any myself.

FP No, I never did either. My brother did, and I just tormented him about it.

de I'm wild with jealousy, I've never had any imagination at all.

FP Didn't you have imagination for disaster?

de You mean the guy coming to shred you? Oh, sure.

FP That was the kind I had. And that still is the one I have most. There's a way in which all these stories are asking, What's the worst thing that could happen?

de Yes, but, strangely, they are the worst thing that could happen. And there's something a little scrumptious about that very thing.

FP Yeah, let it happen. But even when you're a kid, a part of you is thinking, oh please, come shred me up.

de For sure. So—there are connect-the-dot stories. But what other kind of stories are there for you? How else do your stories compose themselves?

FP Well, "Hansel and Gretel" went backwards. Howie and I were having dinner at our friend Charlie's house in New

Hampshire, and Charlie happened to mention a woman who lived next door. A woman I had been to see twenty-five years ago, and spent a weekend at her house, the worst weekend of my entire life. So that story started with trying to reconstruct the past, or reconstruct the weekend. But I couldn't remember anything that had happened. Except the feeling. The feeling of being twenty years old and that my entire life was over. So some start with a feeling.

The others . . . I don't know. "Talking Dog?" I think I ripped part of that off a famous Croatian story about a mystical white dog. And "Ghirlandaio" started with an actual fact of biography, which was that my father used to take me to museums and show me paintings in which people had something medically wrong with them.

de What about "The Shining Path?"

FP Oh. Well, why not just say it? The Pepto Bismol incident actually happened.

de Lucky you! It's such a wonderful thing about being a writer that all the really unbearably horrible and embarrassing things that ever happened to you turn out to have been gifts.

FP But it took twenty years before I could even look at that incident again. What interested me—and it's maybe why it took twenty years—is the passivity. A lot of people have said to me, your stories are so politically incorrect, because the women in them are such passive dishrags.

de I hear that a lot, too.

FP Right. They can't speak up for themselves, and they don't take action, and they let themselves be led around, and people do horrible things to them. And they were me.

de The idea that writing is supposed to reflect some world that doesn't exist is very upsetting to me.

FP Or a better world. Or a world in which people do what they're supposed to do. Or act the way we think people should act.

de Now, you've written a lot of novels. A billion, as I remember.

FP A billion.

de And this is your second collection of stories, so you've written a lot of stories too. Do you know whether you're working on a story or a novel?

FP Of course you have to be really interested in the characters in order to write a story, but you have to be really, really, really interested in them to write a novel because you're going to have to spend two years with them.

de Oh God, I wrote a story about some people that I just hated, and it was agony, because I had to spend all my time with them.

FP Margot Livesey says, perhaps that's why so many people write autobiographical novels.

de !!!!!

FP But structurally, no. Well, yes. I mean, if I know that what I'm talking about is going to begin with the beginning of dinner and end with the end of dinner it's not going to be a novel. Right?

de Well, er, but what about *Ulysses*?

FP Well, that's breakfast, lunch, *and* dinner.

de And, now, these are questions that really make me feel ill. Or mentally ill. But other people ask other people this all the time, and I'm going to ask you: Do you have any interest in the theoretical capacities of the forms?

FP What does that mean?

de I haven't the faintest idea. But I wondered if you might know.

FP Like what it does? Like what is it supposed to do? Like, can we send all my stories over to the Bosnian Serbs right now, and they'll just stop shooting, is that what . . .?

de I don't know, I don't know! But maybe: Are there things you can accomplish with one that you can't accomplish with the other?

FP Tell that to Chekhov: You wrote those stories, but you didn't do anything compared to Tolstoy. I mean, of course not.

de But that does bring me to the only one of these questions I find even slightly interesting, depending on your answer, of course. Which is, do you consider them forms at all?

FP The story and the novel? No. Often one is longer. But sometimes one seems longer, even though it's a story. We've all read long, terrible, boring novels where nothing happens, and then we've read stories by you in which zillions of things happen. More

things happen than in ten ordinary novels, so I don't get it.

de My friend Wall said this wonderful thing the other day. I made him read, I allowed him to read, I suggested he read, I insisted he read, Isaac Babel's "Crossing Into Poland," which is sort of the largest thing that's ever been written, although it's only three pages long. And Wall said—so movingly, I thought—something about the respect for the reader that it showed. That all the thought and selection had been done by the writer. Obviously, of course, one wouldn't wish that *War and Peace* had been a short story, I mean, I'm thrilled to pieces that it's a novel—but it was an interesting way to think about that kind of compression.

FP It's such an incredible act of bravery . . . it is a three page story, but also it's a two-and-a-half-page landscape description. Then a half page of something happened, but the thing that happened already happened before you hear about it. And what you wind up with is the reader feeling like she's just been kicked in the stomach. I mean, it's just so amazing to have the faith, or the knowledge, or the instinct, or whatever it is, to know that you could do that.

de Yeah, that's something I've wanted to ask you about, actually, since I met you. But I'd never dare ask you if I didn't have this tape recorder. I write very slowly, it's true, but you've written exactly five times as many books as I have, so you do work very fast. You read fast; you write fast. And, I've come to think there's a kind of courage involved, particularly in the writing fast, there's a courage involved in inventing things, and I can't locate it. I needed a child to stay home from school in a story I wrote, so I gave him appendicitis. Not an important character, not an important appendicitis—and I sat around thinking about it for weeks and weeks. And none of it seemed real to me, until I had it absolutely nailed down on the page. And that seems like a failure of nerve to me. I mean, how do you just make things up?

FP Well, don't you think it's like walking a tightrope between the World Trade Towers? Is that courage or stupidity? And you'd better not look down, 'cause the minute you look down you're going to go down. You just keep going and assume it's going to be okay, and you find out pretty quickly if it won't work. Or, that it might. A friend of mine talks about this little Jiminy Cricket editor who sits on your shoulder and says it's not going to be okay, it's not going to be okay. And a lot of it is just getting that Jiminy Cricket to shut up long enough for you to do anything. But those things stop me cold. That's what's stopped me in the book I'm doing now. Credibility.

de But your stories and your novels are saturated with the real world. They're very specific, very accurate, and the insane, delicious things the characters do and say are the insane, delicious things

that people do and say right now and in particular milieus. The characters live in specific places, they're affected by specific, and often real, works of art, events, issues, and they have complicated and highly specialized jobs. So, what I mean is, how do you write so convincingly about all these things? Because I, for example, have never *met* anyone who has a job.

FP Don't you have a desperation to know about people's jobs? As soon as I meet anyone who does anything, I'm just grilling them, just plying them with questions. Well, thank God many of them know I'm a writer, so they just think, oh well, she's doing research. I often find myself asking them questions until I see they're getting uncomfortable, and then I stop. So I guess that is research, but it's also prying or curiosity, or, again, desperation.

de Yeah, and of course it allows you to do the thing that really is, I think maybe the basis of good writing, which is to start from first principles—as though you really don't understand anything.

FP What do you mean, "as though"?

de Well, there's that, of course. I notice you've weaseled out of the question of making things up. And I really want you to tell me: Do you actually make things up? For instance, *Household Saints* is a whole long, great big novel about a devout Italian Catholic butcher and his schizophrenic child. Now, you're not any of those things.

FP Well, everyone's been to the butcher shop.

de Francine—

FP Oh, all right. Well, everybody's been to the butcher shop and everybody, I think, has had fantasies of one sort or another about the people who work in the butcher shop. So that's where it started. Okay, research. I read a bunch about St. Therese. Not even a bunch. I read this one book by Vita Sackville-West about St. Therese. Then I did a lot of quizzing of my Catholic friends. But the thing that was most amazing was that often I would write a chapter, and then I would quiz my friends, and they would repeat what I had written the day before. So then I would think, I'm on the right track, I don't have to worry about it.

de You and I have both taught writing. One thing that writing teachers say is, write from your own life. And another thing that writing teachers say is, invent. Of course they're different writing teachers. But in a way, I can't endorse either position. I don't really think you should doggedly strive to write from your own life because I don't think you know what your own life is. And I don't think you should doggedly strive to invent because what does that mean? I mean, how do you invent? So I never say anything, really.

FP I never say either. I think both those things are irrelevant.

de So do I! But what do you mean? Wow!

FP The thing you're most interested in is

beyond invention or autobiography. Or that the ways they come together are beyond invention. For example, *Household Saints*, I thought, was about the whole question of service and devotion, and whether or not you'd give up your life for something else, and whether or not you thought there was something bigger than your life. When I started the book I was pregnant with Bruno, and I was really nervous that I was never going to have a mind or a life again. That I was giving it all up. And also, needless to say, the book is about the terrors of pregnancy. So I went around looking for a situation where those questions of devotion and service and things being out of control and things being in something else's hands would be more central than they were in mine.

de My God. I suspected this of you, that you had ideas.

FP But I didn't know it, exactly. Because where it actually started from was wanting to write about a butcher who had won his wife in a card game. That sense of randomness. And then as it evolved, all these things that had been obsessing me began to work their way into the book. But Catholicism was a way of talking about something else. I mean, it all feels like a way of talking about something else.

de But what other way except some other way could there be?

FP Otherwise you get some stupid essay that doesn't go anywhere.

de I mean how could you just talk

directly about something?
If you could, speech wouldn't
be required.

FP It's all weirder and more mysterious
than it's possible to even . . . it's like
waking up from a dream, and as you
start to talk or think about it, it starts
to disappear.

I was going to ask you, you said the
other day that you were reading Jane
Bowles and you mentioned you're not
interested in the way people behave.

de Well, it isn't Jane Bowles' fault,
really, that I'm not interested. I
just suddenly find myself at this
horrible place in my life where I'm
not interested in the way people
behave. It just seems very, very
trivial to me right now.

FP And what else is there?

de I don't know! I don't know! So I'm
sort of going completely mad these
days. Well, Jane Bowles, of course,
does in a sense cut right to the
chase, whatever the chase *is*. I mean,
her work is *only* profound. And very
funny, and gorgeous. But of course
you have no idea what it's about.

But do you think there's another thing? I mean, do you think fiction is about behavior? Is that what
fiction is? Is it an attempt to
describe human behavior?

FP Oh, God, Debbie! Jesus! Well, I don't
know. I guess since I don't understand
why people do anything, the only
thing I can know for sure is what they
do. So if I just write down what they
do, then somehow the mystery of *why*
they do it will come through what it is
they're doing.

de Let me say I don't think you can
just write down what people do. I
don't think it's possible. Because
the instant you put one word next
to another, aren't you automatically
selecting like crazy? Interpreting,
imputing, hypothesizing, inferring,
distorting . . .

FP Uh huh. But it's also that mysterious
thing of what makes a story. You
know? 'Cause it isn't just what the
characters do. I mean if we just wrote
down what they did, or what we did in a
day . . . that isn't a story. It needs other
things to make it a story, things that
weren't true. Things that were invented, that were grafted on to it. There's
something about the form of a story
that's way beyond what people *do*.

de So what you're saying is that the
selection and arrangement of bits
of behavior is what illuminates the
meaning of each bit of behavior.
And that if you had written for
instance, "The Shining Path," the
story where someone rubs Pepto
Bismol onto a young woman, in
the real context and sequence of
things that actually happened to
you that day, the force and the
meaning of the episode wouldn't
have been revealed. And to show
what it really was, you had to
make up a series of actions—people's actions—that would, in fact,
illuminate the meaning of the
moment. If that was in fact the
moment that interested you.

FP The moment in that story that interested me was when he's rubbing Pepto
Bismol on her and she tries to tell
him that her brother just died. When

something really terrible is happening there's a compulsion to tell it to a stranger. When my father was dying, I would get in a cab to go to the hospital, and I would immediately start telling the cab driver what was happening. It's wanting to feel that there's some human connectedness. In that story, I was trying to think of one of the most alienated moments I've ever had . . . and to take the desire to confess something very immediate and very real and put it into that most alienated imaginable moment.

de It's an interesting reflection on that issue of passivity that we're both raked over the coals for all the time. Young women in the sixties and seventies had been trained to be very passive, and suddenly it was demanded that they be very expressive. So they were constantly finding that they were being exploited. Yet there was some element of tremendous sincerity on the part of the parties involved—or even somewhere in the culture—a longing for the kind of equality that's the real precondition of free action. So there were those moments of strange, ambivalent, ambiguous contact, or intimacy when you found yourself in bed with the guy who could be . . .

FP . . .the axe murderer. There was this feeling that this person could kill me. I don't know this person. What am I doing here? It was also, somehow, I don't know, extreme loneliness, but a kind of thrill. Almost like what you would imagine Goethe meant . . . the

sublime thrill people are always claiming to feel standing on top of mountain tops and looking at the world just yawning out before them and feeling that they're the only one in it.

de So the character has that experience in "The Shining Path," and in a way there is no comparable experience she can have with her boyfriend.

FP Well, he's a schmuck anyway.

de What are you going to do now? You're on this Edith Wharton binge, which has resulted from some strange confluence, yes? What is that word people used to use, a Jungian term . . .

FP Oh, synchronicity. There's an idea whose time has come and gone. But, yeah. I wrote a story about a woman who's working in a library and falls in love with a guy who comes into the library. And before she meets the guy she's compulsively reading Edith Wharton novels. At that point I'd only actually read one or two Edith Wharton novels, but I pretended that I'd read quite a number so I could write the story. But then long, long after I finished the story I started reading all these Edith Wharton novels, and one of them is about a young woman working in a library who falls in love with a guy who comes into the library. And of course, had I actually read the novel when I was writing the story, the character would have noticed that one of them was about her life. But I hadn't.

de You said reading Edith Wharton makes you feel like you haven't done something. What does it make you feel that you want to do?

FP To get to a whole new level of depth. There's a way of getting so deep into that character's mind, making the reader know the character's responses so well—*Anna Karenina* is another example—you know what everyone in that book is going to do before they do it. The same with *The Age of Innocence*. You know exactly what Newland Archer is thinking and feeling, what he is going to do; what he is capable of; what his hopes and fears are without the writer ever telling you.

de Oh, these ravaging ambitions! To make something that's as complex and chaotic and mystifying as reality but more apprehensible. I'm not sure what I think of the whole thing. Why did you decide to write? Or when did you notice that you were doing it?

FP It was the only thing I could do. I mean, not that I could do it. I mean, there's nothing else I can do. I don't mean that necessarily in the noble way. I mean, really, I have not a single other skill. I can barely type.

de Yeah, well, this is all true of me, too.

FP I had gone to graduate school, and I was having a nervous breakdown, although no one even knew, including myself, that that's what it was. I was watching television for twelve hours a day. Clearly, I was not functioning. I knew I couldn't do anything else. It was the only thing that made me—I wouldn't say happy—

but that I liked doing.

de But you did do it. You knew that it was a thing to do.

FP It was just self-entertainment, because I didn't think anything was going to happen. No one was ever going to see it. It was just to amuse me. And that was the best. A pure state which I always wish I could get back to. There wasn't any superego to say this isn't any good.

de There's an analagous feeling I used to have at that happy stage when writing was a completely private activity for me, too—the feeling that something was written just for me. In whatever country, in whatever century, for me.

FP Oh, I know. Like when I read *The Leopard*. Here's this Sicilian nobleman who knew at the end of his life what sentence would make me happy, and what description would make me incredibly happy. And beyond that, how the rhythm of the sentences would make me happy even in translation. Who knows if it's good or bad. Everything dissolves. Time dissolves, and the surface differences dissolve, and you think that beyond anything there's something that keeps running through.

de Oh, wouldn't that be great?

FP Well, maybe some beleaguered passive girl of the future will read our stuff and say, "God, there used to be someone who felt like me! Before all these women got completely together and confrontational and well-adjusted, there used to be someone as fucked up as me!"

Peter Carey, © Marion Ettlinger. Courtesy Knopf.

PETER CAREY robert polito

On an unseasonably sultry October afternoon, I make my way over to the West Village townhouse Peter Carey shares with his wife, Alison Summers, and their sons, Charley and Sam, to discuss his latest novel.

The Unusual Life of Tristan Smith. . . a seemingly whimsical title, reminiscent of Sterne and Swift . . . but whimsy can't fully conceal Carey's fierce—and hilarious—satire of cultural imperialism, and can't fully display the sweep—and dazzle—of Carey's fictional landscape. Creating two entire countries, Efica and Voorstand, and sustaining them with a cavalcade of maps, local histories, dialects, folklore, and a creepy Disneyesque pop culture, *Tristan Smith*, from the shaky vista of the formerly colonized, is the first of Carey's books to register the impact of New York City. Carey, an Australian, is the author of four novels, *Bliss, Illywhacker, Oscar and Lucinda* (awarded the 1988 Booker Prize), and *The Tax Inspector*, as well as a collection of stories, *The Fat Man in History*.

I follow Peter up three flights to a rooftop deck. The previous evening, while introducing Kazuo Ishiguro at the 92nd Street Y, Peter remarked that "recklessness" was the quality that most engaged him in literature: *Don Quixote, Tristam Shandy*, and Dickens as opposed to, he said, *The Eustace Diamonds*. Directly after our conversation he would rush to meet with one of his graduate writing students; earlier that morning he already had worked four hours on his next novel, *Mags*.

The shaded pastoral of Peter's roof proved deceptive—the tape disclosed a squall of police cars, ambulances, motorcycles, and school children we must have overlooked as we talked about Australia, America, and *The Unusual Life of Tristan Smith*.

robert polito Your latest novel, *The Unusual Life of Tristan Smith*, is steeped in questions of national and cultural identity. I wonder if we might start with your own background. You've lived in New York now since 1990—how did you come to be here?

PETER CAREY My wife loved North America and wanted to be here and direct theater. And then there was a job at NYU for me. So we just . . . came. I've made big moves in my life relatively lightly and easily—it wasn't odd, given my history, that I packed my books and rugs and set off for New York. What I hadn't anticipated was how having children makes this move more permanent. I have one absolutely American son, Charley, who was born in New York City. And my other son, Sam, was born in Australia; but he's probably more American than Australian. What do I say to them? OK guys, time to change your accents again? In another life I might be shifting on to the next thing. After having had this rather cavalier attitude towards where I lived, it's odd to suddenly become anchored in New York City.

rp Yet your essay of a few years ago called "Home" sounds more unsettled than cavalier—agitated by feelings of yearning and displacement. You wrote: "I can now see my history as a sometimes pathetic series of attempts to create a home."

PC Yeah, it's true. I began my life as an expatriate at the age of ten. I was sent from this working-class country town to a very posh ruling-class boarding school, Geelong Grammar, which would not easily fit in with anybody's notions of Australia. You might be astonished at how much it was like an English public school. Accents were a little different, but not always all that different, because in the fifties, the Australian ruling class often spoke with English home-county accents. We were brought up to believe that there was something inherently vulgar and second rate in the Australian accent. And to this day I still fluctuate between saying dance, and *dhance*—I said castle my first week of Geelong Grammar, and they said to me, "We don't say castle, we say *khassel*. Only Americans say castle." There was this weird sense of Australia's place in the colonial pecking order. These Australians were acting like nineteenth-century British snobs, looking down on Americans as vulgar colonials. It was grotesque.

rp That little country town where you were born was Bacchus Marsh— what was it like?

PC It was a small town of about four thousand people—one main street with the shops, a lot of farmers, a coal mine, a brick works, and a lot of the people were laborers for a living. In fact, I was just remembering it today because a former classmate sent me our class pictures from 1950 and 1953. They look like they were taken in England at the end of the war. These are real working-class kids: ill-fitting clothes, old, rumpled; but the faces, there are little men in there, staring out of children's faces. My kids' school photos don't look like this.

rp I dressed more like an adult when I was six than I do now—a miniature adult in a suit and tie, a tweed top coat, perched on Santa's knee. Some of that's period fashion, I suppose.

PC These were tough kids; so it was a major cultural leap for me to go from there to Geelong Grammar. I was staggered. No one had fist fights.

rp Really?

PC No one fought, no one fought the whole time I was there. It was amazing.

rp What did your parents do?

PC They owned a car dealership.

rp Ah—the original of Catchprice Motors?

PC Well, I stole the topography of their business for *The Tax Inspector*. And I did worry afterwards that people in Australia would read the book and think that *The Tax Inspector* was thinly disguised family history, and thereby embarrass my sister and my brother. So I went around giving this speech about the nature of fiction: how we draw on things . . . [*laughter*] I grew up in a household that was obsessed with motor cars, selling motor cars. All they talked about day and night.

rp So how did you end up at that boarding school, coming from this background?

PC I'm not always clear about the motives of the characters in my nonfiction life. It was my mother who knew about posh boarding schools. My father would probably rather have not had to worry about the money, but he did, they both did: six hundred pounds a term, in 1953. That was incredible money, as they always reminded me. When I was first published and people started to interview me, I made some comments on my parents' motives, which I regret now. I said going to Geelong Grammar was a reflection of my mother's social aspirations, for instance. You have to be really young and sort of stupid to say those sorts of things.

rp Now you get to say them; but also say they're stupid at the same time.

PC It's true. [*laughter*] Anyway, my mother had her media revenge on me when I won the Booker Prize. It was such an unimaginably big deal in Australia. The tabloid TV shows went out to Bacchus Marsh, thirty miles from the city. She was getting a little old, she was a little forgetful, things were starting to not work well for her, and this is what my mother said on television: The reporter said, "You must be very proud, your son's won the Booker Prize." And she said, "Oh yes." And they said, "Did Peter ring you to tell you the news?" And she said, "Ring me? Why would he ring me? He never rings me." [*laughter*] Which was totally untrue! In fact I rang her the morning after I'd won the Prize. It was about six in the morning in London, and I said, "You know that prize that I told you I might get?" She said, "Yes dear, I know you won it. There were some people here from your work." I said,

"What work?" She said, "You know, with the television cameras."

rp So, as far as she was concerned you were still in advertising. Were you already writing when you worked for an advertising agency?

PC I began writing, and reading, when I got my job in advertising. I'd really not studied literature very much. Although my English teacher at Geelong Grammar says (quite frequently) that we studied a lot of Shakespeare—I did like that. He says Milton, but I don't remember that. I went to university to be a scientist.

rp What kind of scientist?

PC I was going to be an organic chemist; and then I was going to be a zoologist. Along the way I bought the *Faber Book of Modern Verse*, and I got very excited about what I found in it. So I started to write poetry. My bad poetry was published in the student newspaper and I also produced a very inelegant cartoon strip. And then I failed my first-year exams, and got a job at an advertising agency. I had no political critique of advertising, no social critique, just thought it would be sort of an interesting thing to do. I didn't think there was any need to be guilty about selling anything to anyone—my folks sold motor cars. And when I went into advertising, all the copywriters were writing short stories, novels . . . literature just fell into my lap—not eighteenth-or nineteenth-century literature, but Joyce and Pound and Kerouac and Beckett and Kafka. It was an odd way to begin an education.

Most of our copywriting was rejected. We just talked about literature.

rp Was there a transition between writing advertising and writing your fiction?

PC I have a very obsessive personality—the minute I decided that I was going to be a writer—and I decided it quite soon, with no justification—that's how I defined myself. I was a writer. From the start. I wrote every night, and every weekend. And all this other stuff, the copywriting, the suit, was peripheral to my life. I simply became very snobbish; aside from a couple of very literary friends in advertising I wouldn't socialize with anyone from an advertising agency. It was very juvenile. Once again I was an exile. I wasn't really from the place where I lived. It wasn't until after the Booker Prize that it began to look as if I could really live off my writing. But by then I was a partner in a small advertising agency, so it wasn't so easy to get out of it. It was like a large ship that takes a little while to turn around. I was on the train coming back from Princeton with James Lasdun last year, and we were coming through those poisonous swamps, or Meadowlands. It was winter, the end of the day. We were both exhausted from teaching. And I said, "You know James, I used to work just two afternoons in an advertising agency in Australia—that's all I had to do. The rest of the time I just wrote, and I never had to worry about whether my books sold. And he said, "Why did you give it up?" And I looked out the window and said, "I don't know." [*laughter*]

rp As an Australian living in New York you're recreating again that sense you've been describing, of being an exile, an outsider. Do you enjoy being here?

PC I like being here a whole lot. It's when something goes wrong that I can suddenly feel very foreign and very nervous. Like the Sons of Gestapo derailing the Amtrak, or the Texas state legislature deciding that it's okay to carry concealed weapons—these things feel triply scary for me. But no, I really love New York City. I still get high just walking in the streets. I sometimes complain to Alison, my wife, and say, "I've got to get back to Australia. I'm Australian and that's my culture." But if she turned to me and said, "Okay, we'll go now," I wouldn't want to go . . . not quite yet.

rp Do Australians view you differently now that you've moved away?

PC I can't tell. I'm here, not there. But we are descended from people who were cast out, exiled from the center and locked away on the periphery. So when a successful Australian leaves, there's a shiver that goes through the community, that really means, "You think you're so high and mighty, you're better than us." Of course the discourse has become more sophisticated, and perhaps it's not quite as bad as it was. Still, last week's Australian newspapers carried this major story about a literary lunch, one of those lunches where people pay money to eat and hear their favorite author speak. They're normally very polite, genteel affairs. But last week

Frank Moorhouse—a very fine Australian writer—used one of these lunches to actually talk about something important. He complained that it was considered cultural "treason" for an Australian writer to live elsewhere, or to write about matters technically outside the national border. This upset his polite listeners so much that they began to walk out, and it delighted the media so much that it showed up on page three. This was provincial in the best, most exciting sense. I shudder to think about it. And I'm sorry I missed it.

rp *The Unusual Life of Tristan Smith* maps some of these vexations of cultural and national identity, but the geography appears at once invented and familiar. At one end of the telescope there's "provincial" Efica, a former penal colony composed of eighteen small islands; and at the other end is the powerful, culturally dominant and insinuatingly sinister Voorstand. In a sense Efica approaches Australia, and Voorstand the United States—Saarlim City even suggests a sort of *"Blade Runner"* echo of New York City. Yet we're not reading simply allegorized recent history. Were you concerned that the novel maintain its fictional integrity?

PC I spent a lot of time making sure that no one could ever read Voorstand and think "that's America," or Efica and think, "that's Australia." On the other hand, the emotional engine of the book comes from the fact that I'm an Australian. I live in the United States. I'm from a country that—whether Americans know it or not—has this long emotional, culturally and politically complex relationship with the United States.

rp   One of the chilling moments for me in the novel was that line an Efican casually addresses to Voorstand: "You have no idea of your effect on those of us who live outside the penumbra of your lives." As Tristan Smith remarks, "It's the periphery shouting at the center."

PC   I have many American-born friends who travel a great deal and certainly are not isolationist in any cultural or political sense; but they don't, as far as I can see, fully grasp the deep and profound effect of American popular culture on other cultures. You were here on this roof one night having a drink with [Australian novelist] Helen Garner, and Helen was talking about Kinky Friedman and the Texas Jewboys and you guys were all amazed that someone in Australia would have any interest in Kinky Friedman. You bet we knew all about Kinky Friedman in Australia in the early seventies. The powerful can never experience their own power . . .

rp   Americans seem to rarely think about how anyone outside might perceive us—or even, I suppose, how "history" will perceive us. We have a country that originated out of a massive campaign of genocide against an entire native civilization, then sustained itself by slav-

ery of another race, yet still manages an almost spectral innocence about itself.

PC   Yeah, that innocence is extraordinary. A perfect example of false consciousness.

rp   As you write in *Tristan Smith*, again addressing Voorstand, "You stand with your hand over your heart when the Great Song is played. You daily watch new images of your armies in the vids and the zines."

PC   When I read that line to a Canadian audience, I can feel them "get" the line. I mean, they understand about the big country and the little country and they know which is which. Yet I have sometimes been surprised to discover American readers who never saw any connection between Voorstand and the United States. I suppose that one of the things about false consciousness is not having self-perception.

rp   And no sense of irony as a people.

PC   Well, New York is a very ironic city, but I take your point.

rp   The main cultural display for both Efica and Voorstand, speaking of Disney—or irony!—is the Sirkus—these oddly appealing and terrifying animal "stars": Bruder Mouse, the Duck, and the Dog. You told me once that you started *Tristan Smith* while on a trip to Florida.

PC   There was a conference of the American Association for the Study of Australian Literature in Florida. I stayed for a few papers, and then I went off with Alison and Sam to

Disney World. It was something to see Mickey and Minnie walking among the crowds, like royalty, like a king and queen. This happened at a time when I was eager to engage the notion of America in a novel, and at Disney World I started to invent a country that was like an idea of America, not America literally. I started to imagine a country where figures like Mickey and Minnie were the decadent flowering of a heretical Protestant sect. It was like drawing a cause-and-effect line connecting Mickey and the Mayflower. It was an amusing, but also invigorating thought. It created a site for action, an arena in which to engage with my novel.

rp Are there incidents or episodes in the novel that might jump out at an Australian reader but go by an American?

PC You can say *The Unusual Life of Tristan Smith* is most resonant within its own culture, but I think you could say the same thing of Marquez's *One Hundred Years of Solitude*. There isn't a *right* reading of it, but there are things that Australian readers feel in their gut that American readers would not. For instance, there are many Australians who see the dismissal of the Whitlam government in 1975 as having more than a little to do with the American government. I mean, we had a left-liberal social democratic government which behaved, from the beginning, in ways that were unpalatable to America. It was a heady time for us. We recognized China, withdrew our troops from Vietnam—

there's a long and exhilarating list. Australia, finally, began to behave, not as a client state, but as an independent power with a mind of its own. This was a very worrying situation for the United States to face in a country which was, and is, strategically important to it. The Whitlam government irritated the U.S. government, to say the least. It certainly angered and alarmed the U.S. intelligence community. So: Did American intelligence work to destabilize our government? Did your government help bring down the government I voted into power? I believe so. Many Australians believe so. So in a way, the book wasn't really born in Disney World in 1990, but in November 1975, in the moment the Whitlam government was removed from power.

rp The way *The Unusual Life of Tristan Smith* is framed, with the voice of an Efican speaking to Voorstand, the "you" invariably is Voorstand. Could the novel have only been written by someone who moved from a colonized country to an imperial power?

PC I guess. I guess, but I didn't begin by playing it this way. I know the address to the Voorstand reader makes sense in terms of my particular history and psychology. I mean it makes sense that I, Peter Carey, should take on the Efican voice and address my narrative to the Voorstanders. It's like I'm shouting out my apartment window in the Village. But the fact is, I did it to solve a technical problem. I gave an early draft to my editor Robert

McCrum, and he said he thought the characters, the individual drama was working exceptionally well but that he was totally mystified by the history and the politics. All this stuff, which is so important to the novel, wasn't clear to him. And he was dead right. So I sought a way to express this very clearly from the start. So I had my Efican narrator—Tristan Smith—address an imaginary Voorstand reader, and it just fell into place. Tristan could say: "We are like this, you are like that. We do this, you do that." Suddenly I could lay all of this stuff out on the table. I could be clear. I could even hope to be entertaining.

rp Can we talk a bit about those footnotes and the rest of the "apparatus" that accompanies the novel? Because they seem to me symptomatic of something edgier than a smart joke. You provide all these mock references to Efican histories, ranging from something titled *Efica: From Penal Colony to Welfare State* (published by the Nez Noir University Press) to Tristan Smith's own political pamphlet "What Is to be Done?" Then, the book concludes with glossaries of Efican and Voorstand slang. These are very funny, teasing academia, among other targets. But they also convey a powerful, almost tragic sense of the two countries' linguistic strangeness from each other. I'm interested in how you approached the situation of language in the novel.

PC If you are a novelist inventing a country, one of your first questions has to be: How do the characters talk to each other. Are there "guys" and "buddies" in this country? No, that's specific to the United States. A trite, easy expression like "Have a nice day" has its roots deep in the soil of a particular culture. So how would my Eficans and Voorstanders talk to each other? One of my ways to reveal the language of the Eficans was to delve into their French and English colonial past. I began to develop these creolized expressions which would grow from Efican history. Once I began to invent this patois, I could name the trees, the streets. Because I had already done a lot of work imagining what their history was, that history then percolated through their language. The footnotes are there to reveal these historical processes, to add mythological or cultural layers to the narrative in a sometimes amusing way. But you can also ignore them if you wish—the book works without them.

rp There's a sense in the novel that Efica and Voorstand can't speak to each other except through broad cultural spectacles like the Sirkus. The small, avant-garde, left-wing theater company that Tristan Smith's mother, Felicity, runs in Efica, the Feu Follet, seems an attempt to create an alternative culture—and an alternative language—to the Voorstand popular culture that pervades both countries.

PC That was certainly an obsession of

mine. If you're an Australian artist you're engaged in the exhilarating and difficult task of inventing your culture. So the passions that drive the cultural nationalists of the Feu Follet are also mine. Australian writers can have a sense of their own importance that is unthinkable for most American writers. An Australian writer can really name things for the first time. We do all this, of course, at a time when fewer and fewer people are reading novels, and fewer and fewer people can afford the theater. We do it in the face of an all-pervasive popular culture which is not only very popular but has its roots in a foreign—I mean, American—history.

rp As Felicity says, "We have a whole damn country to invent."

PC Yeah, I think that's so. Also Australia still has very little sense of what it has become. It thinks of itself as an Anglo-Celtic place where people might see Paul Hogan as a "real Aussie." Yet there's been this massive immigration since the Second World War, and the effects of this are only just beginning to be felt in the cultural mainstream. So Australia is still in the process of inventing itself.

rp Felicity's theater is an outpost against the ascendancy of the Sirkus. But I wonder if you also had in mind something closer to home. Your wife, Alison Summers, is an accomplished theater director.

PC I drew on Alison's work continually. But I began by thinking about a the-

ater called the Pram Factory, a radical theater collective in Melbourne in the 1960s. At the start I had no idea that theater would be important to me thematically. I was really looking for a political environment, and I certainly wasn't interested in writing about the lives of politicians. Alison is always such a wise and perceptive reader, but in this case she also became a fantastic resource. She'd read a draft of a chapter, and say, "You need to have the *work light* on there." And, "That's called the *pre-light*." And, "If your characters are going onto that set, the set should have *glow tape* to mark the edges in the dark." I love her work and to talk about what she does. I was informed by, enriched by, her life anyway. But that was not why I wrote about the theater.

rp Tristan Smith is hideously deformed—lipless mouth, triangular face, tiny twisted body, strangled speech, club foot and all. He's also kind of Byronic: a terrific acrobat and storyteller, ultimately quite sexy. From *The Fat Man in History* through Benny, the abused child in *The Tax Inspector*, and now Tristan, you often invoke characters who might variously be tagged "monsters." But that's just the starting point for these figures, isn't it?

PC Benny, of course, is physically attractive; but he is, no matter how our sympathies might be engaged, finally evil, monstrous. And I certainly had no desire to engage in a three-year relationship with another monstrous character. But the thing I love about fiction is that it is a totally plastic world. Every word, every "thing" is there to be at the service of the story—I needed to have someone who really wanted to be, for psychological reasons, inside a mouse suit. Then I saw this guy in a wheelchair on Bleecker Street. Physically, he was a tragic ruin in every way, but in his face there were these bright intelligent eyes. I thought, God, there's a person inside there. Tristan was born of that moment. But I did a reading at Mount Kisco this weekend, and three dwarves came to the reading. I was very self-conscious and fearful that they would be offended. Anyway, they liked Tristan. A lot. They were beaming at me from the front row. They asked one of the first questions from the floor—why did I come to write about a character like Tristan? So I said it was the idea, kind of like an equation, and once that was done I had to engage his humanity. He had to stop being an idea and start being a person. With Benny in *The Tax Inspector* I also began with an idea: I wanted to oppose birth and a sexual predator, good sex, evil sex. There seems to me no connection at all between Benny and Tristan. But if there's a pattern here . . . [*laughter*]

rp Some of your reviews have tried to suggest that there's a tremendous bleakness about human relationships in *Tristan Smith* and *The Tax Inspector*. Yet sitting here talking this afternoon, you're one of the happiest men I know.

PC Well, I don't see *Tristan Smith* as bleak. Look at the characters, for instance, Tristan's mother Felicity. She's this beautiful, driven, slightly neurotic woman who gives birth to this hideously monstrous child. And what she gives that child is incredible. She loves him. She's by no means perfect—she shouts and shrieks at him—but those muddy passionate outbursts don't feel bleak to me. Or there's Wally, the ex-prisoner and not very perfect con man. He also loves Tristan. And look at his relationship with Roxanna. She is crazy, if you like, and damaged, I suppose, but I hope their affair is gentle, and touching. Go through the list. There's a very compassionate view of ordinary folk. Perhaps this "bleakness" comes from the political environment, from the degradation of the physical world? Well, maybe you're right there. That's always in my work. How could it not be? But even in *The Tax Inspector*, which is often a harrowing book, the characters are always seen with compassion, and even Benny, the most damaged of the lot, finally respects life—he returns the newborn baby to its mother's arms.

rp You're the favorite novelist of so many women—here in New York, among my Australian friends, even in Taipei, where one bookstore I visited maintained a sort of shrine of your books. Felicity Smith or Maria Takis in *The Tax Inspector* are just two of your strong female figures. There's a disregard—almost contempt, maybe—for American machismo in your fiction.

PC In the real world, these women would not be so unusual, or original. We all know women like these characters. The biographical thing? I suppose one could start talking about my mother. She was certainly a very strong and determined individual.

rp For a whole year, once, you were in the office next to mine, and what I could pick up of your daily working process seemed pretty formidable. As a writer, you do so many things stunningly well. You arrange your incredible sentences in these short Cornell boxlike chapters, but spilling out of the boxes are all these marvelous characters—fantastics, sometimes, out of Fielding, Sterne, or Dickens. And you concoct dazzling plots. What is your process of writing and revising a novel?

PC Well, of course I do all the usual note-taking and planning. Then, I set off for my first draft, but my first draft rarely gets more than fifty or sixty pages before I realize I don't know very much. I go back to the beginning, because the flaw will be with the motivations of the characters. I'll realize that I don't know why they are doing the things I want them to do. I do tend to always build my stories out of what you call "Cornell-like boxes," which I think of as building blocks of story. I think about those little boxes quite schematically—sometimes draw the little boxes—a little square. Inside the square I write what should happen

inside the box. I'll probably have as many as ten different threads of story locked inside the box. So think of the draft as boxes stacked on top of each other. Whenever they get unstable or shaky I go back to the start again. The first draft may have fifty pages, eighty pages with the next, one hundred and twenty with the next, then maybe three hundred. At this very moment I'm on the fifth draft of a novel, about three hundred and fifty pages, and some of the chapters or boxes I've rewritten eight times. I stubbornly commit to those little boxes. That's how I write and rewrite. The motivations of the characters within the boxes will keep on changing, but I am likely to stay committed to a relatively unreasonable action. And I work and work until the action is reasonable. For example, in *Tristan Smith*, Wally the production manager, impatient with everyone's negativity about this baby, leaps from a high scaffold behind the stage down into the audience. He descends like some sort of ludicrous, sacred clown!

rp That's one of the great moments in the novel.

PC I saw it in my mind as an affirmation. I just knew that it was right. But to really believe the moment was terribly difficult. There were so many reasons why he wouldn't do it, and I had to write it twenty or thirty times to discover the real reason for the action. I'm very flexible about writing and rewriting. I love to throw out good writing, but I'll cling to an action, the way a young writer might cling to a

notion when someone—quite right-
ly—says just throw it out.

rp **One knows that a book is yours
just by seeing how the chapters are
arranged through the pages. I'm
guessing you do a fair amount of
research for your novels—all that
old religion behind** *Oscar and
Lucinda*, **say, or for** *Tristan Smith*.

PC Yeah—but it's always less than you
think. I spent less time in the library
for *Oscar and Lucinda* than you'd
probably imagine. At night I tend to
read around the subject I'm writing
about—I'm so self-absorbed and
obsessive, I can't help it. But the most
important thing with research is to
feel confident enough to throw out
ninety-eight percent of it.

rp **The new novel you're writing grew
out of your reading?**

PC I spent a little time recently thinking
about Magwitch in *Great Expectations*,
and my new novel plays with the story.
My character, Jack Mags, returns
home to London in 1837 expecting
to find the orphan he had arranged to
have raised and educated as an
English gentleman. The English gentleman knows he's coming, and runs
away. You see, Magwitch (and Mags)
seem important to me in all sorts of
ways. Magwitch is the first Australian
to go home to London and not be
wanted. He's also, in my version, been
perfectly Australian in that he's abandoned his Australian children in favor
of the superior English product.
Dickens has a considerable degree of
affection for my imaginary ancestor;

but for all that, Magwitch is also this
dark, loathsome other. His money is
vile, unacceptable. Dickens knew what
Australians discovered painfully over
many generations: they cannot go
Home. I thought it might be interesting to give Mags the degree of sympathy Dickens gives Pip. I have also
always been interested in how
exploitative and controlling the best
writers tend to be. And when I discovered that Dickens had practiced mes-
merism, I was electrified. So my
Dickens character—who is not
Dickens, I didn't want to be burdened
with that—is having a mesmeric relationship with Jack Mags, he uses mes-
merism to burgle the convict's soul.
The book has other threads in it,
which have to do with children—
Australian children, lost children, dead
children. Some of this touches on my
more personal nonfiction writing, like
"A Small Memorial," the piece I had
in the *New Yorker* about abortion and
the lost babies in my own life.

rp **Do you see yourself writing more
nonfiction?**

PC Emotionally it is wrenching to write,
but technically it is so much easier
than writing fiction. I am very, very
proud of "A Small Memorial," and it
was only a week's work. Because it's
not made up, it only has to be shaped.
I certainly have plenty to confess but
it would be a little unseemly to make a
career of it. Yet when I think about
the short form, it's the personal essay
that really interests me.

rp **Not short stories?**

PC I can't think of anything I want to deal with in a short story.

rp You've also just published a book for children, *The Big Bazoohley*, that features your son Sam. How did that come about?

PC We were in Toronto, and Sam sleep-walked, went right out the door of the hotel. The door slammed behind him. It was one in the morning, the air conditioning was on, and the door was thick, so we didn't hear him knocking. He set off down the corridor, just knocking on doors until someone heard him. Fortunately, the people were not child molesters or kidnappers. They rang Security and we got him back, but it was really scary. So now I've turned it into something less scary, but when I finished writing it, Sam didn't want to read it. I think he was a little frightened of it. Finally, he read an advance proof, but without the illustrations.

rp What did he think?

PC He said, "Not bad."

rp A character in *The Big Bazoohley* is Philip Lopate, and there's an Una Chaudhuri in *Tristan Smith*. Other novels also feature characters who bear the names of your friends. Are these little hidden homages?

PC Sometimes they're like gifts. Other times, there's my friend Stephen Wall in Australia, I put his name in the books from time to time to check if he's really reading them. He's not such a committed reader, so I keep moving his name further towards the end of the book just to give him some exercise. But sometimes I choose a friend's name from laziness. I'm not disowning the celebratory nature of it, but. . . . That reminds me, I haven't sent Philip the book.

Paul Auster, © C. Dauphin. Courtesy Henry Holt and Company.

PAUL AUSTER joseph mallia

BOMB #23, Spring 1988

Paul Auster has worked in a wide range of genres—a half dozen volumes of dense, highly crafted lyric poems; numerous books of translations from the French, and the editorship of the *Random House Book of Twentieth-Century French Poetry; The Art of Hunger*, critical essays written when he was in his early twenties: a moving, deeply personal yet intellectually rigorous "experiment in autobiography," *The Invention of Solitude; The New York Trilogy*, an acclaimed series of sparse, evocative mysteries; a one-act play, produced in New York (which he refuses to talk about); pseudonymously, a conventional detective story; and, most recently, *In the Country of Last Things*, a post-apocalyptic story narrated from the point of view of a nineteen-year-old woman. What unites his work in such disparate genres? It "has to do with language," Auster says. "It all goes toward exploring the limits of the sayable. It has to do with perception, the connection between seeing the world and speaking the world, what happens in that gap between the two. It is about trying to come to grips in language with things that elude understanding."

joseph mallia In your book of essays, *The Art of Hunger*, you cite Samuel Beckett as saying, "There will be a new form." Is your work an example of that new form?

PAUL AUSTER It seems that everything comes out a little strangely and my books don't quite resemble other books, but whether they're "new" in any sense, I really can't say. It's not my ambition to think about it. So I suppose the answer is yes and no. At this point I'm not even thinking about anything beyond doing the books themselves. They impose themselves on me, so it's not my choice. The only thing that really matters, it seems to me, is saying the thing that has to be said. If it really has to be said, it will create its own form.

jm All of your early work, from the

1970s, is poetry. What brought about this switch in genres, what made you want to write prose?

PA Starting from a very early age, writing novels was always my ambition. When I was a student in college, in fact, I spent a great deal more time writing prose than poetry. But the projects and ideas that I took on were too large for me, too ambitious, and I could never get a grip on them. By concentrating on a smaller form I felt that I was able to make more progress. Years went by, and writing poetry became such an obsession that I stopped thinking about anything else. I wrote very short, compact lyrical poems that usually took me months to complete. They were very dense, especially in the beginning—coiled in on themselves like fists—but over the years they gradually began to open up, until I finally felt that they were heading in the direction of narrative. I don't think of myself as having made a break from poetry. All my work is of a piece, and the move into prose was the last step in a slow and natural evolution.

jm As a younger writer, who were the modern writers you were interested in?

PA Of prose writers, unquestionably Kafka and Beckett. They both had a tremendous hold over me. In the same sense, the influence of Beckett was so strong that I couldn't see my way beyond it. Among poets, I was very attracted to contemporary French poetry and the American objectivists, particularly George

Oppen, who became a close friend. And the French poet Paul Célan, who in my opinion is the finest postwar poet in any language. Of older writers, there were Hölderlein and Leopardi, the essays of Montaigne, and Cervantes' *Don Quixote*, which has remained a great source for me.

jm But in the seventies you also wrote a great number of articles and essays about other writers.

PA Yes, that's true. There was a period in the middle seventies in particular when I found myself eager to test my own ideas about writers in print. It's one thing to read and admire somebody's work, but it's quite another to marshal your thoughts about that writer into something coherent. The people I wrote about—Laura Riding, Edmond Jabès, Louis Wolfson, Knut Hamsen, and others—were writers I felt a need to respond to. I never considered myself a reviewer, but simply one writer trying to talk about others. Having to write prose for publication disciplined me, I think, and convinced me that ultimately I was able to write prose. So in some sense those little pieces of literary journalism were the training ground for the novel.

jm Your first prose book was *The Invention of Solitude*, which was an autobiographical book.

PA I don't think of it as an autobiography so much as a meditation about certain questions, using myself as a central character. The book is divided into two sections, which were written separately, with a gap of about a year between the sections. The first, "Portrait of an Invisible Man," was written in response to my father's death. He simply dropped dead one day, unexpectedly, after being in perfect health, and the shock of it left me with so many unanswered questions about him that I felt that I had no choice but to sit down and try to put something on paper. In the act of trying to write about him, I began to realize how problematic it is to presume to know anything about anyone else. While that piece is filled with specific details, it still seems to me not so much an attempt at biography but an exploration of how one might begin to speak about another person, and whether or not it is even possible.

The second part, "The Book of Memory," grew out of the first and was a response to it. It gave me a great deal of trouble, especially in terms of organization. I began writing it in the first person, as the first part had been written, but couldn't make any headway with it. This part was even more personal than the first, but the more deeply I descended into the material, the more distanced I became from it. In order to write about myself, I had to treat myself as though I were someone else. It was only when I started all over again in the third person that I began to see my way out of the impasse. The astonishing thing, I think, is that at the moment when you are most truly alone, when you truly enter a state of solitude, that is the moment when you are not alone anymore, when you start to feel your connection with others. I believe I

even quote Rimbaud in that book, "*Je est un autre*"—I is another—and I take that sentence quite literally. In the process of writing or thinking about yourself, you actually become someone else.

jm Not only is the narrative voice of "The Book of Memory" different, but the structure is different as well.

PA The central question in the second part was memory. So in some sense everything that happens in it is simultaneous. But writing is sequential, it unfolds over time. So my greatest problem was in trying to put things in the correct order.

The point was to be as honest as possible in every sentence. I wanted to write a work that was completely exposed. I didn't want to hide anything. I wanted to break down for myself the boundary between living and writing as much as I could. That's not to say that a lot of literary effort didn't go into the book, but the impulses are all very immediate and pressing. With everything I do, it seems that I just get so inside it, I can't think about anything else. And writing the book becomes real for me. I was talking about myself in "The Book of Memory," but by tracking specific instances of my own mental process, perhaps I was doing something other people could understand as well.

jm Yes, that's how it worked for me. "The Book of Memory" dwells on coincidences, strange intersections of events in the world. This is also true in the novels of *The New York Trilogy*.

PA Yes, I believe the world is filled with strange events. Reality is a great deal more mysterious than we ever give it credit for. In that sense, the *Trilogy* grows directly out of *The Invention of Solitude*. On the most personal level, I think of *City of Glass* as an homage to my wife. It's a kind of fictitious subterranean autobiography, an attempt to imagine what my life would have been like if I hadn't met her. That's why I had to appear in the book as myself, but at the same time Auster is also Quinn, but in a different universe.

The opening scene in the book is something that actually happened to me. I was living alone at the time, and one night the telephone rang and the person on the other end asked for the Pinkerton Detective Agency. I told him that he had the wrong number, of course, but the same person called back the next night with the same question. When I hung up the phone the second time, I asked myself what would have happened if I had said "Yes." That was the genesis of the book, and I went on from there.

jm Reviews of the book seem to emphasize the mystery elements of *The New York Trilogy*, making it out to be a gloss on the mystery genre. Did you feel that you were writing a mystery novel?

PA Not at all. Of course, I used certain elements of detective fiction. Quinn, after all, writes detective novels, and takes on the identity of someone he thinks is a detective. But I felt I was using those elements for such different ends, for things that had so little to do with detective stories, that I was somewhat disappointed by the emphasis that was put on them. That's not to say that I have anything against the genre. The mystery, after all, is one of the oldest and most compelling forms of storytelling, and any number of works can be placed in that category: *Oedipus Rex*, *Crime and Punishment*, a whole range of twentieth-century novels. In America, there's no question that people like Raymond Chandler and James M. Cain are legitimate writers, writers who have contributed something important to the language. It's a mistake to look down on popular forms. You have to be open to everything, to be willing to take inspiration from any and all sources. In the same way that Cervantes used chivalric romances as the starting point for *Don Quixote*; or the way that Beckett used the standard vaudeville routine as the framework for *Waiting for Godot*. I tried to use certain genre conventions to get to another place, another place altogether.

jm The problem of identity, right?

PA Exactly. The question of who is who and whether or not we are who we think we are. The whole process that Quinn undergoes in that book—and the characters in the other two, as well—is one of stripping away to some barer condition in which we have to face up to who we are. Or who we aren't. It finally comes to the same thing.

jm　And the detective is somebody who's supposed to deal with the problems we have in maintaining a conventional identity. He deals with the messy edges of reality. Like, "My wife, she's not doing what she's supposed to."

PA　Right, exactly. Or, "Somebody's missing." So the detective really is a very compelling figure, a figure we all understand. He's the seeker after truth, the problem solver, the one who tries to figure things out. But what if, in the course of trying to figure it out, you just unveil more mysteries? I suppose that's what happens in the books.

The books have to do with the idea of mystery in several ways. We're surrounded by things we don't understand, by mysteries, and in the books these are people who suddenly come face to face with them. It becomes more apparent that they're surrounded by things they don't know or understand. So in that sense there might be some psychological resonance. Even though the situations aren't strictly realistic, they might follow some realistic psychology. These are things that we all feel—that confusion, that lack of knowing what it is that surrounds us.

jm　I saw the protagonist dropping into a kind of necessity, suddenly, and putting personal life aside, driven by some extraordinary hunger. It has almost religious undertones to it. I remember reading a review by Fanny Howe in the *Boston Globe*, and she said that the book is a kind of gnosis—"grace among the fallen."

PA　"Religious" might not be the word I would use, but I agree that these books are mostly concerned with spiritual questions, the search for spiritual grace. At some point or another, all three characters undergo a form of humiliation, of degradation, and perhaps that is a necessary stage in discovering who we are.

Each novel in the *Trilogy*, I suppose, is about a kind of passionate excess. Quinn's story in *City of Glass* alludes to *Don Quixote*, and the questions raised in the two books are very similar: What is the line between madness and creativity, what is the line between the real and the imaginary, is Quinn crazy to do what he does or not? For a time, I toyed with the idea of using an epigraph at the beginning of *City of Glass*. It comes from Wittgenstein: "And it also means something to talk of 'living in the pages of a book.'"

In *Ghosts*, the spirit of Thoreau is dominant—another kind of passionate excess. The idea of living a solitary life, of living with a kind of monastic intensity—and all the dangers that entails. Walden Pond in the heart of the city. In his *American Notebook*, Hawthorne wrote an extraordinary and luminous sentence about Thoreau that has never left me, "I think he means to live like an Indian among us." That sums up the project better than anything else I've read. The determination to reject everyday American life, to go against the grain, to discover the more solid foundation for oneself. And in *The Locked Room*, by the way, the name

Fanshawe is a direct reference to Hawthorne. *Fanshawe* is the title of Hawthorne's first novel. He wrote it when he was very young, and not long after it was published, he turned against it in revulsion and tried to destroy every copy he could get his hands on. Fortunately, a few of them survived.

jm In *Ghosts*, Blue, in effect, loses his whole life in taking the case, and the narrator in *The Locked Room* goes through that terrible experience in Paris . . .

PA But in the end, he manages to resolve the question for himself—more or less. He finally comes to accept his own life, to understand that no matter how bewitched or haunted he is, he has to accept reality as it is, to tolerate the presence of ambiguities within himself. That's what happens to him with relation to Fanshawe. He hasn't slain the dragon, he's let the dragon move into the house with him. That's why he destroys the notebook in the last scene.

jm And the reader feels it. We're inside him.

PA The one thing I try to do in all my books is to leave enough room in the prose for the reader to inhabit it. Because I finally believe that it's the reader who writes the book and not the writer. In my own case as a reader—and I've certainly read more books than I've written!—I find that I almost invariably appropriate scenes and situations from a book and graft them onto my own experiences, or

vice versa. In reading a book like *Pride and Prejudice*, for example, I realized at a certain point that all the events were set in the house I grew up in as a child. No matter how specific a writer's description of a place might be, I always seem to twist it into something I'm familiar with. I've asked a number of my friends if this happens to them when they read fiction as well. For some yes, for others no. I think this has a lot to do with one's relation to language, how one responds to words printed on a page. Whether the words are just symbols, or whether they are passageways into our unconscious.

There's a way in which a writer can do too much, overwhelming the reader with so many details that he no longer has any air to breathe. Think of a typical passage in a novel. A character walks into a room. As a writer, how much of that room do you want to talk about? The possibilities are infinite. You can give the color of the curtains, the wallpaper pattern, the objects on the coffee table, the reflection of the light in the mirror. But how much of this is really necessary? Is the novelist's job simply to reproduce physical sensations for their own sake? When I write, the story is always uppermost in my mind, and I feel that everything must be sacrificed to it. All the elegant passages, all the curious details, all the so-called beautiful writing—if they are not truly relevant to what I am trying to say, then they have to go. It's all in the voice. You're telling a story, after all, and your job is to make people want to go on listening to your tale. The slightest distraction or wandering leads to boredom, and if it's one thing we all hate in books, it's losing interest, feeling bored, not caring about the next sentence. In the end, you don't only write the books you need to write, but you write the books you would like to read yourself.

jm Is there a method to it?

PA No. The deeper I get into my own work, the less engaging theoretical problems have become. When you look back on the works that have moved you, you find that they have always been written out of some kind of necessity. There's something calling out to you, some human call, that makes you want to listen to the work. In the end, it probably has very little to do with literature.

Georges Bataille wrote about this in his preface to *Le Bleu du Ciel*. I refer to it in *The Art of Hunger*, in an essay on the schizophrenic Wolfson. He said that every real book comes from a moment of rage, and then he asked: "How can we read works that we don't feel compelled to read?" I believe he's absolutely correct: there's always some indefinable something that makes you attend to a writer's works—you can never put your finger on it, but that something is what makes all the difference.

jm In other words the writer has to be haunted by his story before he can write it.

PA In my own experiences I've often lived for years with the ideas for books before I could manage to write them. *In The Country of Last Things* is a novel I started writing back in the days when I was a college student. The idea of a young woman writing letters from the edge of the world, from some unknowable place . . . it got under my skin and I couldn't let go of it. I would pick up the manuscript, work on it for a while, and then put it down. The essential thing was to capture her voice, and when I couldn't hear it anymore, I would have to stop. I must have started the book thirty times. Each time it was somewhat different than the time before, but the essential situation was always the same.

jm In the same way that some reviewers classified *The New York Trilogy* as a mystery, there were many articles about this book that classified it as apocalyptic science fiction.

PA That was the farthest thing from my mind while I was writing it. In fact, my private, working subtitle for the book was *Anna Blume Walks Through the Twentieth Century*. I feel that it's very much a book about our own moment, our own era, and many of the incidents are things that have actually happened. For example, the pivotal scene in which Anna is lured into a human slaughterhouse is based on something I read about the siege of Leningrad during World War II. These things actually happened. And in many cases, reality is far more terrible than anything we can imagine. Even the garbage system that I describe at such length was inspired by

an article I once read about the present-day garbage system in Cairo.
Admittedly, the book takes on these
things from a somewhat oblique
angle, and the country Anna goes to
might not be immediately recognizable, but I feel that this is where we
live. It could be that we've become
so accustomed to it that we no
longer see it.

jm What are you working on now?

PA I'm coming close to the end of a novel
called *Moon Palace*. It's the longest
book I've ever written and probably
the one most rooted in a specific time
and place. The action begins in 1969
and doesn't get much beyond 1971.
At bottom, I suppose it's a story about
families and generations, a kind of
David Copperfield novel, and it's something that I've been wanting to write
for a long time. As with the last book,
it's gone through many changes. The
pages pile up, but God knows what it
will look like when it's all finished.
Whenever I complete a book, I'm
filled with a feeling of immense disgust and disappointment. It's almost a
physical collapse. I'm so disappointed
by my feeble efforts that I can't
believe I've actually spent so much
time and accomplished so little. It
takes years before I am able to accept
what I've done—to realize that this
was the best I could do. But I never
like to look at the things I've written.
The past is the past, and there's nothing I can do about it anymore. The
only thing that counts is the project
I'm working on now.

jm Beckett once said in one of his
stories, "No sooner is the ink dry
than it revolts me."

PA You can't say it any better than that.

LUISA VALENZUELA linda yablonsky

Luisa Valenzuela is and always has been unafraid to be a woman who writes biting political satire that is also highly charged erotic literature, all this in her "phallocentric" country of Argentina. Nothing, however, has more value for Luisa Valenzuela than memory. Perhaps because the governments her country has survived so often try to rewrite its history, imposing a collective amnesia on the people.

The daughter of writer Luisa Mercedes Levinson, Luisa Valenzuela grew up under Peronism in the fifties within Buenos Aires' most important literary circle, the world of Borges and Sábato, Bioy Casares, and local poets and publishers, who gave her the opportunity to have her first short story printed when she was eighteen.

To date, she has published five collections of stories, among them *Up Among the Eagles, Strange Things Happen Here*, and *The Heretics*; and six novels, including *He Who Searches, Clara, The Lizard's Tail*, and the upcoming *Black Novel with Argentines* have been translated into English. Just before Christmas, Ms. Valenzuela was visiting New York. While in Buenos Aires there was a brief attempt at a military coup, as demonstrations continued against President Carlos Menem's impending pardons to the generals who, during the Dirty War of the 1970s, were responsible for the tortured deaths of at least 9,000 people. Against this background, we began talking about her first short story, "City of the Unknown," which opens with a girl's discovery of a man who possesses "a voice that could raise the dead."

BOMB # 3 5, Spring 1991

linda yablonsky If you could raise the dead, who would you go after?

LUISA VALENZUELA Cortázar and Borges. First Cortázar, because he had such an inventive mind. And perhaps more, out of my heart . . . Cortázar had an eye for things you couldn't see at first glance.

ly You were only seventeen when you wrote "City of the Unknown," and yet it has such a mature sexuality and a very developed imagination.

LV The imagination was very developed then. I don't know about the maturity.

ly Was that story based on a particular longing, or incident?

LV What happens when you revive the

Luisa Valenzuela, © Enrique Molder.

dead? That was the question that triggered the whole story.

ly Terrifying idea, actually. You bring it up again in "Up Among the Eagles."

LV That's much later, "Eagles" was written ten years ago.

ly In that story, it's not that the dead are being revived, but that they're very present.

LV The dead are present in life, constantly.

ly You say that if we stopped writing, history would stop, time would stop. In "Up Among the Eagles," there's a lot of talk about controlling time, aging and not aging.

LV It's a different concept of time—the Iroquois, and many other native American languages, don't have tenses. There's no notion of a past or future, verbs are always handled in the same tense.

ly Do you worry about aging?

LV Oh yes, as everybody else. And I get furious—except that the more you live, the more you realize it's so much in your mind.

ly It's so strange, the image you see in the mirror and your self-image being so totally different, and the older you get, the more distance there seems to be.

LV Except, sometimes, you catch yourself in the mirror being who you think you are. Is the mirror lying?

ly We're running out of a lot of things, one of which is time, time

keeps getting compressed. These two stories of yours were written years apart and yet they both share this sense of stopping time to keep things the same, creating history by recording events and people: the sense that without the record, there would be no history.

LV I'm very worried about memory, about the fact that you tend to repeat the past if you ignore it. And Argentina's always trying to obliterate your memory, so there's all this talk of pardons and amnesties for the generals implicated in the tortures, as if one could make a clean slate of past horrors.

But I insist that you can't simply obliterate memory. If you say nothing happened, you can't move. This is something that has been in the back of my mind for ages, and it pops up in different stories. It finally has to do with reviving the dead—which is again, the other impossibility. You cannot kill the memory or revive the dead. You have to accept the time law as we know it.

ly In what direction do you think the Argentinean government is going, and what do people have to say about it?

LV The people have to say everything they can, if they can, because they are very hungry at this point.

ly Literally, hungry?

LV Literally hungry. But anything is better than another military coup, so nobody says too much for fear of getting the military back, which would be worse, decidedly. The economic problems, I don't think, can be solved one way or the other, but at least there is liberty. It is a very strange government: playing the game of the populists—and having an extremely right-wing capitalistic policy. They are using a very obvious double standard and very obvious lies, so obvious that there's nothing you can do about it. It's not that you can't denounce anything, it's that everything's being denounced every day, so everything has lost its value. Nothing happens.

ly **What sort of people in Argentina become members of the military?**

LV There is an odd historical situation here. It used to be the upper classes. The military of the last century were the cultured people, they went to important military academies, they knew languages, translated Dante— they were very intelligent. And little by little, we got more dogmatic. I suppose people who go into the military now—except for the poor, who have nothing else to do but join—are those who believe they are the owners of the truth and are ready to impose it by force. I once gave a talk at West Point.

ly **Really? You didn't!**

LV I was talking in front of all these West Point cadets, and suddenly, out of my mouth, without thinking, I said, "I don't understand what you are all doing here. If I were in Argentina, I would know that you all wanted to be President." [*laughter*] In Argentina they all want to take charge, it's a question of power. That fascinates me. What is this madness called power?

Did you read the *Desert of the Tartars*, by Dino Buzzati, the Italian writer? It takes place in a military post, a frontier bordering the so-called desert of the Tartars. And they are all the time waiting for the enemy to come, and there are strict military rules in this fort. Only the enemy hasn't come for two centuries, and there is no enemy, there is only desert. But they can't recognize that reality. One day, somebody goes out and when he comes back refuses to announce the code word. He is shot and killed because they had to create something to justify their existence. All this has to do with the phallocracy.

ly **Would you consider yourself any kind of feminist?**

LV I'm a born feminist. I'm not a dogmatic feminist.

ly **Have you personally been confronted with a lot of violence in Argentina?**

LV No, not much nowadays. You see more in the streets of New York. Things in Buenos Aires are calm. It's very disturbing, because you know they're not calm. It's impossible for them to be calm. There was this military uprising the other day and people thumbed their noses at the fighting. The minute the rebellious military tries something they get horrible abuse from the public.

ly **How can they?**

LV The public verbally insults them. It's just fantastic. One time a bunch of dissident military tried to take over the city airport and the people who were going on their vacations pushed them out of the way. Life goes on and private citizens don't allow this to stop them anymore. We are no longer afraid. We've seen too much during the dictatorship.

ly But are the citizens armed?

LV No, I hope not. Some are, unfortunately. But, this is pure chutzpah.

ly So, you've picked up a little New Yorkese, I see.

LV Yes, I lived here for quite a while—eleven years.

ly Do you want to tell me a little bit about how you grew up?

LV It was a very literary house, and Borges and Sábato, Bioy Casares—mainly Borges, and all these big shots in Argentine literature—were there very often, and I thought it was all very fascinating, but not for me. I wanted to be a mathematician, an artist or a painter—anything but literature. I had always wanted to be an explorer. You don't know how much of an explorer a writer is when you're young. Literature seemed so passive, and ironically, they were practically all very apolitical. Ironically, because this was during Peronist times, and all of these writers were out of a job because they'd been censored and kicked out of work. My mother organized paid lectures and readings in our home so that these writers could earn a living. I didn't think I was political at all, myself, but I thought there had to be some action in all this, and there was

no action. So I went into journalism. In journalism, you move.

ly And what were your first forays into journalism?

LV Travel pieces.

ly The title of one of your novels is *He Who Searches,* there's definitely a seeking in your writing.

LV There's a seeking in my life, in general.

ly Are you religious at all?

LV No. Yes. Yes, but not of any religion. I believe in the sacred aspects of life and that level of thinking. So I read a lot about religions. But I don't believe in God.

ly I was just going to ask you.

LV But there is a sense of the sacred in the world, in nature. Westerners don't know about dualities, simultaneity. This is a very Asian concept, the sacred and the profane, you cannot separate one from the other, the sacred couldn't exist without the profane.

ly All of your stories in *Strange Things Happen Here* start with some human intimacy that grows in the historical context, the canvas of events that surround it and give it another dimension. I noticed you don't give names to a lot of people in your stories.

LV These stories were written very quickly, triggered either by something I was told or something I overheard. It's a collective mind, in a sense. I want to make them archetypal . . . a name is a very heavy burden. Sometimes, I don't want to put this burden on certain characters. Some don't need a name.

ly "The Censors" really twisted me up inside, that obsession.

LV It was so self-defeating, such a male story in a sense. That book [*Strange Things Happen Here*] wasn't censored because—God knows. I think, censors don't have a sense of humor.

ly I'm sure they don't.

LV They were doing a video two months ago in Argentina, and they asked me to read any story. I started reading "The Best Shod" [*in which the beggars of Argentina, helping themselves to the plethora of new shoes worn by the dead bodies lying around them, become the best-shod beggars in the world*]. And suddenly, I realized I couldn't read that one. Not because it would be censored, but because it's so painful. So much of it had really happened. Seen from a distance it's a metaphor, but at the other end, it's no longer a metaphor.

ly Your writing has a very strong interior voice, much stronger than whatever is on the narrative's surface. It's almost as if you're whispering under your breath.

LV I'm glad it comes out in translation.

ly I feel when I'm reading your stories, that I'm hearing what really goes on in your mind, even when you're talking about people outside yourself.

LV Because the narrative itself makes the good connections, the proper associa-

tions. The narrative per se knows more than what the writer knows, or whatever has been told to you. Whatever has been told to you is full of holes and omissions and things that are hidden. A narrative line will make all these things pop out in the open. You will discover them while you're writing. That's what fascinates me about writing.

ly Do you spend most of your time writing?

LV I wish I did.

ly So what do you spend most of your time doing?

LV Daydreaming. Worrying. Feeling guilty for not writing. You have to go through that phase, now I've learned.

ly Do you ever use a tape recorder?

LV No, never. I can't, because I need the physical act of writing. Now I'm using a computer at times, but it's not the same. I write generally with a fountain pen.

ly Do you live on your writing?

LV No, I don't. I do with my lectures, and other things.

ly What did you teach here?

LV Funny enough, I had a writers' workshop in English.

ly Do you teach in Argentina also?

LV No, no. This is an American operation!

ly Have you ever thought about going into politics?

LV Oh no—oh no! The only thing I do with politics is denounce whatever's going on at that horrible level. I think it's the worst . . . I don't believe in darkness, least of all in politics.

ly You're very sharp with the political satire.

LV I know I'm sharp, but it's scary because I sometimes become prophetic.

ly Do you find that life imitates art in this case?

LV No, I find that art puts two and two together—that's all. And again, it obeys a narrative order. There always is a narrative.

ly To life.

LV To life, in general. And in writing, the narrative is then cut into pieces of time and place and convenience, whatever is hidden or forgotten or not said. And in writing, the narrative reconstruction builds this whole edifice again and there you have prophecy. You have everything, because that is a real narrative.

ly Are you saying you think things have definite beginnings and middles and ends, so to speak? Or is life continuous?

LV There is a continuum, and there are links to things. But nothing pops up out of the blue, in fact. Things are linked—there is a chain. And that chain can be seen in the narrative, because the narrative needs a chain. Otherwise, it's sheer luck, serendipity. We don't live in a plotless novel. The novel of our lives has a very rich plot! And the only thing a writer does is follow that plot as best she can.

ly What's your home life like now? Are you living alone?

LV I'm living alone. I have a part-time dog, and I'm living in the middle of a park. I'm surrounded by wonderful, very nice old trees. People are around.

ly You never feel lonesome?

LV No, I like it.

ly You don't miss the intimacy of a family?

LV My daughter's around, friends are around all the time.

ly But not a man?

LV Oh, yeah, sometimes. But then it becomes . . . I don't know. Things are as they are. I have always quarreled with my men.

ly You have?

LV Yes, yes. I was often quite violent. You wouldn't believe it.

ly Well, no—not sitting here. Although I can see your anger on the page.

LV Yes, I don't like to be invaded. I feel invaded easily. I need my privacy more than anything else. And then I travel all the time.

ly What made you move back to Argentina?

LV New York was becoming too hectic. I was dreaming in English, I was thinking in English—I didn't want that anymore. My novel, *Black Novel with Argentines*, took me five years and it was very hard to write. It takes place in New York. It is a very dark piece, a very gutter-like

book, with very, very deep unconscious levels, really hard stuff. I
thought that in a sense I was writing
a farewell to New York.

ly Oh, I can't wait to read it.

LV It's very strong. And there is a crime,
and again, it's a search, not a search
for criminals, but more a search for
the motive of the crime. And there are
two Argentine writers, so it has to do
with writing, it has to do with confusions, and it has to do with the S & M
scene in New York—with all the
boundaries you cross, in all senses. It
was hard to write. I didn't want to
write it half the time, so then I wrote
this other one [*National Reality from
the Bed*] very quickly.

When I'm writing a novel there is
a different state. It's like being in a
trance. So when you're reading the
novel, you're inside this other situation. Life has another dimension.
Everything that comes into your life
has something to do with another.
There's this conflict, there is a voracity, there is vampirism when you're in
your novel.

ly Vampirism?

LV Yes, because when I write I become a
vampire. I suck cold blood from anything for a novel.

ly How do you know when to end it?

LV Oh, it abandons you.

ly It abandons you? Oh!

LV That's it. And you feel awful sometimes. A novel has to have a life of its
own. This is when you know you are
writing well.

ly Could you compare the attitude
toward work between New York
and Buenos Aires, say?

LV Oh, yes. This is one of the reasons I
left. Because I started *believing* in
workaholism, and everything was so
desperate, and things had to be done
perfectly right, and I started believing
this New York thing. I saw myself
absolutely caught in this trap. And I
ran away. I said: This is not true! I
need to respond to the first principle of
pataphysics that says you never have to
take serious things seriously. And here
I was, taking things seriously. So I left.

SUZANNAH LESSARD AND HONOR MOORE
betsy sussler

Born just before the turn of the century, Margarett Sargent was an exuberant socialite, iconoclastic wit, audacious lover—and mother and wife—from Brahmin Boston. A uniquely talented and professionally recognized painter, she exhibited in New York and Boston, but abruptly stopped making art in her mid forties. Suffering from severe depression, using alcohol to quell the growing conflict between her creative and social drives, she spent the last years of her life in and out of sanatoriums undergoing shock treatment or travelling with a chauffeur through Europe, estranged from her family and isolated from friends and colleagues.

Stanford White was the leading neoclassical architect at the turn of the century. His energy and output were gargantuan: He designed the Washington Square Arch and Park, the original Madison Square Garden and the Players, Metropolitan, and Colony Clubs, as well as palaces for the robber barons of the Gilded Age rich—the New York society we know best from Edith Wharton's novels. His lifestyle was as frenzied as his output—long junkets in Europe buying art and antiquities for his clients, designing and orchestrating extravagant dinner parties and balls, rebuilding and designing the grounds for his wife and family at Box Hill, Long Island, and maintaining a tower high above midtown New York where he entertained privately. In 1906 he was murdered, shot in a public restaurant by the delirious and jealous husband of Evelyn Nesbit, a young woman Stanford had seduced when she was sixteen. Stanford's affairs were revealed at the trial, and the ensuing scandal was subsequently romanticized and glamorized over the decades by biographers, historians, and, of course, Hollywood.

As juicy and highly entertaining as these stories might seem to the public, the dramatic and painful effects for immediate family members are another matter. Family stories handed down, or ones never discussed but revealed by outsiders, form a family's identity as much as time, place and individuals. Honor Moore's biography of her grandmother Margarett Sargent, *The White Blackbird*

Suzannah Lessard, © Sidney Frissel Stafford. Courtesy The Dial Press.

(Viking), and Suzannah Lessard's rumination on her great-grand-father and family in *The Architect of Desire: Beauty and Danger in the Stanford White Family* (The Dial Press), are provocative and shimmering revelations of both the myth and the truth of these two larger-than-life figures and the legacies they left their families. We sat down over tea this summer, just hours before Suzannah and Honor were leaving New York for vacation in Italy.

betsy sussler I felt that you were both haunted by your subjects: Honor, by your grandmother Margarett Sargent's talents as a painter and beautiful socialite, and her ulti-mate decline into depression; and Suzannah, with your great-grand-father Stanford White's dramatic talent and lifestyle, and his mur-der. Were these hauntings?

HONOR MOORE It was a haunting for me in that my grandmother's life was a trap door I was certain I'd fall through. I felt sure that if I became creative, as I wished to do, that I would become alcoholic, promiscuous, manic depressive, in and out of men-tal hospitals, and a casualty of years of shock treatments. It didn't look good.

SUZANNAH LESSARD In my case, there was a story and a romance that was very colorful and ebullient, and there was also an avoidance that was disturbing. A feeling of unfinished business.

bs An avoidance in that within the family the murder was never dis-cussed?

SL Stanford himself was never discussed. But in fact we lived in this very power-ful, vivid, and beautiful context which had been created by him so that he was everywhere there. And then there was silence about him to the extent that anything said was a denial of the very glamorous myth that was held elsewhere in the world. What was mysterious to me was how the family continued to be disturbed by the very name of Stanford White. It didn't make any sense, because it was a sophisticated and cosmopolitan fami-ly, not a prudish one—a bohemian family by my time. And one very tol-erant of all kinds of behavior. Therefore, why would they be upset about this glamorous, bohemian, sexy guy? Most mysterious of all was that I seemed to be wired with the same ner-vousness about him.

bs Do you think that by discussing the scandal, that your family would have uncovered an evil that they didn't want revealed? No one knew really what happened between Stanford and Evelyn.

SL Well, there were different layers, dif-ferent generations knew different things. My grandfather knew, he lived through the trial. And my grand-mother knew. And then there was what they communicated—or failed to communicate—to their children, my mother's generation. My mother and my uncle Bobby didn't learn

Honor Moore, © Inge Morath/Magnum. Courtesy Viking.

about it from them. My uncle learnt about it for the first time while he was in the Coast Guard in World War II; and my mother learnt of the story from a Smith cousin.

bs This is not unusual, that members of subsequent generations are the last to hear the details of a family scandal.

HM What occurs to me as you're talking, is that the myth I grew up with was a very negative one. Margarett was demonized in our family. I learned, when I was growing up, to be frightened of her, so it was more a question of finding out what the real woman's life was, which actually turned out to be less "crazy" than the myth. I never knew when I was growing up that she'd had a real career as an artist.

bs But hadn't you grown up among her paintings?

HM No. There was one drawing in our house. No paintings. I didn't know she'd ever done a painting until I was an adult. I thought maybe she'd dabbled. I had no idea.

bs But she had a reputation, and she knew and befriended Betty Parsons, Jane Bowles, Berenice Abbott . . .

HM I knew none of that. Those were all friendships I learned about when I began to research the book.

bs What first compelled each of you to start these books?

SL It was at the center of my writing life. After I got to the *New Yorker*, William

Shawn said to me, "We're here to publish what you write, not to tell you what to write." And at first I didn't believe him; I thought, that's ridiculous. This is a job. And I went ahead and wrote articles that I thought of as *New Yorker* articles. But something deep in my psyche heard what he'd actually said, and I began to develop a combination of a focus and a block. Every subject that I picked up would start off fine, no matter how neutral, and then after a while started developing troubles. It was as if the article had tethers attached to it: long, long tethers that were attached to a whale that started swimming, the minute I started writing, in the direction of what I thought of as New Zealand, which was a place I had never been. In other words, I knew the direction, but I didn't know where I was going. So I'd be a little ways in and then the piece would get pulled by the whale, and shortly thereafter a terrible conflict would develop. Sometimes the subject matter was close to home, sometimes it was far from home, but it didn't matter. It was as if my psyche found a way, out of any material, to develop a conflict that was archetypal for me. And finally it got so bad, and it was taking me so long to write anything that I decided that I was going to believe what Mr. Shawn said, "We're here to publish what you write." So I decided to follow the whale. One morning I sat up in bed, looked out my window, and I picked up my pencil and immediately started what is now the opening of the second chapter in the book, "Lower

Fifth Avenue, this is my neighborhood." It started moving like a spiral, and I noted all the aspects of the neighborhood that were family references starting with Washington Square Arch, which is Stanford's; and then I saw a little bit of the Hudson out the window and my mind went right up the river to Rokeby, which was the seat of the Chanlers, one of the clans that is now a part of the book. And so it went, that morning, directly into the family story. But then for many years I remained in conflict about it because I wanted to write a love letter to the family, I wanted to restore it to what it had been for me. And at the same time I needed terribly to tell the truth. I feel that what I've done is a restoration and not a destruction of the family. It's a restoration because it grounds the family story in reality rather than fantasy and denial. But for many years I was unable to proceed because I didn't have all the information I needed in order to come to terms with my own life, much less all the information about Stanford's.

HM What happened to me was that in 1969 I was struggling to write poems in New Haven, and going out with a guy who was a writer. You know, I was going out with him because . . .

bs You were young and you went out with the person you wanted to be.

HM Right. And I sat up in his little office and started writing about my grandmother. It was the first coherent thing I'd ever written. It had voice and image.

bs But then what happened? That was 1969 and this is 1996.

HM I saved the piece and more or less forgot about it. It was about meeting Margarett at Prides, her house and studio north of Boston, after she no longer lived there full-time. Eventually, after I began to write seriously, I tried to use some of the material in a poem about her. I was obsessed. I used to go to those exhibitions of women artists in the seventies and look for her on the walls. Literally. But I never found her, and I could never finish the poem. Finally in 1980, Janet Sternburg was editing an anthology called *The Writer On Her Work* and she wrote a very interesting letter. It didn't say, "Write about being a woman writer." She asked, "Who influenced you? Who was it that made you become a writer?" And I wrote the essay, "My Grandmother Who Painted," in which I quoted that first piece I'd written about Margarett. *The White Blackbird* starts with a part of that essay Sternburg commissioned in which my mother berates me—I'm twelve years old—because she's afraid I'll grow up to be like the mother she's terrified of.

bs I do believe that any writer has one subject about which he or she must write, that imperative sets them free—to write.

HM Like Suzannah, I had to get free. It was as if Margarett's example was a family curse that I had to break: My grandmother stopped painting, and my mother died at fifty after publishing one book and left me her writing in her will.

bs She was telling you what you had to do.

HM That's right—but I also had to get past my version of what the crisis was that stopped Margarett cold at forty-five

bs Both of you ground your books in places that have an animistic quality. They're family seats. Do you think places have souls?

HM Prides was not a family seat. It was the house where my mother grew up, but it was charged with the same kind of negative force that Margarett was, and it was sold as quickly as possible after she became incompetent enough not to notice.

bs It was your mother's family home. It was imbued with some kind of spirit . . .

HM It was imbued with the demonic spirit of family stories about Margarett. I did not go there. I went there only once as a child. When I was growing up, our "family seat" was the farm where my father grew up in New Jersey.

bs So Prides was in fact a place that was a mystery to you, whereas Suzannah, you grew up at Box Hill in St. James?

SL Mmm-hmm.

bs One of the things that drew me to your book was the description of the land; it felt very much as if it contained the souls of your family. Did you feel their personalities lingered in Box Hill?

SL Oh yes. Clearly.

bs Stanford White didn't just design the house. He designed the landscape as well.

SL A lot of the landscaping of the place was on that plateau, the twenty-five acres where the dwellings are. And even then down in the lower woods, there's a temple designed by Stanford. The Beaux Arts design tends to transcend—in a way becomes the landscape rather than a superimposition.

bs In the book you refer to a wildness to the land, the ruins, the overgrowth . . .

SL The earlier landscape. Yeah, there were layers to the landscape.

bs Like Rome, where the present is built upon layers of the past.

SL That's why Rome was so familiar.

bs Suzannah, you said when you first started to write this book you looked out the window and started moving from Stanford White's architectural sites in your neighborhood up the Hudson to your grandparents' home. It's as if the land and its sites were narrating to you.

SL Yes, very much so. At first I found it impossible to describe my life as a child in my home, all I could describe was the interior of the house. And in a different way, describing the land was almost like an objective correlative for what I felt. I think this is very common in families where there is silence and pain, where there are emotions that are tied up and communication between people is very faulty. People don't know how to communicate love to each other. They transfer it to the land and the land becomes the loved thing, and the custodian of family love.

bs And history.

SL And history. What happened for me in the process of writing the book was that for a long time writing about the land was the only way that I could write about any of this, and gradually it led me toward the essence, which of course is not about the land at all. I had to break through, I had to liberate myself from that because as long as you stop there and just say the land has mythic quality and a soul, you haven't really cracked the riddle.

HM You get stuck in the aesthetic.

SL You get stuck in metaphors, and it's a substitute for feeling.

HM I had that experience a little about the land, it was more about Margarett's paintings, her drawings, anything with her handwriting on it. Everything had a talismanic quality.

bs Although Honor, you use a very interesting device, you start many of the chapters by describing one of her paintings as a way of getting into her psyche.

HM I didn't intend to do that. I was eager to make the book readable and compelling and there was this problem with transitions—going from 1920 to 1921, for instance, or from a given January to a given August. At a certain point I no longer had her written diaries—she stopped keeping one at

twenty-one—but I did have a visual record. She shifted her medium from the verbal to the visual. I struggled with the loss of her written narrative, until one day—and I remember the moment, it was winter and I was at my computer—I realized that I could simply translate her images into language, something I often do in poems.

bs A psychological language.

HM Well, I think of it more as phenomenological. I set up a slide projector by my desk, and put up a window shade on the wall, and I would project a painting. I really went at it as if I were writing a poem—that is, I began to write, letting Margarett's image give me both language and the rhythm of my language. The reason I resist the term psychological is because I did not think of Margarett in an analytic way as I wrote, and I don't use analytical language in those passages.

bs I'm thinking of psychological in terms of character study, character development.

HM Well, I didn't think about that. I simply wrote those descriptions when the narration seemed to call for them—sometimes at the beginning of chapters, sometimes at other crucial points in the story. Much later they came to represent Margarett's inner life, and reinforced the conflicts between her artistic search and the banalities and strictures of the social and domestic context in which she lived. My attempts to enter her paintings through language heighten the tension of the prose. When I was in the final stages of revision—when a book really takes over and creates its own form—I realized that Margarett had, with her paintings, given the book its particular character, that she had somehow led the way.

bs Suzannah, I felt that you discovered a new form in *The Architect of Desire*, somewhere between biography, memoir, and rumination. When I told you this you said that that was very much decided by the content of what you had to write, and what you had to write decided the form of the book.

SL Well, that sounds more intentional than it actually was. The material had a life of its own with its own demands. I felt like I was a stenographer. For years I was too tortured to talk about it. Nothing happened. And I'd write and rewrite and rewrite, as if looking to crack a safe with certain combinations of words as if the words were dice. I had this feeling that if I threw the right combination of words, that they would crack *something* open. It was this latent feeling. Of course, words can't do that. I needed to crack open. This futile struggle ate up my thirties. At forty, I finally stopped. And then five years later, with great horror because it had taken up so much of my life, it came back. It was in a little writers' group that Honor, Kennedy Fraser, Louise DeSalvo and I had put together. I started again with that first passage and they all said, "It's great, keep going." What they told me was that it reached them, that they could feel that there was

something very vital that was happening with those words. I didn't have to keep throwing the dice. What was your question?

bs We were talking about devices and form, how you use the descriptions of your family place in the same way Honor uses her grandmother's paintings—to get into an interior state.

SL Well, I would make a distinction, because when Honor is interpreting the paintings, she's interpreting the work of an articulate person, not words, but a painting by Margarett. That's much more direct. She's in a dialogue with Margarett. Whereas when I'm writing about the land, the land isn't really talking to me, it's complete projection. Not only my own projection, but what it became through the generations. My perception of the land is very influenced by my mother's perception of the land, and by my great-grandmother's perception, and by my perception of their perceptions. It was very wound up in what other people had told me to see and feel. When land becomes so terribly pregnant with meaning, when there's probably some kind of pain bound up with it that hasn't been expressed, you need to pursue that pain and find the cause in order to have real human communication.

bs I have to ask you both something which might seem out of left field. The English believe that we don't have a class system, which always surprises me.

HM Americans don't believe we have a class system.

bs Do you think we have a class system?

HM Absolutely. It's not a system in the way that the British think of it. But we're brought up here to believe that there are no classes. I said something about the upper class, and a friend said to me, "Oh you mean upper middle class?" I said, "No, I mean upper-class." It's a genuine experience, it's a genuine ghetto of shared history, values, education, religion. My parents rebelled against their class. They took great pains to have themselves removed from the social register, which was apparently very difficult. And we went to live in downtown Jersey City, where my father, an Episcopal priest, had an inner city parish. And we were sent to public school.

bs If your grandmother had been able to leave her class, and I'm not suggesting that a woman in that time or place could do that . . .

HM Well, some women did.

bs But if Margarett had left her class, do you think her life would have been more successful, or easier?

HM Let's put it this way, I think that it's possible her life would have been different. There is compelling evidence that making art gave her a kind of balance. There is no one reason she stopped making art, but in the convergence of events, experience, and circumstances in which she stopped, there are forces which have to do with

her conflicts about how she was meant to function as a woman in that class.

bs Both of you talk about this in your books. Stanford White married into the class he aspired to and then proceeded to become one of the biggest proponents, in terms of building their mansions and planning their parties, of the Gilded Age rich.

SL Stanford came from a long line of Calvinist preachers with early New England roots but never much wealth, by Gilded Age standards. But there definitely had been what might be called financial substance. His grandfather had made a fortune in clipper ships, for example, and then lost it when he failed to switch to steam. Stanford married into the Smiths, a country gentry family with roots in place so deep it was extraordinarily indifferent to the vagaries of its own fortunes. And these things are important because the Gilded Age is perpetually nouveau riche, even a century later. The old Yankee class that my great-grandmother Chanler belonged to was very refined, austere, unostentatious, with quite strong values and identity. There are those nuances. But there is that sense, in Stanford, that came from his father of feeling resentful, or somehow diminished by these unbelievably wealthy people who converged on the scene at the turn of the century and swept away a lot of the old standards, and also swept away some of the older families' stature. Henry James writes about this in such great nuance and detail.

bs There's always the class that's had their money for a long time, built their values, built a certain kind of security in who they are and how they want to present themselves to the world. The upper class marries into the noveau riche, the rising class, so that they can maintain their lifestyle, and the rising class in turn raises their social standing. You both talk about taste and lifestyle and you both talk about it a little as a trap, that feeling of entitlement, which both Margarett and Stanford had. Or am I misreading?

HM I didn't say it in so many words, but in the essay in the Wellesley catalogue for Margarett's painting show, Ann Higonnet said, "What would drive you to work, if you already had the things that most people work to get?" I think Margarett had an intuitive and temperamental understanding and reaction to the suffocating life that she was born into. Art was her ticket out, it was the only way that she could alter the aesthetic context that she was born into. All her battles were fought on the sexual and aesthetic plane. And there was her interest in becoming friends with people who were different from her—Fanny Brice, and Vivian Pickman who married into Boston society but had been a showgirl. And there were other people who Margarett gravitated towards who led bohemian lives within an upper class context.

bs Suzannah, at the end of *Architect of Desire* you describe how Edith

Wharton couldn't come to a plot line for *The House of Mirth* until she understood that it had to do not only with the destruction that was being wrought by the Gilded Age rich and their thoughtlessness, the havoc that they wreaked, but also what that havoc did to the good. I believe you think this about the Smiths, that they were good, they had a strong identity and values, regardless of wealth. Whereas Stanford White courted this danger, this chaos. Is that true?

SL That isn't a formulation I would call exactly right, that the Smiths are good and Stanford is bad. But I definitely do see Stanford as someone whose life is hard to understand because it seems he never had consciousness of his own course of destruction. There's an absence of consciousness and responsibility. And without that consciousness there's no drama, no story, there's no real narrative, any more than there's a narrative of the cyclone. The only way you describe the meaning of the cyclone is to say it destroyed this village. As I said in the book, you can never compare Stanford to the destructive characters in *The House of Mirth*, because he did a lot that was good. He was a creative force, he designed a lot of architecture and the city still benefits from much of it. I don't think he wanted to hurt his family, but it was a tragedy that he did, and that it has reverberated down through the generations. He never took responsibility, or he wasn't able to arrest that course.

bs But that particular love triangle was so loaded. Stanford's ex-lover, Evelyn, marries Harry Thaw, a man with an obsession for Stanford White. And Thaw seemed insane to begin with.

SL But, I would say that the threesome, Harry, Stanford, and Evelyn, were all caught in a trap of compulsion. Of the three it's only Evelyn who tried to escape. It's really only Evelyn who had consciousness, who gives the story a moral.

bs You think, in what way?

SL Because she struggles against the blind force of her fortunes, and that gives it some moral shape. If you had three people hurling mindlessly along in their force and ending with death and mayhem . . . If you didn't have her struggle, if you just had this young girl who's devastated and becomes fixated on this man and marries a man obsessed with that man because she can't have him any longer . . . You really have no human story at all. I see it as a struggle toward meaning. A struggle to own one's life, to become responsible. And I think Evelyn did, of the three, more than anyone else. She wanted to get out and have a career. She didn't want to be fixated on Stanford, she didn't want to be married to Harry Thaw. She wanted to be an actress. In this context you can see her provocation of Harry to shoot Stanford as a brilliant move. With one stroke, Harry is off to jail and Stanford's dead. Bam. She's free. Except that she wasn't.

bs We don't often think of beauty as being connected to violence. And yet both of you bring it up. How do you think beauty is connected to violence?

HM What comes to mind is that Margarett created beauty in order not to be violent. I see her as having created the house and grounds at Prides as a kind of refuge. Prides was beautiful, but not without conflict. Her painting actually has wholeness *and* conflict because her temperament inhabits it. Her painting speaks to her situation. Once she started doing the gardens and the house, it was more about creating beauty in order not to be weeping or gnashing her teeth. But that didn't really work.

bs The paintings are beautiful, but definitely violent. The way color is applied, the way Margarett delineates physiognomies . . .

SL Margarett's paintings include shadow. Beauty without shadow is what's dangerous. One of the things that was confusing about growing up in the atmosphere of Stanford was that the aesthetic contained no shadow. The aesthetic was one of harmony, joy and rationality, and that form of design doesn't acknowledge the dark side of life at all, as Gothic architecture does, for example. In the family past there are painters, who, in their personal lives suffered deeply. But they have painted wonderful pictures of their lives—their children in the gardens, the kitchen . . . communicating this serenity. They're beautiful paintings of a beautiful way of life. I love those paintings, but they're not the truth. And I don't know how important the truth is in art. I don't think that it always has to be there. But what we're talking about here, when we're talking about beauty and danger, is that Margarett Sargent had danger in her paintings, and I grew up in an aesthetic where danger wasn't acknowledged. But we lived in a dangerous atmosphere.

HM Perhaps her paintings were "lost" because of that danger, because people did not want to look at them.

SL In some ways I think that coming to grips with that kind of darkness *and* danger is anti-domestic. That indeed families are in some ways right to reject that. I don't know if it really can exist in the bosom of domestic life which, one hopes, is at its best serene and happy and joyful. There is something destructive about that too, something difficult and egotistical in a certain noncommittal way because there's a line at which that serenity no longer holds true. Honor, in the case of your family, I don't know if you'd say that the inability to acknowledge that dangerous aspect within the family reflected an inability to deal with things the family should have been dealing with.

HM Yes, I would say that Margarett carried that truth, and that that is why I grew up thinking of her as dangerous. Though we never had a real conversation about the danger of that truth, I believe she would have spoken to me openly about it if I had not been too frightened to ask. She would really talk about what happened and would

tell you what was going on in life.

bs I loved that passage! "Papa, what's a den of iniquity?" And Margarett's husband says, "Who asked you that?"

HM "Oh, Uncle David. He says you live in one." [*laughter*]

bs You both interviewed members of your families. What was their reaction to your inquiries? Was it difficult for people?

HM I had two long interviews with one of my uncles and at the end of them he said, "I feel as if I've been in psychoanalysis." He had a great deal of pain as a consequence of having Margarett as a mother. Margarett's chauffeur, Charlie Driscoll, who became her close friend and witnessed some of her worst suffering, believed she should be left to rest in peace. He only agreed to talk to me when I burst into tears— for my sins, the tape recorder was off for the entire interview! Oliver Smith refused to talk because he said he was writing his own book. I wrote him letters, I begged, but to no avail. Years later, I was seated next to him at a benefit dinner party. He knew about the affair with Jane Bowles. And I thought, Oh my god, I could ask him again for an interview. Right then and there he turned to me and said, "The story is this . . ." and out it came. I couldn't take out a pen, I had no tape recorder, I just had to turn on my brain. But usually people adored her and wanted to talk.

bs She was demonized yet adored?

HM She was demonized in the family and marveled at by most other people who knew her. Kenward Elmslie told me there are three people in his experience whom he considered larger than life: Frank O'Hara, John La Touche, and Margarett Sargent. And people who knew her as a friend or a cousin might have disapproved of her but they thought she was fabulous.

bs They didn't need the kind of love from her that her children did.

HM People who reported on her drunken states were people inside the family, and generally people outside the family did not see her like that. There were some exceptions as the disease progressed and things got worse. It was as if she had comfort and happiness elsewhere but not in the life she'd constructed.

bs Suzannah, this is a quote from the end of *The Architect of Desire*: "One cannot easily break the habit of looking for protection from that which is powerful. One cannot in one motion cast one's lot with the unprotected. One cannot in one day learn to see a sanctuary and strengthen in that." What do you see as your sanctuary?

SL When you identify with the strong and the strong are inimicable to your well-being, you think you're safe but you're not really safe, and you can't find anything approaching real safety until you cast your lot with people who share your experience. Even if those people are the most unprotected and unpolitically powerful people, still you're not

going to have any strength until you acknowledge that bond because that's where your selfhood lies and that's where the truth lies—that's your only solid ground. You can't be in reality until you do that; and as long as you're not in reality, you're not safe.

bs Which brings me to my last question. Honor, the first quote in your book.

HM The Gnostic Gospel.

bs Yes, of Thomas: "If you bring forth what is within you, what you bring forth will save you. If you do not bring forth what is within you, what you do not bring forth will destroy you." Did you both have revelations about the past?

HM I didn't have one single revelation but there came a time in the writing of the book when everything became clear. I knew what I was writing was true. But of course truth can be an illusion.

bs That old paradigm.

HM But the book certainly represents my truth, and I did feel that I had represented Margarett. The night after I wrote her death I dreamt I was with her in a hotel, both in the dream and watching it at the same time. Margarett was on a bed with a gorgeous black sheath and I was asking her questions. I would say what I thought had happened and she would say, "Yes, yes, absolutely." But I had a survival reason for writing Margarett's story: to distinguish my life from hers—so that I didn't have to live out what her life had always told me I must live out. The revelation that came in writing was that she, too, was a woman and an artist, and that as women and as artists we had a lot in common. In that sense, as I wrote, Margarett became a companion.

bs Suzannah, did you have a revelation?

SL Well, there's the revelation in the book where my sisters and I got together and we realized that we shared these memories of our father at night in the cottage. That was a very, very big revelation because I'd been struggling for so long, I knew something was very wrong. I was very close but when that happened, it established a context for my experience. I realized that it wasn't some isolated incident but that this was the context in which we lived. So if there was one moment that was it.

bs Is there anything either of you wanted to say that we didn't cover?

HM Suzannah and I have talked about the notion of reconfiguring the family and one of the unexpected gifts of the book—among my brothers and sisters, cousins and aunts, uncles and parents—was that they have been so

grateful to have Margarett's life set out. One of my uncles said it justified a lot of the suffering in his life at the hands of his mother, that that suffering was in some degree mitigated by the fact that he could see the whole life and see what she had suffered. At the recent opening of a show of Margarett's paintings, two of my sisters came with infant daughters. Their great-grandmother was an artist, not a madwoman. I really wasn't expecting this shift in the energy of the family. It has changed how the family experiences itself and that's powerful. This kind of work can restructure a family because while families are made up of people, they are also made up of myths and psychic realities that we're only dimly aware of. When we break those open, you can't know what's going to happen.

bs You can set loose demons or you can set loose angels. Suzannah?

SL It seems that reconfiguration of family realities is something that a lot of women are working on. It's wonderful to feel a part of a movement, of the evolution of the consciousness of women entering the frontier of their own experience with words.

Tobias Wolff, © Marion Ettlinger. Courtesy Knopf.

TOBIAS WOLFF a.m. homes

His is the taut, trim, prose of an athlete. Intricate and highly compressed, Tobias Wolff's explorations of our emotional and moral infrastructure are psychological travelogues, beginning in one place and ending in another. His first story collection published in 1981, *In The Garden of the North American Martyrs* was the handbook for aspiring writers. Tobias Wolff was the man who had mastered the story, who knew how to contain and control it and simultaneously, when to let it run. I studied that book top to bottom, backwards and forwards, along with the volumes that followed: *The Barracks Thief* (1984), *Back in the World* (1986), and his two stunning memoirs *This Boy's Life* (1988) and *In Pharaoh's Army* (1994).

The Night in Question—Wolff's newest collection of stories just out from Knopf, once again puts us in the hands of a master craftsman. Tobias Wolff watches himself and the world from a certain distance—always observing, taking it in, piecing things together. The result is an intensely compassionate, rich, and wry prose style that shows us ourselves in all our graceless glory.

Tobias Wolff and I met for the first time during the telephone calls that were this interview. When we spoke we were each on summer vacation, each by a lake looking out on the water. Liberated by the anonymity of the telephone, I felt I could ask Wolff all the quiet questions about what it means to progress as a writer, to mature. Our conversation left me feeling that what seems impossible might actually be possible—gaps can be bridged, progress is constantly being made.

a.m. homes How has the process of writing changed for you over time?

TOBIAS WOLFF I'm not sure it has. No, it probably has. Let me say that I am now a little more reconciled to my peculiarities as a writer. When I first started writing, in my teens, I could write eight pages a day. And I believed that all eight pages were deathless prose. Now I am reconciled to writing a paragraph or two that I'll end up keeping.

amh I wonder whether it gets harder and harder on some level.

TW Every successful piece of writing you do, I mean successful as art, illuminates even more greatly the difficulties of what you do. You're always trying to top yourself. You don't want to do what you did before again and again. You get tired of certain conventions. You want to do other things, so you're creating the difficulties as the very condition of your art. It's a way of keeping it exciting for yourself, but it also makes it increasingly harder.

amh How do you know when you're finished with a story?

TW When everything necessary is done, and I feel as if even another word would be superfluous—would, in a manner of speaking, break the camel's back. That sense of completion comes about in different ways, and plot is only the most obvious of them. You should feel, when you've finished a story, that it has achieved a life independent of yours, that it has somehow

gathered up the golden chain that connected you. This feeling is not always reliable. I often go back and revise endings that I was pretty sure about when I set the last period to the page. In writing, of course, everything is subject to revision. But I am guided, however roughly, by inexplicable instincts like the one I have just attempted to describe.

amh In your story "The Chain," and in "Bullet in the Brain," events spiral and flip out of control, one bit of wrong thinking folds into the next in an effort to clarify or correct the last. Is this a recurring theme with you?

TW Some of my writing is about folly, and the capacity folly has for reproducing itself, how it multiplies. How a bad idea becomes ten bad ideas, becomes a hundred bad ideas. Stories are a good kind of theater for folly.

amh A minute ago you mentioned your peculiarities as a writer—how would you characterize them?

TW Oh, I'm not the best judge of that at all. I can say something about my intentions, though even those are finally beside the point when the work is finished. But I'm looking at the story or the book from inside, and I'm often unaware of what is plain as day to people regarding it from the outside. For example, a graduate student at SUNY Albany sent me an essay of hers concerning the terrible fate of dogs in my work, together with some speculations about my motives in writing about them in this way. She had plenty of evidence from my work—dogs shot, burned, even eaten. Yet in all honesty I'd never been aware of this . . . pattern, if you will, or peculiarity. I guess you'd be justified in calling it a peculiarity. And I'm glad I was unaware of it, because otherwise I might have avoided it and not written some things that I'm pleased to have written. That's the danger of excessive self-consciousness—it either becomes very constricting, or leads to self-parody of the worst kind. Like X. J. Kennedy's poem about the goose that laid the golden egg. She sticks her head up her rear end to observe the process, then gets stuck in that position. His poem concludes, "If you'd lay well, don't watch."

amh I'm interested in the idea of writing from a moral point of view. In one of the *In Pharaoh's Army* interviews you said, "It seemed to me that I was responsible for a moral accounting. A book like this has to be a personal moral inventory."

TW When I talk about the "personal moral inventory" it's not so much about the immorality of the war itself, but the sense of how an ordinary person is complicit in the ongoing folly of his time. Even with honorable intentions and a certain measure of innocence, you can become a part of the very thing you fear and despise. And this shows up in my fiction. It isn't a question of the stories being moral fables, "Don't do this because something terrible will happen." It's more an exploration of the moral sense that dominates our lives for bet-

ter or worse, the constant effort of trying to find the right thing to do in complex situations. I can't imagine not having that kind of reckoning in my work because it's at the center of our lives. Everyone I know is puzzling things out, trying to figure out the right thing to do. We're all in a web of connection to friends, family, community, and the moral sense is what determines how we honor those connections. To leave that out of one's fiction seems to me to be impossible. It's going to be there, so it's better that it not be there by default, but that you have some edge of consciousness about its workings.

amh We were talking before about how events in your stories spiral, how wrong-headed thinking multiplies, for instance, in your story "The Chain."

TW Here's a man who's trying to find the right thing to do. He isn't just trying to get even, he's trying to do what is right in this situation. He acts out of love for his daughter, through rage at the wrong done by the indifference of others, and from a sense of the wrong of being too timid in the face of evil. All these good motives are at work in what ends up being an absolutely catastrophic mistake.

amh One of my favorite stories in the new collection is "Casualty." I was fascinated by the structure, the nurse who essentially ends the story isn't there at the beginning. This is very conservative of me, but I always think the people in the beginning of the story must be the same people around at the end of the story.

TW It does seem unfair, to spring a new character on you at the end. In the case of "Casualty," I had her in mind from the beginning. I didn't want too narrow an understanding of who gets hurt in this war. The word casualty usually refers to soldiers, but the damage ripples out in every direction, and touches all these people and harms them deeply. I had her in mind all the time I was writing that story, but how could any reader know that? Now if I had done that to evade the consequences of the story for the characters who were there at the beginning, B.D. and Ryan in particular, then I think her late appearance would be a mistake. But their stories are pretty well settled when she shows up.

amh It's interesting that she was always in your mind—it works that she doesn't appear to us until later, it makes the story keep going.

TW She is very much a part of their story, but she isn't present until their circumstances compel her to enter. Then the story becomes as much hers as theirs. At one point I was thinking of calling it "The Nurse's Story." It would give people some sense that this was coming. I did realize that it was a gamble to introduce her so late, and give her so much weight. But her presence brings something essential. There's an almost romantic obsession with soldiers in most writing about war. It may not mean to be romantic, but it ends up that way because it

views soldiers in isolation from the consequences of what they do and what is done to them. You don't see how they're situated in a web of relations, how one person's suffering bleeds into other lives. That is what is missing from so many of these war narratives, and why the nurse was so important to me.

amh I love the part when she slips the one dying guy's hand into the other's, that's just so lovely. How has the way you write about Vietnam changed over the years?

TW I couldn't write very much about it in the beginning. I have one very short story in my first book which touches on it. I'm still hesitant to write about it.

amh Why, do you think?

TW It's one of those things you just don't want to get wrong. There's a way of writing about Vietnam that is extremely stale: the helicopters; the jazzed-up soldier lingo; all the acronyms; deadpan talk about killing. There's a strong pull exerted by the conventions of war fiction in particular. That's why I ended up writing about it in a memoir, because I thought I could resist those pressures more successfully by being faithful to my knowledge of my own situation, of the effect of that situation on my character and nature. I wouldn't just be writing about what everybody already knew about.

amh I've always been fascinated with the Vietnam War and I wonder where people who've been at war put the experience?

TW What do you mean?

amh Where does it fit inside you? How do you reconcile it? Does everybody who has been in the war have side effects from it?

TW I don't have post-traumatic stress syndrome. But I have no question that others do have it. It comes about through prolonged exposure to combat, which I did not have. I had some, but not very much, very little, compared to most of the people I knew. I got lucky—the place I was sent that year was quieter than many other places. The luck of the draw, really. It was bad enough for me. I had my stomach full of it and then some. But nothing like what happened to others. I was very lucky, and lucky not just in terms of surviving it, but lucky in that when I got home I was still healthy enough psychologically to have a reasonable life. But a lot of people weren't.

amh Are you by nature very aware?

TW Cautious you mean?

amh I'm thinking about situations in which a person has to be aware of their surroundings, of their safety, and then about being a soldier, where something could happen at any moment, a sniper, something falling out of the sky, a land mine—and what that does to you.

TW It had effects, there's no question about it. Nobody gets away scot free from something like that. I certainly have a healthy sense of the dangers of

this world. One way I do notice it is that I worry about my kids. One of my boys just started driving and the other will start driving in another month. I try not to think about it or else I'll go crazy. Nevertheless it's there. One of my boys likes to go for long walks at night, and although we live in a reasonably safe neighborhood, it's bordered by an unsafe neighborhood. I hear myself "Mother Henning" him all the time on this.

amh I have the feeling that you are a wonderful teacher and a good father. How have you transcended the experience of your own father?

TW How do you learn to be a father without being your father?

amh Exactly.

TW It has always come naturally to me to be affectionate with my kids and to enjoy them. They certainly make it easy. I have great kids. They're funny, they're good company. They always have been. It just hasn't seemed like hard work to me, to tell you the truth. One thing of course that makes it easy is that I have more time than other people do. I teach, and I work at home. When my kids come home I'm there. They can come up and talk to me. I'm not under the kind of pressures that make it hard for most people to be the kind of parents they want to be and just don't have the time to be.

amh But you also remade your experience of family.

TW Oh, I was always pretty nervous about the whole idea. It's sort of like writing. You approach it very warily and then when you're in it, it teaches you what to do. But yeah, I had real doubts about my abilities to pull this thing off. But the moment children arrive, you're so busy with them, you find yourself doing the right things. Most of the time, anyway. I hope.

amh I'm curious to hear your thoughts on the differences in your experience of writing nonfiction and fiction.

TW I hold myself to very different standards when I'm writing fiction and nonfiction. I have to be able, with a straight face, to tell myself that something is nonfiction if I say it's nonfiction. That's why, although there are autobiographical elements in some of my stories, I still call them fiction because that's what they are. Even though they may have been set into motion by some catalyst of memory.

amh Why do you think people want everything to be true?

TW They're uncomfortable somehow with imaginative reality, which is a very powerful reality against which we have few defenses. They're perhaps unaccustomed to art, and the assumptions of art. I'm not really sure.

amh Do you think it's an American thing?

TW I think Americans are more accepting if they think it's nonfiction. Is it an American thing? No, my guess is it isn't. Writers and artists have always done what they could to seduce the audience into a sense that what they're looking at is genuine. That's

the great power of movies, isn't it? They give you the feeling that what you are looking at is life happening before your eyes. Writers invite that kind of approach to their work. We want people to believe it while they're reading it—we want them to enter our world fully.

amh I'm curious about how we grow up, the progression of things. You're fifty-one now—you seem incredibly stable—what about a mid-life crisis? Are they inevitable? Do you have to have one? Do you feel one coming on?

TW I had mine when I was in my teens, that was my mid-life crisis.

amh Right, precocious.

TW I'm grateful to have had the life I've had. First of all, I feel lucky to be alive. I feel lucky to be sane and whole, to have a life as a writer. What a privilege that is, and one that for years and years I thought I would not have, that this would be something I would just do on my own all my life. That I would probably have to end up doing something else, and do this when I could. It still astonishes me that I've been able to have a life as a writer. I don't teach a lot, but I love the teaching that I do. And I meet people like you. What's to complain about?

amh I don't know.

TW I do feel sometimes—which may be the kind of propellent for a lot of these absurd chapters in the lives of people my age—a sense of having become too comfortable, of being an old shoe and wanting to push myself to thinner air. But I find ways of getting around that. I drive too fast. I ski the black diamond slopes, and I play cutthroat softball. I'm being facetious. But that restlessness is still there. I don't think it's in a virulent state, I don't think I'm going to destroy my life in obedience to it. It isn't at its deepest level philosophical. I know I have found the ground on which I must make my peace, through these people I live with and not through change of circumstance or a dramatis personae.

amh *In Pharaoh's Army* you write about joining the military to get at an experience. And I think about you having settled down, teaching and living this seemingly stable life; from where do you get experience now?

TW In *The End of Alice* you write very powerfully and persuasively from the point of view of a pedophile. Am I to think therefore that you must have experience with pedophilia?

amh I actually know nothing about it, which is the funny thing. I did a lot of research.

TW You know that old chestnut of Flannery O'Connor's, about anyone who survives adolescence has enough to write about for the rest of their lives. There's a strong, very early story of hers in *Double Take* magazine called "The Coat," written from the point of view of a black woman. She wrote it when she was in her twenties, at the University of Iowa. How the hell did

she know to do that? In the end, the writer's task is not to accumulate experience, but to develop a consciousness that can see the world with some accuracy and fitting sense of drama.

amh As a child you lived with you mother in relative poverty. Then you went to boarding school, and then into the U.S. Army, and then off to study at Oxford in England; did you feel comfortable in all those settings or were you an outsider?

TW I felt right at home when I went off to that boarding school because I had wanted so much to go there. It was funny to be happy in this place where all the other kids wanted to be home. But it was much more peaceful than my home life. And it was intellectually alive, there were people talking about ideas and books in a way I'd never even known you could, except through my brother in the brief time we'd spent together before I went off to school. So I was quite happy and at home in that place. But God knows there were transitions to be made. I was aware of there being class tensions at Oxford, but as a Yank I was outside of those considerations. And I really felt as if I belonged to a community when I was there, an artistic and intellectual community. Those were the people I knew at Oxford, and they were not consumed by questions of class. Artists and intellectuals are their own class. These were people who were committed to writing, and reading, and understanding. And we talked incessantly. My real education came not so much through the classes and tutors, as through my time with my friends. The pubs closed at ten, so we'd buy some booze and sit around somebody's room and just talk, talk, talk, talk, and I've never forgotten that. The sharpening effect on the mind, the awakening was so exhilarating that questions of class and economic status really didn't play much of a part. I started writing in a disciplined way, as soon as I got to Oxford, and that was very important to me. I was reading, making friends, travelling—it was a God-given time.

amh Were they amazed that you had been a soldier?

TW We didn't talk about it very much. First of all, I did not have a way of talking about it that did not make other people extremely uncomfortable. I had this compulsion to rub peoples' noses in the horror of it, to tell them the worst things. But I would tell them in this cruel laughing way. Because the minute I started on that subject I'd go back to being a soldier, and that's the way soldiers handle it. I began to see how discordant a note this struck whenever we started talking. Most of my friends learned not to talk to me about it, and I never brought it up, I never brought it up.

amh But that in itself is fascinating. I'm always amazed by splits in people.

TW Well, I still have plenty of those.

CARYL PHILLIPS graham swift

I first met Caryl, or Caz as I've come to know him, a few years ago at a literary jamboree in Toronto. We spent a lot of time in a place in downtown Toronto called the Bamboo Club—one of those places that has since acquired a sort of metaphysical status, because whenever Caz and I have met again in some far-flung corner of the globe, it seems our first instinct has been to find out where the "Bamboo Club" is. Caz, I confess, is a little bit better at finding it than I am.

Caz was born in 1958 in St. Kitts, one of the Leeward Islands in the Caribbean. He came to England when still a babe in arms and was brought up and educated there. In more recent years, he has traveled extensively and has made his temporary home in many parts of the world, including his native St. Kitts. In keeping with his nomadic inclination, it could be said that one of the main themes of his work is that of the journey or, put rather different-ly, of human displacement and dislocation in a variety of forms. The journey behind his first novel, *The Final Passage* (1985), was the one Caz himself took part in, albeit unwittingly—the immigration in the postwar years from the Caribbean to England. The journey that lies behind both Caz's last novel, *Higher Ground* (1989), and his new novel, *Cambridge*, is a more historic, more primal and more terrible journey, the journey of the slave trade westward from Africa.

Caz has maintained, however, a keen interest in Europe or, to be more precise, in Europe's pretensions and delusions about the place of European civilization in the world. His book of essays, *The European Tribe* (1987), was devoted to the subject. In *Higher Ground*, a novel in three parts, we travel from Africa in the slave trade days to North America at the time of the Black Power movement, only to end up in a Europe still nursing its wounds from the last war. In *Cambridge*, Caz has reversed the direction of this journey to

Caryl Phillips, © Jerry Bauer. Courtesy Knopf.

bring a European consciousness face to face with Europe's global perpetrations. He does this through the person of Emily, a woman of the early nineteenth century who escapes an arranged marriage by traveling to her father's estate in the West Indies (her father being an absentee landlord); there she is exposed to, and, indeed, exposed by the effects of slavery and colonialism.

Like its predecessor, *Cambridge* is a novel in three distinct parts, the first and longest of which is Emily's own account of her journey and her observations when she arrives. From what seems at first to be an inquisitive, self-consoling travelogue there emerges a drama revolving around a handful of characters: Emily herself; Brown, an Englishman whom we understand has somehow ousted the previous manager of the estate; the Cambridge of the title, a negro slave who has suffered the singular and equivocal fate of having lived in England and having been converted to Christianity; and another slave, Christiania, who, despite her name, indulges in decidedly un-Christian rites and appears to be on the verge of madness.

The second part of the book is Cambridge's own account of how he came to be Anglicized and Christianized. The third, written in the form of a report (which we guess to be far from reliable), describes how Cambridge comes to be executed for the murder of Brown. And the brief epilogue of the novel tells us the effect of all of this on Emily. These last few pages are particularly astonishing. Coming at the end of a novel of enormous accumulative power, they pack a tremendous punch and, written in a prose of tense intimacy, they show how facile it is to assess either Caz's work as a whole, or his heroine, by any crude cultural or racial analysis. Caz is interested in human beings. Emily's plight at the end of the novel plainly has its cultural and racial dimension, but it's essentially one of personal trauma—psychological, sexual, moral, and (a word Caz will no doubt love) existential.

graham swift How did *Cambridge* arise? What was the germ, the idea behind it?

CARYL PHILLIPS You know that period when you've finished a book and you don't know what to do? We generally have lunch during these periods in that place around the corner from the

British Library, as one of us is pretending to be "working" in there. Well, true to form, I was doing little more than scrambling around in the British Library, having just finished *Higher Ground*, and having a month and a half on my hands before I was due to go down to St. Kitts. It was during this period that I happened upon some journals in the North Library. One in particular caught my eye. It was entitled "Journal of a Lady of Quality," and written by a Scotswoman, named Janet Schaw, who at the beginning of the nineteenth century traveled from Edinburgh to the Caribbean. What attracted me to this story was the fact that she visited St. Kitts. Right beside what was once my brother's place, up in the mountains in St. Kitts, is a broken-down great house. Janet Schaw described going to a dinner there when it was the centerpiece of one of the grandest plantations in the Eastern Caribbean. I began to realize then that there was a whole literature of personal narratives written primarily by women who had traveled to the Caribbean in that weird phase of English history between the abolition of slavery in 1807 and the emancipation of the slaves in 1834. Individuals who inherited these Caribbean estates from their families were curious to find out what this property was, what it would entail to maintain it, whether they would get any money. The subject matter began to speak, but that's never enough, for there's another and formidable hurdle to leap; that of encouraging a character to speak to

you. At the back of '88 when we used to meet, I was concerned with the subject matter and research, but as yet, no character had begun to speak.

gs And how did the character of Cambridge evolve?

CP Actually, he came second. Emily, the woman's voice, came first, partly because for the last ten years I'd been looking for a way of writing the story of a Yorkshire woman. I'd grown up in Yorkshire and I had also read and reread *Wuthering Heights*, so I had this name in my head, Emily. Emily, who wasn't anybody at the moment.

gs The novel's called *Cambridge*, but Emily certainly has more prominence in terms of pages. I wondered whether you'd ever thought of Cambridge as the main character, or indeed if you'd still think of him as the main character?

CP No. Emily was always going to be the main character, but Cambridge was conceived of as a character who would be ever-present. He doesn't appear often in the narrative, in terms of time, but he's always in the background of what she's doing, and what she's saying, and what she's thinking. And then, of course, in the second section of the novel, he has his own narrative.

gs There's a lovely irony to Cambridge's narrative. We've had many pages of Emily and then we get Cambridge's account: Emily figures in Cambridge's mind merely as that Englishwoman on the periphery—scarcely at all, in fact.

CP There is a corrective in having Cambridge's perspective. Cambridge's voice is politically very important because it is only through painful application that he has acquired the skill of literacy. There are so few African accounts of what it was like to go through slavery, because African people were generally denied access to the skills of reading and writing. Reading and writing equals power. Once you have a language, you are dangerous. Cambridge actually makes the effort to acquire a language. He makes the effort to acquire the skills of literacy and uses them to sit in judgment on himself and the societies he passes through.

gs Did your feelings about Cambridge change as you wrote the novel? He is a very ambiguous character.

CP You know you cannot be too judgmental about your characters. Novels are an incredibly democratic medium. Everyone has a right to be understood. I have a lot of problems swallowing most of what Emily says and feels. Similarly, I have difficulties with many of Cambridge's ideas and opinions, because in modern parlance he would be regarded as an Uncle Tom. But I don't feel I have the right to judge them.

gs Emily seems to be a mixture of tentative liberal instincts and blind prejudice. And it could be easy for us, with our twentieth century complacent hindsight, to judge her quite harshly, but you are very sympathetic—and we can't do anything but sympathize with her, pity her. I wonder if your feelings about her changed as you wrote her long narrative?

CP [*pause*] Maybe.

gs Did you have the end in mind even as you wrote the narrative?

CP No. No. I think she grows. She has to make a journey which begins from the periphery of English society. I could not have told this story from the point of view of a man. She was regarded, as most women of that time were regarded, as a "child of lesser growth" when placed alongside her male contemporaries. She was on the margin of English society, and I suspect that one of the reasons I was able to key into her, and to listen to what she had to say, was the fact that, like her, I also grew up in England feeling very marginalized. She also made a journey to the Caribbean for the purpose of keeping body and soul together, which is a journey I made ten years ago. So in that sense, looking at it coldly now, through the prism of time, I can understand why I would have listened to somebody like her and why she would have entrusted me with her story. And through the process of writing . . .you are right, I did begin to feel a little warmer towards her. She rose above her racist attitudes.

gs She became alive in her own right.

CP Because she was courageous. It may be a small and somewhat unpleasant thing in the context of 1991 to find a woman expressing some warmth and affection for her black maid, but in the early nineteenth century it was remarkable that a woman, and particularly this woman, was able to confess to such emotions. A nineteenth-century man couldn't have done this, for men have a larger capacity for bullshit and for self-deception, even when they are talking only to themselves. I am not sure that I would have trusted the narrative of a nineteenth-century man engaged in the slave trade. The only time I read men's narratives which seem to me to be lyrical is when the men, nineteenth century or otherwise, are in prison.

gs Emily, in a way, is about to be sold into a kind of slavery—her arranged marriage—which gives her a perspective on what she sees. Is that how you saw it?

CP Yes. I didn't want to push it too hard, for the two things are obviously only analogous on a minor key. However, an arranged marriage to a widower who possessed three kids and a guaranteed income was a form of bondage. Emily finds the strength, the wit, and the way out of this. I admire her for this. What makes her grow are a series of events which are particularly painful and distressing for her. As I have already stated, part of the magic of writing is that you cannot be too judgmental about a character. You have to find some kind of trust, some form of engagement. You attempt to breathe life into these people and if you're lucky they breathe life into you. You love them with passion;

then, at the end of two or three or four years, you abandon them and try and write another book.

gs You said a moment ago that men could only become lyrical when they are in prison. The second part of *Higher Ground* actually consists of letters from prison in a very distinct male voice. In that novel generally, you seem to depart from your previous work in using strong first-person voices. In *Cambridge* again, there is an emphasis on first-person narratives. Was that a conscious decision or did that just happen?

CP It was conscious. There are any number of stories to tell. You are populated with the potential for telling stories from now until doomsday, for these things are circling around your head. But it seems to me that the real test of a writer's ability is the degree to which that writer applies him or herself to the conundrum of form, to the task of imposing a form upon these undisciplined stories. I had written two novels in the form of the third person and somehow I couldn't address myself again to such a manner of telling a story. It was as though I had to find some way of expanding my repertoire. So the first part of *Higher Ground* is written in first person present tense, the second part in a series of letters and the third part is in the third person, but with these rather strange flashbacks. Each segment of the novel demanded a different point of attack. It was a way of breaking out of what was becoming, to me, the straightjacket of the third person. We used to talk about this when you were writing *Out of This World*. I remember you saying that there was an intimacy about the first person which you found attractive. Well, me too. And like you, I am interested in history, in memory, in time, and in the failure of these three things. It seems to me, at this stage anyhow, that the first person gives me an intimate flexibility which I can't find in the third person.

gs Nine-tenths of *Cambridge* is written in a pastiche of nineteenth-century language. Certainly, the final few pages of it are in your language, the language of the twentieth century. This sense of a language that can talk about certain things suddenly bursting through Emily's own language in which she can't, is very volcanic. It is a brilliant conclusion to a novel. I wonder if we could broaden things out and talk more generally about your writing. You say in *The European Tribe* that you knew certainly you wanted to be a writer while sitting by the Pacific in California with the waves lapping around your ankles . . .

CP Alright, alright! The summer of my second year in college I traveled around America on a bus until my money ran out in California. And I went into this bookshop and bought this book, *Native Son* by Richard Wright. There weren't many black people writing in England. So it never occurred to me that writing as a profession was a responsibility. But when

I was in the States, I discovered such people as Jimmy Baldwin and Richard Wright and Toni Morrison.

gs Do you think it was necessary to go to America to become a writer?

CP I was slouching towards a writing career. Being in the States shifted me into fifth gear and out of the very slovenly third that I was stuck in.

gs How old were you when you first went back to St. Kitts?

CP Twenty-two. I had written a play, *Strange Fruit*, in 1980, which was done at The Crucible Theatre in Sheffield. And with the royalties from that, I went back to St. Kitts with my mother, who had left in 1958 when she was twenty. It was strange, because I had grown up without an overbearing sense of curiosity about the Caribbean. My mother hadn't been back either. She held it in her memory. But when we arrived in St. Kitts, many of the things that she remembered were no longer there: her school had burnt down, people that she knew had died, and someone she dearly wanted me to meet had long since emigrated to America. For her, it was like a ghost town. But for me, it fired my curiosity about myself, about England, about the Caribbean. Naturally, the "rediscovery" confused and confounded me, but that was no bad thing for, after all, writers are basically just people who are trying to organize their confusion.

gs Your first two novels were very much about the Caribbean, com-

ing from and going back to. How much was that actually paralleling your life and exorcising your own feelings about the Caribbean?

CP My first novel, *The Final Passage*, was published in 1985. I had started it some five years earlier, on the inter-island ferry between St. Kitts and Nevis. I looked back at St. Kitts and began to write some sentences down. I wanted to try and tell the story of the journey from the Caribbean to England, which seemed to me to be, in terms of fiction in this country, an untold story. People had written novels and stories about the journey, but not people of my generation. The second novel, *A State of Independence*, although not autobiographical, fol-lowed the emotional contours of my life in that it dealt with the problems of returning to the Caribbean and thinking, they are not sure if I am one of them, and yet feeling that I am not sure if I am one of them either. However, I have certainly not exor-cised my feelings about the Caribbean. I have no desire to do so. The reason I write about the Caribbean, is that the Caribbean con-tains both Europe and Africa, as I do. The Caribbean belongs to both Europe and Africa. The Caribbean is an artificial society created by the massacre of its inhabitants, the Carib and Arawak Indians. It is where Africa met Europe on somebody else's soil. This history of the Caribbean is a bloody history. It is a history which is older than the history of the United States of America. Columbus didn't arrive in the United States. He

arrived in the Caribbean. The Caribbean is Marquez's territory. He always describes himself as a Caribbean writer. It's Octavio Paz's territory. It's Fuentes's territory. The Caribbean for many French and Spanish-speaking writers has provided more than enough emotional material for a whole career. For me, that juxta-position of Africa and Europe in the Americas is very important.

gs But now it's not just Europe, America has moved in. How do you feel about that? You are living in America now, teaching here at Amherst.

CP The reason I am living in America is because, like yourself, like many peo-ple, business occasionally takes me to the United States. When I'm not here, all I have to do is turn on the TV, or open up the papers, and I am bombarded with images of America. In other words, over the years I have come to think of myself as somebody who knows America because I have some kind of a relationship with it. I even spent some time in Alabama for my sins. However, I'm not sure that anybody can seriously claim to "know" a country as large and as diverse as the United States. It seemed important, given the opportunity of spending a year or maybe two years in the United States, to make a concerted effort to get to know a part of the country more intimately. That's really why I'm living here. Furthermore, the Caribbean is now, to some extent, culturally, an extension of the Florida Keys and I really want to understand a bit more about American people rather than simply imagining them all to be characters out of "Dallas," or a nation whose soul is reflected in the studio audience and guests of the *Oprah Winfrey* show.

gs I've one last question and it's quite a big one. We always have a lot of fun together; whenever we meet we have some laughs. Yet your work doesn't exactly glow with optimism. You are very hard on your characters; most of your central characters are lost people, they suffer. Pessimism seems to win though. Is that ultimately your view of the world?

CP I am always surprised that people think I am a pessimist. *Cambridge* is, to some extent, optimistic. Emily grows. Okay, she suffers greatly, but she still grows. It's the price of the ticket, isn't it? The displacement ticket. Displacement engenders a great deal of suffering, a great deal of confusion, a great deal of soul searching. It would be hard for me to write a comedy about displacement. But there is courage. Emily has a great amount of courage. As does Cambridge. And in *Higher Ground*, there is faith. I don't necessarily mean faith with a religious gloss on it. I mean the ability to actually acknowledge the existence of something that you believe in, something that helps you to make sense of your life. You are right when you say that the characters are often lost, and that they suffer. But I would like to claim that the spirit and tenacity with which my characters fight to try and make sense of their often helplessly fated lives is in itself optimistic. Nobody rolls over and dies. If they are to "go under," it is only after a struggle in which they have hopefully won our respect.

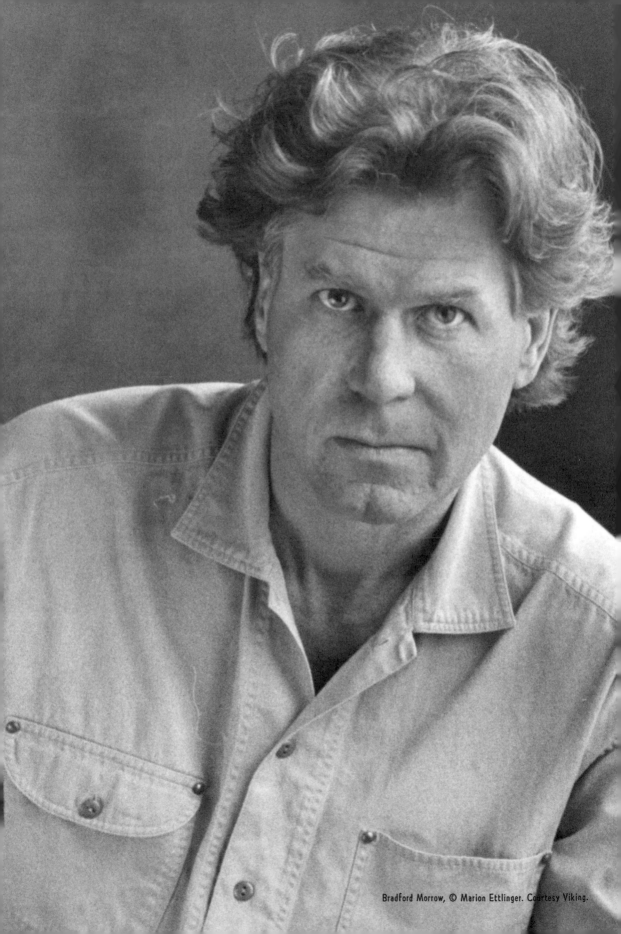

Bradford Morrow, © Marion Ettlinger. Courtesy Viking.

BRADFORD MORROW jim lewis

BOMB #51, Spring 1995

He is a good friend, but I know next to nothing about his past. He'll begin a sentence, "When I was a musician," or "When I was a medical assistant in Honduras," but I never have been able to figure out exactly what he was doing when. I do know that a dozen years ago he founded *Conjunctions* and has edited it throughout its impressive history, somehow finding time along the way to write three extraordinary novels: *Come Sunday*, *The Almanac Branch*, and his latest, *Trinity Fields,* the story of two close friends who grow up together as the children of scientists at Los Alamos, part ways during the years of the Vietnam War, and then meet again to confront each other, their history, and their fate. It is a beautiful, admirable book.

jim lewis I wanted to ask you about going to the Trinity Site near Alamagordo.

BRADFORD MORROW It was an astounding experience. Here, I brought something to show you.

jl Am I going to get cancer from this?

BM Well, plutonium has a half-life of 24,000 years or so.

jl And what is that exactly?

BM It's radioactive trinitite.

jl Which you carry around in your pocket.

BM I'm having a lead box made for it; it'll go in that. The Public Relations Director at White Sands Missile Range will tell you it's so safe you could live at ground zero, but the clicking of a Geiger counter might suggest otherwise.

jl Was this a backwards-looking research trip for *Trinity Fields* or are you working on something new?

BM Actually it was forward looking: I don't know how many novels will come out of *Trinity Fields*, but it will at least be a diptych. At the end of Trinity, Ariel, the narrator's daughter, is given a diary and a key, which I find irresistible.

jl So, going to Trinity was a part of finding what Ariel would find out?

BM When I inhabit a character, I have the opportunity of seeing the world twice:

I, myself, get to see it, but I am also allowed to see it through fictive, narrational eyes, at the same time. So I'll visit a place that already has a resonance for me, a timbre. That's how characters become manifest in me; it's partly through the language that appears when writing. A novel occurs under your fingertips but it also occurs in the field. *Trinity Fields* involved spending a lot of time in Los Alamos; I'm a member of Los Alamos Historical Society. And, I spent a lot of time in Chimayo, up and down those roads. The book was heavily researched. For the Laos passage, I put in hundreds of hours talking with Colonel Roger Daisley who was head of a highly covert task force in Laos called the Ravens, including flying with him over defunct volcanoes and green mountains that resembled Southeast Asia. I interviewed other surviving Ravens from our secret war in Laos. That was my form of research, not so much sitting in the library reading books, though I did that, too.

jl All of your novels seem to be set in New York and someplace else. A character will start out in New York and end up going farther and farther away, and the book will end with him or her at the farthest distance from the city.

BM To what degree they're autobiographical, I suppose those are my trajectories. My wobbly place in the world, in New York and elsewhere. I come from elsewhere, and even though I've been in New York for fourteen years now, it still feels like a way station. But then, when I'm elsewhere, I want to get back. So, I suppose the novels manifest this in-betweenness. It's a beautiful curse in a way—bad for roots, but good for branches.

jl You grew up in Denver?

BM In a dusty suburb of Denver called Littleton.

jl What were your folks doing there?

BM This all goes back to my grandmother's tuberculosis. Our family migrated west in the early twenties because my grandfather Morrow wanted to place his dying wife in a tent city outside Chicago. Then he got it in his head that her tuberculosis might be retarded by the clean air of the high Rocky Mountains, so they traveled to a hamlet called Oak Creek. She died, and he set up a medical practice there, and became Mayor of this tiny coal-mining town. When he retired, he moved down to Denver. My mother's side of the family are farmers from Nebraska who lost their homesteads in the Depression and migrated to Colorado seeking work. I was conceived in the back of a Plymouth on Pike's Peak. And I grew up in Denver. Once I was fifteen I went on an American Medical Association grant to Honduras, and never went back home again. After that I was itinerant—Europe, all around America—until I moved here. These years in New York are the longest stretch of time I've ever been in one place.

jl So explain to me how *Trinity Fields* got started.

BM Insomnia. I was staying at an adobe near Tesuque, New Mexico, with friends, at the end of a long reading tour for my last novel, *The Almanac Branch*. One night, I noticed these amber, twinkling lights in a long string up along the western mesas at the foot of the Jemez Mountains. They were entrancing. Here was a desert, all dark, and this vast spray of constellations and stars overhead, and then this peculiar man-made amber twinkling going on in the foothills. I asked my host about them the next morning and he said, "Oh my God, that's Los Alamos." I said, "I'd love to go there." But they weren't willing, so we wound up going to the desert chapel of Chimayo instead that day, twenty-five miles in the opposite direction. The seed was planted. Chimayo is an extraordinary, mind-boggling, pure, and inspiring place. The Santuario was built about 1818 by Hispanic Catholics in a valley that's been sacred to the Indians for thousands of years. The soil is said to have magical properties, healing properties, and the Indians, the Tewa and their ancestors practiced geophagy for years there before the Catholics. This little place is the Lourdes of America, but instead of drinking miraculous water . . .

jl You eat dirt.

BM You rub *tierra bendita* on you and are cured that way. Somehow it all got fused in my head that day: the death-magic of Los Alamos and life-magic of Chimayo, the rationality and science of the hill and the faith and reli-gion of the valley. I had seen Chimayo for the first time when I was nine years old, and had also been up to Los Alamos and Bandelier Canyon. I just felt very inspired by the proximity of such a pure, simple, powerful place as Chimayo, and this postmodern high-tech place, this—what to call Los Alamos?—this other kind of mecca.

jl Almost like a monastery itself.

BM Yes. Every major physicist on earth went there in the forties to develop the atom bomb. They all lived in total iso-lation for the twenty-seven months it took to complete both the plutonium and the uranium devices that were eventually detonated at Trinity, Hiroshima, and Nagasaki. The two poles of death and life, community and isolation, drew me, too. You know, you still have Pueblo Indians at San Ildefonso, dancing the corn dances their ancestors danced, work-ing their fields. And just up on the hill, you have the place where chaos theory was developed, where neutron showers rather than rain showers were what were valued most.

jl How did they settle on Los Alamos?

BM Oppenheimer chose it. As a kid, he'd gone to New Mexico and loved it. The Manhattan Project people needed a place that was isolated and protected, and the mesa was perfect. Also, they needed to be away from large population centers, in case something went wrong.

jl He seems like a really interesting character, Oppenheimer.

BM One of the most remarkable Americans of the century.

jl Son of a bitch, apparently.

BM He was a son of a bitch? Oppenheimer?

jl Yeah.

BM I don't know; I am ambivalent about him. The way this country treated him, the way he was beat down by Senator McCarthy and by the reaction against nuclear weapons, is scandalous if typical. He became a scapegoat figure. His brilliance in helping put that project together was awesome. But they did make an atom bomb, a fact Oppenheimer himself came to regret.

jl I didn't mean a son of a bitch for building the bomb. I just got the impression that he was maniacal, extremely vain and overbearing. Did you talk to anyone who knew him? Are any of the scientists or the military people still alive?

BM Edward Teller, the father of the hydrogen bomb, gave a piano concert up at Los Alamos last year. He played the untuned grand at Fuller Lodge. Unlike Oppenheimer, Teller is someone for whom I harbor no fondness. But yes, a number of the scientists are still alive.

jl One of the interesting things about *Trinity Fields* is that, even though part of it is set in Los Alamos, you never talk about the actual making of the bomb. The bomb is brought up as an issue, but the story of how it was made and the people who were involved in it is almost assumed.

BM Well, I figured Richard Rhodes had already done that so brilliantly in *The Making of the Atomic Bomb* that I didn't need to do it. At a certain point, I had read so much on the making of the atomic bomb that I felt I could build one in my basement. *[laughter]* But I wanted to write about growing up in America in the post-atomic era by focusing on two boys who not only were raised in the shadow of it, but right at the epicenter where the whole project had taken place. Brice and Kip didn't build a bomb, their parents did. That's as close as I needed to get. The narrator, Brice, has a naïveté, an innocence, that carries into his adulthood. It's interesting: the sequestration in which Los Alamos was founded has provided for a kind of brilliant naïveté which is evident when you meet scientists and mathematicians who are still working there. Their minds are extraordinarily active, but there's a kind of unworldliness to them that seems childlike.

jl The Institute for Advanced Studies is like that, also.

BM Although you can feel Princeton nearby when you're at the Institute. At Los Alamos, you really are away from everybody. You cross the Rio Grande at Otowi Bridge, and drive up the same road Enrico Fermi, Segre, Neidermeyer, Bohr and Oppenheimer all drove up. Going up that road was really one of the most astounding emotional events I experienced when I was starting this book. This commu-

nity was brought into being for a specific purpose; it didn't exist before. I
mean, a boy's ranch was there.
William Burroughs and Gore Vidal
both went to it. There are photographs of them in the Historical
Society office.

jl That is perfect. They were there at
the same time?

BM No, different years. In the photo of
Burroughs' class, you can see him sitting in the lower left-hand corner. He
looks so unhappy. He's staring at his
feet as if he were wishing he were anywhere else.

jl Why is it called Trinity?

BM There are conflicting theories about
that. One is that Oppenheimer
named it Trinity Site because he'd
been reading a poem by John Donne
with the line, "Batter my heart, three
person'd god." He was a great admirer
of the *Bhagavad-Gita*, and there is a
moment in the narrative when Vishnu
is manifest in his multiarmed form
and says, "I am become Death, the
destroyer of worlds." So, another theory is that he named it for the three-
spirit Hindu godhead.

jl That line that Oppenheimer spoke,
right after the bomb went off,
about becoming death, the
destroyer of worlds, always struck
me as kind of bullshitty. It seemed
so . . .

BM Prepared?

jl Prepared, designed for what was
very self-consciously a historical

moment. Who was it who said,
"Now we're all sons of bitches?"

BM That's the great line, and it strikes me
as totally unrehearsed. It was Kenneth
Bainbridge, the director of the Trinity
test: he turned to Oppenheimer and
said, "Now we are all sons of bitches."
He wasn't wrong.

jl So what's it like when you get up
there?

BM Trinity Site? It's a scratchland of
mesquite and creosote and rabbit
brush. It is Billy the Kid's old stomp-
ing ground, really desolate land.
Desolate, beautiful, towering skies,
little water—the *Jornada del Muerto*,
the journey of death. And
Alamogordo, which is young as towns
go—founded in 1898 by a railroad
entrepreneur named Charles Eddy—is
snuggled up against the Sacramento
Mountains. You set out in the morning from the Otero County
Fairgrounds and there's a pleasant
group of people with turquoise
Alamogordo Chamber of Commerce
T-shirts on, and two hundred cars car-
avan out under military police escort,
with their lights on, like a big funeral
procession. It's about three hours in
through White Sands Missile Range
which is very eerie, with telemetry
bunkers and radar installations dotted
around the landscape.

jl I love this vocabulary. I mean,
"telemetry": what a great word! I
was jealous of *Trinity Fields* because
I've always wanted to have an
excuse to use the word "ordnance"
in a sentence.

BM Write a war book. Then you can have all the ordnance you want. Well, you can have emotional ordnance, of course.

jl I'll use it metaphorically.

BM Anyway, you can't use cameras on the way in, so I took many pages of notes which, whenever the MPs came by, I hid under the seat, just in case.

jl Is there still research going on there?

BM All the time. Since the Trinity blast, there have been 40,000 missiles fired on this range. The Cruise missile, the Stealth fighter and bomber programs were developed there. So you arrive and walk the last several hundred yards and suddenly a black lava stone obelisk rises from the center of the shallow crater marking ground zero. To me, it's one of the most emotionally startling, disturbing, moving national monuments in this country.

jl Especially because nobody can see it.

BM Only twice a year, on the first Saturday in April and the first Saturday in October.

jl Like the plaque on the moon.

BM After the plaque on the moon, this is the most hidden monument we've got. Only open nine hours a year. I can't think of anything more humbling than standing in this place where the world changed. Because when that bomb worked, we were at a new historical era. We wrested the apocalypse away from God and had it at our own disposal. You can see san-

itary scale-model reproductions of the Fat Man and Little Boy devices at the Bradbury Museum in Los Alamos. TNT tonnage equivalents are given on the exhibition plaques but no mention of casualties. We're still in denial about our newfound demonic potential.

[break]

jl Now, I want to talk about your near death experience. I know that in August you nearly died from perotinitis.

BM I was in such extraordinary pain that my memories are really specific, and mostly interior. The experience was not anecdotal though I remember an orderly in the emergency room in this little hospital upstate touched my side and I did a double jackknife and screamed. He said, "If I can't touch you, I can't help you, champ." And I said, "Don't call me champ." [laughter] I remember that.

jl I've never felt extreme physical pain. Is it like regular pain, only more so?

BM Regular pain, which hurts and is annoying and disturbs your normal mental processes and which you hope to get out of your life as soon as possible, is different for me from the pain I experienced at the brink of death. That pain was fully occupying. It was me, that pain. My consciousness became active in a brighter, different way: I wasn't against the pain so much as inside it.

jl Does it reach the point where it almost gets abstract?

BM No, it's very concrete. [*laughter*] What gets abstracted is the sense that something exists outside that pain because it becomes so completely a part of your existence while you're in it, there's no consideration of what might lie outside the envelope. You simply begin to think inside of it. You view other people from inside the fleshy border of your body as if you're one universe and they are another.

jl So it becomes a proprioceptive fact.

BM It's not that you have a pain. You have become an organism that is pain. You feel yourself as a physiological complex in which everything has gone wrong. It's a moment at which I abandoned hope, and therefore, fear wasn't part of the experience either. Which is, in retrospect, one of the most astounding aspects of the whole thing. At the end of a hundred-mile ambulance ride to the city, I remember coming across the George Washington Bridge and looking up at those big silver spans, and thinking, this is how you die. I was more fascinated by it than afraid of it. It just seemed very normal and natural and things were falling into place. I couldn't get up and help myself; no one could help me. It was peculiar in that I was so intellectually and imaginatively conscious and alive but my body was falling away. Suddenly, I was in this amazing free-fall. Time became bendy and warped and peculiar. It was a great experience. I mean, I've come out of it sharpened, honed. Your purpose can't help but become focused, refo-

cused. I got ripped to the roots. Everything had to be reevaluated. Everything. It's been like a small, personal atomic explosion; there's a green, glassy trinitite on the bottom of my being. It's like a green monocle through which I can look up into the universe and review everything. Things re-fused; other things were unconfused. Friendships were strengthened. My work seems to have a meaning to me now that it didn't before. I have to say, I'm not as convinced as I was before all this occurred, of the eradication of the imagination, the consciousness, or the soul, after physical death.

jl Oh, you're not going to start getting all pious on me, are you?

BM No, I didn't go gooey. [*laughter*] I'm just as crinkly and cranky as before. It was just one of the noticings that occurred when I was that sick: I was still able to perceive what was going on with me, and I remember thinking, how could the mind be this active when the body is this distressed?

jl All right, let's talk about Vietnam. One of the first things that struck me about your treatment of Vietnam in *Trinity Fields* was your description of the Pathet Lao dropping yellow rain on the Hmong. I was under the impression that the notion that the stuff was a form of chemical warfare was a pet theory of the right wing. The left, in this country, always maintained that it was just bee droppings. But you seem to endorse quite strongly, in the book, the idea that there was, in fact, a great deal of chemical warfare. Not that you shouldn't believe anything that isn't left wing, but I was curious about how you came to that conclusion.

BM Well, I have a left hand and a right hand. And the fact is, the Hmong people are being eradicated by military extremists in the Pathet Laotian regime and the Hmong are neither left nor right. They're mountain people, farmers, who've been itinerant for four thousand years, and basically have been pushed from mountaintop to mountaintop by whomever was in power at the time: the Chinese, the Cambodians, the Vietnamese. It's true they were funded by the CIA; we gave them weapons and helped them to sell heroin so they could have funds to fight the Pathet Lao and the NVA [North Vietnamese Army]. But the Hmong got tricked by the Americans the same way they're being systematically eradicated by the Lao. So you'll find that the right wing is just as anxious to embrace the bee droppings theory of yellow rain as the left wing is, because neither conservatives nor liberals much want to deal with the war anymore. It always comes down to money, finally, and there's not enough potential commerce or money in Laos for us to bother with it, yet. I think Vietnam has opened because there's sufficient commerce promised that enough money would be lost by both countries if ties weren't reopened. So the Hmong meant more to me than left or right; they just seemed, again,

innocents, in the same way the physicists in Los Alamos were, insofar as they became part of a machinery larger than themselves. The Hmong became pro-democratic extremists in the fringe of the CIA, out of a need to survive. And you can't expect them not to fall prey to things they don't really understand or can't control. In the end, we deceived and abandoned them, and it was a Republican president who did it after two Democrats got it going.

jl There's this kind of vice that afflicts people, for example, who write about the police a lot: they become cop groupies. They very quickly lose all their objectivity, and become so infatuated with the romance of police work that it becomes very clear whose side they're on. Given all the time you spent with the Ravens, how did you keep yourself from doing that?

BM Don't forget, the narrator of *Trinity Fields* is an antiwar activist who studied law so that he could get other antiwar activists out of jail, and he's essentially a liberal. So I was no more tempted into a romance with the elite Air Force spooks known as the Ravens who fought clandestinely in Laos, than I was into a romance with the antiwar activists I talked to, as I was writing the Columbia riot sections. I think the journey for me as a novelist was just that: as a novelist, I got into it as much as I safely could, without going native.

jl Is there a name for . . . ?

BM Yeah, "going bamboo". But the novels I like reading and the novels I seem to write tend to be anthropological by nature: they explore how the culture works at a macrocosmic level, as well as an individual level. So I try the best I can to ensure that the novel expresses itself, that the form fulfills itself properly.

jl And yet the narrator has your initials.

BM I noticed that. [*laughter*] But I don't relate any more personally to Brice than I do to Kip, or Jessica, or Ariel, or anyone in the book. What's dicey about writing a novel that has politics as one of its facets is that you've got to remain true to your characters and to the fiction itself, but at the same time, you can't sell your own political views down the river. And, I think it's apparent by the end of *Trinity Fields*: I don't consider this government, or any other government, to be much more than made up of generally ambitious, often selfish, sometimes cruel people. What interests me as a novelist is how individuals live a life in the shadow of these larger, monstrous, grotesque dancing figures, how you live a life in the presence of people who really aren't good. And there are people in the world who are really evil. That's part of what the book's about.

jl Do you have a theodicy? Why do you think people become evil? Because they're weak? Because they're malevolent? Because they're ignorant?

BM Because they're incapable of empathy. And because they're full of fear and therefore overprotect themselves, and become selfish and greedy. If you can't empathize and embrace, you can't understand, and if you can't understand, you're on your way to becoming evil.

Edmund White, © Jerry Bauer. Courtesy Knopf.

EDMUND WHITE   ALAIN KIRILI

Double Portrait of the Artist: A Conversation

During a very pleasant dinner at Edmund White's apartment in Paris, I proposed we simply continue our conversation rather than conduct an interview. Edmund had just been to see my sculpture show at Galerie Daniel Templon. And I was deeply immersed in reading his extraordinary biography, *Genet.* I have long been a fan of Edmund's novels, *Forgetting Elena* and *A Boy's Own Story* being my favorites. And, being a Parisian who now lives in New York, I was curious about this American living in Paris. We did continue our conversation, on a December afternoon shortly after our dinner, again at his home.

BOMB # 47, Spring, 1994

EDMUND WHITE Do you always work with music playing?

ALAIN KIRILI Never with music. I like to memorize it and absorb it, but when I create I really need silence, total concentration. How about you?

EW I always work with music.

AK You write with music?

EW With music, yes. I always have, my whole life, and my father did too. We lived in a house that was flooded with music from dawn to dusk. My friends who are composers think I'm crazy, because they can't bear music. Of course, that's because they listen to it so carefully that they don't want it as a background. Virgil Thompson once said to me, "I think you like music for the reason lots of writers do, because it gives you something to resist, so that you can concentrate better."

AK It's a kind of challenge.

EW That's right. When you worked with Roy Haynes, [creating clay sculptures while he was drumming], did you take your inspiration from what he was drumming, or were you working independently?

AK I pushed my gestures, making them a little quicker than what I'm accustomed to. That was the main stimulation Roy gave me. The strange thing is that he did follow what I was doing, but at other moments he would move even quicker, anticipating me, and I would follow up what he was doing.

EW   So sometimes he took the lead, and sometimes you took the lead. You were definitely interacting back and forth.

AK   Yes, certainly, we were interacting. You told me last time that you knew Mingus. Could you tell me more about your interest in jazz and in Mingus particularly?

EW   It's more in Mingus than in jazz *per se*. I don't know that much about jazz. As a twelve-year-old boy, I used the money from the first job I ever had to buy a record player and my first record, which was by Chet Baker. I met Mingus in New York, in 1962 or '63, right after I got out of college. Two girls I went to school with, Ann McIntosh and Janet Coleman, were helping him to edit his book, *Beneath the Underdog*. They would invite him to parties, and I would always see him there. I spent New Year's of 1963, '64 and '65, I think, in his apartment. The most beautiful moment was this: one New Year's Eve we were all screaming and carrying on, and he said, "Be quiet! Listen to the silence. I could orchestrate that!" He wanted to notate it, he felt he could write all that down. And it's true, once you're very quiet you hear the creaking of the building, the traffic, you can even hear the furnace in the basement.

AK   I think it's great that you care to read artists and write about them. You recently wrote a beautiful text on Ross Bleckner.

EW   I've written on Philip Taaffe and Richard Prince, too . . . and Duane Michaels, and Robert Mapplethorpe, and different photographers.

AK   Tell me about your interest in a book that is crucial to me, Jean Genet's *L'Atelier d'Alberto Giacometti*. This is a book I like to give as a gift.

EW   What's great about that book by Genet is that he doesn't try to sound like an art historian. He doesn't talk about art history. It seems to me that all most critics know how to do is trace influences. So they say, this artist is a little bit of this or that. Genet was capable of that kind of criticism, and when he wrote about an artist he didn't like very much, for example, Leonor Fini, he resorted to that kind of art historical talk. But when he wrote about an artist he really loved, he invented a whole new language for discussing him. As when he proposes that the statues of Giacometti should be offered to the dead, and that they should be buried. He talks about the wound each person must have in order to have a sense of beauty.

AK   I thought it was remarkable—and I like the way you emphasize this in your biography of Genet—that a novelist, a writer should have such an appreciation for the differences between a sculpture in plaster and a sculpture in bronze. Genet spoke about how great it was to see the original plaster, and that Giacometti's didn't lose anything when they were transferred, cast, in bronze.

EW That's right. He said he thought that the bronze was pleased . . .

AK Yes, exactly.

EW Genet was a writer who would travel to look at paintings and sculptures. He would go to the Hague, to Germany, he would travel all over the world, actually, to look at works of art.

AK The thing I find most interesting and remarkable—especially considering the different sexualities of Genet and Giacometti—is the way Genet raises very direct questions that are definitely not typical of art criticism. Genet talks about Giacometti's cult of prostitutes, he asks about Giacometti's lifestyle, about the way he lives; it gets very intense when he asks about the *poules*, the whores.

EW People say Genet would not have liked a biography—and it's true he probably wouldn't have, since he lied so much. But on the other hand, when he wrote about Giacometti he didn't write about him in a formalist way. He talked about very human things. And interestingly, in *L'Atelier d'Alberto Giacometti*, he gives little bits of conversation between the two of them, as in the wonderful exchange where Giacometti says to him, "How handsome you are, how handsome you are . . . like everybody."

AK As an artist, I think it's intriguing to think about how you, being an artist yourself, a writer, were affected by the writing of this biography. How is this project situated in your life, in your development? After your first series of novels, you have devoted seven years to the biography of another writer. Can you predict what effect this will have on you? How did you absorb or assimilate this experience, how will it affect your next books?

EW It's hard for me to know because I'm writing them now. But I think the best example Genet provides is that of doing something in the strongest, simplest possible way. Making a big, bold gesture. For example, I've just finished writing a short story, and I like to think it's less confused and more direct, simpler, than anything I've written before. I don't want to write in Genet's style—I think it's idiotic to copy somebody's style. But you can copy their example, which is the example of someone who goes to the limit. If one definition of a successful work of art is something that has fully exploited all the possibilities within the invented genre, then Genet is certainly successful in those terms. You couldn't do anything more along the lines he was pursuing.

AK So the example he provides is that sort of radicalism, or intensity, taken as a stimulation, as a challenge. What's the title of your next book?

EW I'm writing several different books. I'm writing a novel called *The Farewell Symphony*; I'm writing a book of short stories called *Skinned Alive*; and I'm writing a book of essays called *The Burning Library*.

AK We spoke a little bit about the collection of essays, *The Burning Library*. Could you tell me more about it?

EW It's essays from the late 1960s until now, some of which are art essays. Since I'm a writer who publishes so much in Europe and in little magazines all over the world, I don't think there's anyone, not even my mother, who has seen everything I've written. So there will be a lot of surprises for people, because there are little art essays I've written for *Parkett*, in Switzerland, or for instance, I wrote a catalogue essay for Robert Mapplethorpe when he had an exhibit in Holland, I wrote about Prince the singer and Richard Prince the artist. There's a long interview with me that was done for *The Paris Review* and that's probably the best interview I've given. So there's all kinds of things. There's also a lot about the history of the gay liberation movement. In 1970, I had already started writing about that subject in essay form, and I continue to do so up to the present. So there are essays on everything from the very beginning of the gay liberation movement to the whole question, now, of political correctness.

AK Political correctness is a subject that's tough to address.

EW How do you feel when Robert Rosenblum says, in his essay about you, that you are an artist who's recuperating the past, who is a very cultured artist, one who is linked to great artists of the past?

AK Well, I think of myself as an artist who is not amnesic. Certainly, one of the reasons for living in New York is to appreciate a different way of life, a dif-

ferent culture, but also another ethic—and, thus, not to take the French way of life as natural. There is no such thing as a "natural" way of life. For me to be a foreigner helps me evaluate the different traditions that we, in the Western world, are still confronting.

EW Do you say, "them" when you look at French people, or do you say "them" when you look at Americans? I mean, do you find Americans easier to understand now than French people? Do you find yourself more of a sociologist studying the French, or studying the Americans?

AK Well, at this point, I feel like a foreigner everywhere. I feel that very deeply, a sort of irreducible *étrangeté*, or foreignness. How about you?

EW I actually feel now that Americans are harder for me to understand; I'm more interested in studying them than French people. I don't go to America very often, only three or four weeks every year, and when I do, I'm always thinking: Oh, that's what they are doing now, that's what they think, et cetera. For one thing, American culture seems to evolve much faster than French culture.

AK What's intriguing for me is that I've come to a similar point. I've lived in New York for twelve years now, and France has started to become more and more foreign to me. And when I come here, to France, I've started to feel the difference in their speed of evolution, or whatever, almost like a foreigner. And in fact I like that disconnection. [*laughter*]

EW One thing that always strikes me as a big difference between America and France is this: I've a friend who's an art dealer who told me an American woman walked into his office and said, "Last year I had no money and I was living in one room; now I have millions of dollars and I'm living in twenty rooms. I don't know anything about art, so I want you to buy lots of art and put it on my walls." And I thought, that would never happen in France. First of all, people don't make money that quickly. Secondly, if they made it, they'd pretend they'd always had it. They'd never go in so naively and say, "Please tell me what I should buy." And if they had just made new money, they'd want to buy old paintings. They wouldn't want new paintings, they would want it to look as if they were from an old family with ancestors.

AK How many years have you been in France?

EW Twelve years.

AK What made you decide to live in Paris? What was it you liked?

EW Well, I like the fact that it is so calm here. People don't bother you too much. And I also like being slightly out of it, in terms of America. I like being close to other countries in Europe.

AK It's a base.

EW Yes, a base. I go to England, to Switzerland, Italy, Germany, a lot—especially England, maybe once a month. I have more friends in London than in Paris. So London's

really . . . I just don't like the city very much. I also feel the English like me more if I live in France than if I were to live in England.

AK [*laughter*] What do you like about Paris itself?

EW I like the beauty of the place. I like the food. I like the calm. I think that French people are very difficult to get to know, but once you do they're the best friends, the most loyal friends, because they have a cult of friendship in a way most people, most countries, don't. And even if France has very few great writers right now, it has lots of great readers. In other words, there are many extremely cultured people who read for the pure pleasure of it, and who have read everything. I know lots of people like that here, and not many in New York.

People in New York are very *intéressé*, they're looking out for their own interests, they're always networking, they all want to climb the ladder. You never know whether they like you for yourself or because you can help them with their career. Whereas here, I don't think people are like that so much. When I first arrived in Paris I wanted to give a party and invite all the journalists and all my friends. And a French woman, a friend said, "We don't do that in France—you have two parties, one for your friends, one for the journalists, but you don't mix them." But in New York you mix everybody.

AK Very true. In New York you feel that the notion of network often involves people who share the same background, in terms of universities and so forth.

EW Here too, with the Grandes Écoles, Sciences Po, and all that.

AK Do you think that affects the writer? That sort of school?

EW Camus said that America is the only country where writers are not intellectuals. It's true that here in France you tend to meet people who are writers. And when you dig a littler deeper it turns out that their father was an editor at Gallimard, that they're from a grand bourgeois family, or their great-grandfather was François Mauriac, or they were ranked number one at their school, or they were a professor of philosophy and now they're a novelist. In other words, there's a profile of people who live in the fifth, sixth, and seventh arrondissements, who all know each other, who tend to have a private income, and who tend to have a very exalted idea about art, and who want to be *hommes de lettres* in the sense of wanting to combine writing essays with writing novels, who read everything and are *au courant* with everything. Someone like Marc Chodolenko, for instance, who is a friend, who won the Prix Medicis many years ago—every time I go to the Louvre he's there. He's always there, studying everything. He has never written a word about art, he never will, it's just that he wants to know all about it. I mean, there are these culture vultures. But in America I have many students of writing who go on to become writers, and their

mother's a nurse or their father's a truck driver. They become writers but they're not intellectuals; they haven't read very much. They're from modest families. Maybe that's why American fiction is so vital and gutsy.

AK This is what is all the more extraordinary about someone like Genet. He's self-taught. He knew how to create his network, by being somewhat protected by Cocteau, but at the same time he came from . . .

EW Nowhere.

AK Exactly. From nowhere.

EW I think it helped in his case that there was the war. There was such chaos during the war, so many people were compromised by being collaborators, that suddenly there was an opening up in French culture that allowed a lot of talented nobodies to emerge. I don't think they would have risen before the war. There are certain great exceptions. Céline, for example, was not from an important family; he was just a great writer. Obviously there are always going to be the "genius" exceptions. But I think the chaos of the war actually helped Genet to write, and then to be published and recognized.

AK With regard to what you said earlier about Rosenblum's statement that my work has a memory or a heritage, I myself dealt with post-war chaos, being from the first generation after the war, a generation that had to make connections all over again. When I was a twenty year old in Paris, there were no major artists ten or fifteen years older than myself, representing the previous generation, that I could meet. Yves Klein was dead, Dubuffet was totally inaccessible, and thus the generation between me and the artists I could meet was an American generation. That's how I met Robert Morris and Rauschenberg; it's one of the main reasons I went to New York.

EW I see . . . I wonder, I feel that one of the historical movements you connect with is abstract expressionism. But abstract expressionism itself was anything but a historical movement. It was interested in discovering the new, in pulling a vision out of the guts. It was very improvisational, like jazz, and it was heroic in that fiercely romantic and individualistic way. Even when someone like Robert Rosenblum can link it with the northern, German tradition, I don't think American painters thought in those terms. They themselves thought they were doing something brand new. And I know in your case when you do modeling that is nonfigurative, that this represents something new as well.

So my question is, how important is it for you to do something brand new in a kind of heroic way, like the abstract expressionists, and how important is it for you to see yourself in a tradition? Or is this a false dichotomy

AK No, I think the answer is something I can observe in your case too. You gave me an answer earlier about Genet that's very similar to what I want to say now. You said that Genet provided

a heroic or radical example that stimulates and pushes you in your work. Similarly, for me, the power of transgression that occurs in abstract expressionists, their "heroic" sense of urgency, is absolutely crucial. It's their sense of urgency that's important for me, something they possessed more than anyone else at the time, excepting perhaps the jazz players. There is probably, as you have mentioned, a great connection between Charlie Parker and Jackson Pollock. What they shared is the sense of urgency.

EW I think that's right, actually. Phillippe Sollers, when he wrote about your sculpture *Commandment* when it was installed in Paris, said that you were more recognized by the Americans than by the French. Would you say that's true now? Was it true when he wrote it, in 1985 or 1986?

AK For the most part it's still true now, if only because the community of artists is so much larger in New York. Personally, you know, my priority has always been to have the respect and concern of my *confréres*—what's the word?

EW My colleagues.

AK Yes. So in some ways I feel I'm more a part of the New York art scene than of the one in Paris.

EW Is there a Paris art scene?

AK Is there a Paris art scene . . . That indeed is the question.

EW Didn't you say once that you sculpted while listening to Sollers recite from *Paradis*?

AK That's right. Something very helpful for me is to hear the French language. It's hard for me to escape French. It's my mother tongue, and I've never really mastered English; I don't have that Nabokov-like talent in language. Are you going to write in French some day? You speak it well enough, eh? Would you find it stimulating to write in French, or merely inhibiting?

EW [*laughter*] I think I would just make mistakes. It's easy to make mistakes, especially if you have never been trained in a language. I never studied it to write it. I suppose I could if I worked with somebody.

Samuel Beckett, obviously, only became a great writer after he began to work in French. If you look at *Watt*, the last book he did in English, and then the trilogy, the first books he did in French, there's a tremendous leap forward—and it comes from writing in French. In his case he was a descendent of Joyce, he was Joyce's secretary, and in a way was too clever, knew too many words, had too many ideas. He was overrefined. But by writing in French he was forced to concentrate and simplify. I think that helped enormously. At the same time, he made another change; he began to write in the first person and say I, which he'd never done before. Those two things, I think, simplified and gave tremendous strength to his writing.

But in my case, I don't have the problem of being too clever. Writing in English is a problem already. It's not that I write too well, but that I'm always trying to write well enough. Gertrude Stein said, when she lived in Paris, that what she liked about it was that she felt she was the only person in the world who spoke English, that she was alone with the language. I like that part. I like writing in English in Paris.

The story I just wrote takes place in the Midwest in 1957, and I find that all those words we used to say in 1957 come back to me; I have a perfect memory for them. The longer I'm away from that world, the more crystal clear it becomes to me.

AK Speaking of such clarity, it's true that living in New York, I have a better, clearer appreciation of what is specifically French. I'm much more aware of this now than if I had stayed in Paris all this time.

EW You made me laugh the other day when you talked about the work ethic. You said that when you first arrived in New York, you were impressed by how hard everybody was working. But I found that what I like about Paris is that I don't work so hard. I relax more and I practice the art of the *flâneur*. I spend hours walking around looking at books and things like that, without worrying about wasting time, which I used to worry about all the time.

SAPPHIRE kelvin christopher james

BOMB # 57, Fall 1996

Written in a young girl's unschooled voice, *Push* is a harrowing story of a brutalized child's journey to redemption and relevance. It's a searing indictment. A sensational read.

We met for lunch at Barocco. I got there early and chose us a quiet corner table, then waited reading the menu, sipping white wine. Right on time Sapphire walked in. Our eyes met and I went over. We hugged each other in greeting. A good looking woman, rich brown skin accented by a dark red dress, well fitting, a neat firm body. Close-cropped hair bearing a nice round head. Big bold eyes. Rude lips of a matter-of-fact mouth that'd laugh or scream or testify with passion. I felt good with her.

kelvin christoper james *Push* is a very dark, Dickensian book. It's mired in humanity. The characters do the worst to themselves and to each other. Its success surprises me, as recent writing seems to be moving towards the gothic. Did you consider this when writing *Push*: Be a winner by breaking the trend?

SAPPHIRE What I considered was that we were going to enter into a person's life who was being damaged, but who was not *intrinsically* damaged. We're going to enter into and watch the growth of someone who has been emotionally crippled. That was the focal point of the novel. I wasn't interested in writing a dark, horrible story—a case history or a crime novel—but in how, through all these impediments and all these trials, a human being could still grow. And why they could. I didn't get an answer in writing the book, but it has to do

with human nature. It's human nature for young people to grow and learn. So we enter into *Push* with Precious doing a natural thing; it only seems bizarre because so many bad things have happened to her, but she just wants what any other kid wants. She wants to live. She wants a boyfriend, she wants to learn, she wants nice clothes . . .

kcj That's why I said Dickensian. I see Oliver Twist and Nicholas Nickelby, but Precious goes through worse times than they did in every way.

s Part of what's so wrong in this story is that we're not in a Dickensian era. Those things shouldn't be happening in a post-industrial society.

kcj Your character, Precious Jones, and her life could be considered a caricature of white people's guilt in producing such disgusting

Sapphire, © Joyce Ravid. Courtesy Vintage Books.

social conditions. Are you turning this guilt against them? Is this a social-conscience novel?

s The novel definitely has areas of social commentary. I don't really see it as an indictment of white people, I see it as an indictment of American culture, which is both black and white.

kcj What if it's white people who control the culture?

s This morning when I woke up to feed my cat, it was me that fed my cat. I had a choice of whether I was going to pet him or kick him. No white people were there. Even within slavery, in our most deprived state, we had choices. Yeah, we're looking at some people who are horribly, horribly oppressed. We can say that Precious' mother and father, and many of the people in the culture, find themselves in a steel box, that's how bad the oppression is. You can sit there in that steel box, you can kill yourself in that box, or you can turn on your young and kill yourself that way. Even when the choices are limited, you still have choices. To me, it is an indictment of the people who created the parents, but it's also an indictment of the parents. We can see in other circumstances where Precious interacts with people who have choices. The EMS man could have looked at her and said, "What the fuck?" and walked out. He chose to be a human being and say, "I don't understand this, I don't know about these people, but here is a child giving birth. Push." He saved her life.

kcj He's the only sympathetic male in the story. Other than Mr. Wicher, who is a wimp.

s Mr. Wicher's not a sympathetic male. He's a wimp who is terrified, like many inner-city teachers. He's using Precious to police other students.

kcj But he's the one she says she wants to marry . . .

s Of course, she's in fantasy land, and she misunderstands his using her for love. She needs that misunderstanding, the conjecture of fantasy relationships. All this man wants is for her to keep beating up the other kids to keep them from bothering him.

kcj Am I on the mark when I find that most of the people who take care of Precious have dreadlocks and a Caribbean quality?

s I see Precious very much as an individual and as my creative child character; but she can also be a symbol of African Americans. And her first challenge towards growth is that her own xenophobia is called into question. Before the Hispanic man saves her life she says, "What is this spic doing here?" Even as ignorant as she is—she cannot read and write—she comments on him having an accent. Her narrowness, which is created by oppression, reinforces her own oppression. We see that if she is to grow, if she is to overcome her condition on any level, she will have to accept help from people who seem very different to her. Only to a very narrow minded, up-from-the-South black culture would a West Indian or an Hispanic person be so different. But to her they are. Any type of expansion of a human being's life has to do with an expansion of consciousness. There are several points in the novel where Precious could have said "No." She could have said "No" to the man when he first came to help her. She could have said "No" when she found out Miss Blue Rain was gay. But she keeps saying "Yes." She keeps entertaining what I think is a very African mentality: she is able to embrace dual paradigms. Precious says, "I believe in Farrakhan, but I also believe in Alice Walker and Miss Rain." We see a multiple consciousness which is very different from a Western reality.

kcj Africans have many gods . . .

s Yeah, in the same way you have Africans who believe in Yoruba and polytheism, and then say, "I'm Christian." We see the best of her roots come forward in being able to accept this consciousness.

kcj She doesn't accept the Jewish woman, her teacher Mrs. Lichenstein, the one who first comes to her house and challenges her.

s Precious can't appreciate Mrs. Lichenstein, but the reader can. The reader can understand what it means for a white woman to leave her neighborhood and come stand on Lenox Avenue and ring that bell, and be polite while Precious is screaming, "Get out of here Mrs. Lichenstein . . ." Precious cannot understand that gift until much, much later. Precious has attitude, but that's what keeps her alive. Attitude.

kcj You have convincingly portrayed the more horrible experiences of Precious' life. Do you have an opposite moment that might not have been written into the book?

s I think she has many happy moments in the book.

kcj She's going to die. She has HIV.

s We're all going to die. Miss Rain might die before Precious dies. Precious just knows when and how she will die. Or, maybe she'll catch a bullet on the way home from school.

kcj And what will happen to Precious' baby boy, Abdul?

s Well, we're all hoping that Newt Gingrich and Bob Dole don't get in, because then we know that Abdul will be slated for the orphanage. Now, we know that the white, middle-class, and gay males with HIV are living twelve years after diagnosis. Precious is very healthy; she has no preexisting conditions, no other STDs, she was diagnosed early . . . She may have been infected at sixteen. Add twelve years to that and what do you get?

kcj Okay, so she could live to her mid-twenties. Maybe until thirty.

s Thirty years. And how old will Abdul be?

kcj He'd then be about ten.

s Ten years with your mother is a lot of time to be infused with some deep love, and you know that she's a child who knows how to love. He would never forget that. So in the best world, Precious would live to be about thirty. That would mean that she would be able to see Abdul through elementary school, and have him recite his Langston Hughes, and be there. He may, if they had proper care, be part of her hospice experience and therapy, and learn what was happening to his mother. That would be the best thing. In the worst world, if she were to become homeless, and had to go back to the shelter, where the people have TB and stuff like that, she would get more sick and die in two or three years; and he would be put into foster care, where he would be raped and abused.

kcj Is Precious a child who never had anything? Not even sunshine, and the normal days of happiness?

s Well, that's a lot. Have you ever been in prison and then you got out? You hear them talk about how they enjoy just walking. Here's someone who has had an almost parallel deprivation. Precious never had a friend, so just to go downtown with her schoolmates Rita and Rhonda is a high point. I imagine Rhonda will start taking her to church at some point.

kcj Let me tell you something. I read this book with a box of Kleenex next to me. It is so horrid where she lives. Every little touch of kindness that she feels breaks my heart. It's such a despairing happiness. I want her to have regular happiness.

s Well, the novel is on us. People ask me stupid shit like, "What's going to happen to her?" You know what's going to

happen to her! The literature program really existed—I used to teach there. Not anymore. The halfwayhouse really existed. Harlem Hospital—Koch wanted to close it. And they closed Seidenham Hospital. If you remove all the medical care, all the educational facilities, then you know what's going to happen to her. Part of my job as a citizen of America is to see that that doesn't happen. To see that the literature programs stand, to see that the Harlem Hospital stays intact.

kcj So you write these stark stories . . .

s That's part of it. And also, we're having to look at how black culture looks at women. I would like for her to have a boyfriend, but I couldn't just make one up. I would like for someone to love her for who she is. I would like for us to be able to look at somebody's soul and love them. I want that for her.

kcj When and why did you start writing, and what were your influences?

s First I started writing in journals, and then I started writing poetry. My very early influences were people like Sonia Sanchez, Jayne Cortez, Don L. Lee— that whole black arts movement. Although I wasn't a part of it.

kcj They're predominantly straight people, is that deliberate?

s That was San Francisco, where I was living when I first started to write. But I wasn't exposed to writers in real life until I started taking dance classes. One of the master dancers in the class was Ntozake Shange. I'm a young woman and I'm like, "Oh my God!" I never saw nothing like this before. It's much more a feminist woman's consciousness.

kcj And the women looked exciting and vigorous.

s They were at the top then. They were doing with words what Tina Turner used to do with her body. And I saw Tina in her prime. She was the most sexually and physically assertive when she was in that Ike and Tina Turner thing. I saw her at the Five Four Ballroom, in the early seventies with the Ikettes. I'd never in my life seen a human being move like that. And these women were doing that with words. Ntozake would come out there and do her thing, and that was a primal influence that freed me. But Don L. Lee and Sonia Sanchez—as a bisexual I didn't exist in their world. At that time Sonia Sanchez was in the Nation of Islam—I admire that, but I can't go there. I'm moving a bit more to the left.

kcj Beyond the physical geography of New York City or San Francisco, where are you from in America?

s I'm from a secret world. I was born and literally spent the first years of my life on an army base. My mother and father met in World War II. My mother was born in 1920, a child of the Depression who graduated from high school, which was a big thing in those days. Then in her twenties she ran away and joined the WACs, the colored WACs, it was a segregated unit.

kcj She ran away to war?

s She wanted to escape poverty and working in a factory. She didn't do any combat. You know what I mean, they dated the soldiers. My father left the rural south, Texas, and joined the army. They met each other and married—all of my siblings were born on an army base. I didn't really leave the military life until I was twelve years old. It was another world that I have not yet seen in literature. It was not the ghetto or the rural South, and it definitely was not that fly-in-the-buttermilk, black-person-in-the-suburbs experience. This was raw. The white people there were in the Klan, and the black people there were escapees from poverty. And then you had years and years of war. My father was in World War II and Korea. It was the military. I was raised like that. And then we got into normal life. At twelve I moved to South Philadelphia, a large, urban black environment.

kcj Another life in the scene.

s Exactly. Even as bad as life in the military was, and I can't describe how bad it was, during Truman's time they had desegregated the armed forces, so you couldn't overtly act out the racist stuff. Even when I was in Texas, the army base schools were integrated while schools outside—you know, they were using firehoses and shit. There was a court order to integrate and they wouldn't do it, but at the base we were already doing that. So then I get to Philadelphia. I remember my first year there, 1963, they had a race riot. For the first time I was exposed to an urban situation . . . I already had internalized that as a black person I'm an outsider. But on the army base, we never had a chance, as blacks, to divide into light-skinned or dark-skinned, or educated, or any kind of faction. We were under siege. But in Philadelphia, the black Northerners made fun of my accent. That's the most basic thing you have, your physical self and your speech.

kcj Nobody likes you. You're an outsider even when you're inside.

s Exactly. But then from Philadelphia we moved to Los Angeles, another large, urban environment. And that became the rest of my life. Now, I can't be anywhere but a city.

kcj Would you now write a gentler, kinder novel, or do you still have material from this world that you want to explore?

s I don't see things getting gentler and kinder. If I go forward, I will go more and more into depth. In this novel I made some big assumptions about my readers, that they would understand certain things. I feel comfortable with that. You can't write explaining everything to the outsider.

kcj Yeah, some people have said that it is a negative version, right?

s Yeah, but my next book will not be a response to that criticism. I feel that I gave a big picture. It's not my job as a writer to satisfy you. I'm not trying to jack you off. We're living in a culture where people are constantly screaming about family values, but I don't think

we'll win the battle. The only time more children have been out of the control of their family was that Dickensian period of orphanages. What does it mean in terms of the race and class that I come from—that large masses of my children, metaphorically, are being raised by the state? In foster homes and in jails and in poor schools? That's something that intrigues me deeply. Even though I'm examining Precious, I'm also examining the family.

kcj How do you respond to skeptics, and how do you respond to envy at your success?

s I have lived a very isolated life. I know people are envious of me, I can feel it. But I basically have kept myself away from people. I was upset that my life all of a sudden became so public. I'm used to my work being out there, but not me, literally. Now I'm starting to renegotiate my physical reality, trying to be and make myself safer. And if you're envious, I'm glad you're envious. I'm so glad I got something. Hey, I'm a black woman, and I'm forty-six years old, you know what I mean? I could write about scrubbing floors because I've scrubbed floors; I could write about turning tricks because I've turned tricks. I did a lot to get where I am. But I'm glad for what I have and I'm not ashamed of it. I'm the type of person who, even when I had little, I put it to good use.

kcj So, now that you are well paid by publishers, lauded by the critics, and read by the masses, how do you feel to have arrived: satisfied, justified, or just impatient?

s Number one, I'm real serious, and I've always been serious. And I've always been serious about my time, knowing that time equals life. I have a brother who is no longer here, my parents are dead, and I understand that one day I'll be dead too. I don't want to waste my time and I don't want to waste my life. I deserve to be paid for my work. I am a little skeptical of the critics, but I'm glad for the positive critical reception. I was on 125th Street on Saturday, and a young girl came up to me and said, "Are you Sapphire? I read your book. It's the best book I ever read." That meant something to me. I was in the xerox shop xeroxing a manuscript, and there was this brother in there with his gold chains and his jeans and he looked like he was getting ready to do a rap concert instead of xeroxing, like he was supposed to be doing. I was mad, and I said to myself, "Now if this was a white girl he'd be xeroxing faster, why is this guy taking so long to xerox my shit?" And then he turned around to me with tears in his eyes and he said, "Lady, did you write this here literature?" I said, "Yes, I did." He said, "This is some bad stuff." That was before the book was published, when I was xeroxing the galley. Stuff like that, no one can take from me. The black middle class who are embarrassed because of the subject matter can't take that from me; the negative black journalist in the *Wall Street Journal* can't take it from me. That's something. And that has been holding me.

kcj How does Precious learn to care for Abdul? Where would she learn care from? Nobody ever cared for her in a consistent way. I can see the possibility of a cycle of abuse happening.

s Two things happened, Precious got removed from her house when her mother attacked her and they sent her to a halfway house. We get some intimations that Precious has a positive relationship with the house mother. Often in these halfway houses the women literally go around and teach the girls how to nurture. Part of abuse, not sexual abuse but physical abuse, comes from not knowing what to do. So I see Precious as literally learning the things to do. Early childhood sexual abuse is, to me, like a car accident. We have, say, five people in a car that crashes: one person is killed, one person is paralyzed from the waist down, one person gets up and walks away, one person has psychic trauma for the rest of their life. Different people react differently to abuse. We see that one of the things Precious does, despite being abused, is fantasize about being loved. Some children who have been through that abuse fantasize about cutting the ears off a rabbit, or killing the family cat. So we see that she is pulled by a desire for love and affection. It's in her makeup to love. That's not to say that that love might not turn into something else, but it could be nurtured. She goes to a meeting of survivors. When I went to those meetings, women who were psychiatrists and therapists were not there to counsel people, they were actively seeking help on a peer level. We were examining some of the best literature on abuse and post-traumatic shock. That was the type of environment Precious goes to when she goes to that little tacky meeting. That's one of the first things she'll learn, that she, more than other people, is in danger of abusing her child. This is beyond social services. What you see here is the self-help network. The Body Positive meeting, and the Survivors of Incest Anonymous meetings are not funded by the state.

kcj What do you do when you're not writing?

s I'm very obsessive about writing, so I do a lot of writing which is not writing; journal-taking, notes, and so on. I like to read, and I'm now taking myself back to African dance class, and I'm going to Haitian dance class tonight.

kcj With all of this love you have in you, what about adopting a child? Taking care of something other than a cat or a dog, another human being?

s I have friends who have adopted, and this is the first time where I've felt psychologically healthy enough that I could do it. At a certain point you reach a lack of selfishness. I would like a baby but that's not the best thing for the world. The best thing would be for me to adopt a six or a seven-year-old.

kcj It gives somebody a chance.

s Yeah, and they have seven and eight-year-olds, little Abduls, who nobody will ever take. That is definitely something that I'm letting in, it's part of

my healing. Coming in from the outside. For the longest time I had an outsider mentality. My brother was a paranoid schizophrenic who was murdered. He manifested the outsider, and I identified with him deeply. He was all the way out there. But literally, I don't want to live out there. Part of the past 20 years has been about coming in and seeing myself as part of the human fabric, I'm not so different. Like when the nurse told Precious, "You're not so special. It's a lot of motherfuckers who are out there homeless. Get a grip, little girl . . . " So that's my thing too, everybody has been pained. When Precious learns to really read and starts reading about Bosnia, she'll understand that this is a world condition. It will either destroy her or empower her. I could see her on television talking about HIV. I could see her doing the very best with what she's been dealt. And I can also see her going to her primary caretakers, her housemother, her teacher and saying, "How do I prepare for my death?" They had a beautiful article in the *New York Times* once, a young white woman with a terminal disease was trying to find adoptive parents for her child. This is what conscious people do. You don't run around on a train shaking a cup; that's not my girl. There's a way that we're all being dealt this shit, how are you going to deal with it? That's what this book is about.

kcj Do you love Precious?

s I love her. I love everybody in the book, but I love her the most. Everyone says, "Well, the other people

in the book aren't as developed."
Okay, so what? I'm giving voice to the children that I saw.

kcj Has this book made you a stronger person?

s It has made me stronger. No matter how strong you are, outside validation . . . I've watched black women, and I haven't seen the same thing in black men, but black women over and over will go to the mirror with positivity and say, "I am beautiful, I am strong." And then when they go down the street it's like, "You black bitch." It hurts them. Even though the females can't make her beautiful, Precious stops being ugly when she comes to Ms. Rain's class. In that world she gets to be with other women who are older than her, so they are able to embrace her. She's not competition, but she's also not the fat joke that she was with the little kids. She gets some sense of herself. I see them schooling her, telling her how to do her hair, taking her downtown . . .

kcj What about women in sports? I believe you get an advantage that men already know from playing sports, that feeling of support. You hit hard, but it's in the game. It's not you I'm trying to hurt, but the opponent.

s That's one of the early things that can be done to empower women. To learn how to kick ass, and to learn how to compete with other people without killing them. What women learn is that competition can kill you, but what you learn with team sports is

that at the end of the game, we shake hands. At the end of the male-female competition, you've lost the man. But with team sports, there's something communal.

When I teach writing, I teach everyone how to write. The slave narratives are some of the most important American literature we have. Most of it is not high art, but it's part of what someone like Toni Morrison can read and make into high art. Most of the time when you listen to those Library of Congress folk recordings, they're not appealing, but when Muddy Waters listens to it, it goes farther. If those other people hadn't put their voices out there, our experiences wouldn't be documented. If we say that only a certain people can write, then we're left with less. For seven years I encouraged women to write their stories, so I've got an idea of the collective cosmic pain of women, as opposed to just my own story. As a teacher, you can't get by me without writing.

kcj It's important that you depersonalize your story. In the first book, *American Dreams*, most of the poems were your stories . . .

s I needed to depersonalize, but I had no right to tell anyone's story until I told my own. I felt I could write about Precious's mother and father raping her because I talked about my mother and father raping me. I'm not making a class statement. I'm not saying that this is what the nigger parents in Harlem do, and what the Cosby parents or the army parents don't do. I felt that once I laid my things out, I could enter into other people's lives. I was not coming towards the book as God, I was coming as the wounded writer, and that gave me an authority that I wouldn't have had if I was not stating where I came from.

kcj You couldn't imagine this story of Precious, it would be cruel and wicked to put this upon a regular black family.

s I don't think that this is what only black people do, you can't generalize. This is human behavior. This is something that has been going on since time began, and part of becoming conscious is attempting to root out the behavior that no longer serves us. In a society where it causes psychological and emotional breakdown, and the children end up crackheads, then I say stop fucking them. My friend works in homeless shelters and with all of them, over and over, it's the same story: the mother's boyfriend raped them. What we're dealing with is a nation of people in post-traumatic stress. We now know that when the men went to Vietnam and got shot up, they came back unable to cope. Part of what Precious describes and lives in is post-traumatic stress, a reaction to trauma, and you don't grow like that. It's warping us.

kcj I feel embarrassed by the black men in this story.

s Well what about Precious's Mama? She abuses her too.

kcj She's also victim of the black man.

It's not a racist thing, but I prefer to see the white males in authority; the money holders, the buyers and sellers of culture and humanity, as the bad guys—the people who care about money and bottom-line profit before humanity. And now we have the black male who is usually a victim, who never had money or authority when he came to this country, as the guy who is fucking this whole family up.

s One of the myths we've been taught is that oppression creates moral superiority. I'm here to tell you that the more oppressed a person is, the more oppressive they will be. As a friend of mine, Black Magic Rainbow, a lawyer and writer explained, the white, sadistic master came to me and said, "Lay down Sapphire, I'm gonna fuck you." Don't you know that's what he did to Kelvin, and Michael, and John? Don't you know that part of the black male experience in slavery was repeated rape by white men? So this is what we enter in with, trying to make a family? This is our baggage?

kcj How would you help a black man out of it? You're not against black men, are you?

s I'm not at all. Part of it is what we see at the end of the book, with Precious not being separated from her son. That's the most important thing, that early childhood development is nurturing. I was in Atlanta and a group of black men were reading and one of them started to cry. He talked about being abandoned by his father. A white person might ask me why Farrakhan is in the book. Well, to Precious he's a positive male role model of today. Twenty years ago I might have put in Malcolm X. A woman cannot give another woman, cannot give a man everything. Somewhere there has to be a positive male. Precious needs male interaction. We need to start thinking of how we can help children like Precious interact with their babies. We must begin to teach young men and women to begin to interact positively with each other. And not to let children be raised alone. Precious is not going to be able to give that boy a father. Where is the young black men's organization where Precious can take him to spend the day? Where can he learn how to be a man?

kcj Do you mean like big brother stuff?

s Exactly. That's how I would start, to get black men and women involved. If push came to shove I wouldn't care if it was an Asian man or a white man that came up there to take Abdul out to play.

kcj So you see it as totally beyond race?

s It's going to have to go beyond race. If we leave it there, then we're going to be lost. We're going to have to open up.

kcj Now what about sexism? What about the fact that we separate people into straight and gay?

s I think some of that is being approached in New York. I think there has to be more interaction if possible. For whatever reasons, my gay characters, Jermaine and Ms. Rain,

chose to be a part of their Harlem community. But if I was her mother and I saw Jermaine get beat up one more time, I would say, "Take off the necktie and go downtown. Don't stay up here and get killed." Just like I wouldn't go hold hands with a white boyfriend out in Howard Beach. We're talking about practical, life-saving things. I do think that any outsider has something to teach, and in the black community, the bisexuals and homosexuals have been the outsiders. Look what happened to James Baldwin—the oppression was so great he had to run. He didn't leave here because he was black, he left here because he was a gay man. He went away where he could be accepted and loved.

kcj He took France, and a white lover.

s He took someone who could see him as beautiful. He said again and again that his own father used to look at him and say, "You're ugly."

kcj Something you said, that we should leave this culture in America, and go other places to see where we can be loved, and then come back. If we didn't come back, then all of the art, all of the feeling, all of the sensitivity would go away. We can't abandon this place.

s There are a lot of different ways to leave. Precious only goes downtown; but she travels. Even by going to school, she's sitting with a West Indian woman, a Spanish woman, a gay woman, a bisexual woman, her world gets bigger.

kcj And she has to relate to all of them.

s She better.

kcj Because they are her support group.

s It's only white culture that can't see Precious as a child. I was being interviewed and I referred to Precious as a little girl, and this white woman said, "Who are you talking about?" I said, "Precious: she's a child." She's a baby.

kcj That's what I thought was so harrowing about the book. Because this is a child I'm reading about, and I am such a pussyfoot, I can't deal with that stuff.

s I know that although I'm in the middle of my life, I'm just at the beginning of my life as a writer. I'm not being false and humble, I know that *Push* is not as well written as *The*
Bluest Eye, it's not as powerful as *The Color Purple*, but my girl doesn't die, you know what I mean? American solutions, the solution to rape and abuse used to be to go crazy and kill yourself. Now the American way is to go on television and embrace talking about it. We have to move forward. We can't stand still.

kcj We have the President's wife making this statement, "It takes a village." And so, in a way Hillary Clinton has gone out of American solutions. And whether we as Americans accept and employ this solution, that's another step. I think *Push* is a wonderful book. You're itching at us, and forcing us to scratch. I think that you're a wonderful person. And of course you would be, writing a book like that.

Frederic Tuten, © Laurie Lambrecht. Courtesy William Morrow and Company.

FREDERIC TUTEN bruce wolmer

Frederic Tuten is a writer whose many admirers treasure hard-to-find copies of his published stories and sections from his work-long-in-progress, a novel based on the French comic book character Tintin. They pass among themselves xeroxes of his trenchant critical essays (on David Salle, Peter Brook, R. B. Kitaj, Alain Resnais) and, in 1986-87, they looked forward to each month's *Artforum*, when that magazine published his serial novel about the art world, *A Canvas of Episodes*. They quote Tuten's phrases to each other at dinner parties and tell new acquaintances, "There's this terrific writer you should really know about." Tuten's work has won the praise of Joseph McElroy, Edna O'Brien, Raymond Queneau, and Iris Murdoch. His first book, *The Adventures of Mao on the Long March* (1971), a serio-ironic, *collageiste* meditation on art, revolution and love—the novel as Godard film—was praised by John Updike as providing "an intelligent, taut and entertaining change in the conventional novel." If *Mao* prefigured the hyper sensuous, pastiche-and-parody sensibility of the past decade, his new book, *Tallien: A Brief Romance* (just published by Farrar, Straus and Giroux) is warmer, more subjective, disabused yet rooted in history, ours and his. Susan Sontag says of it, "*Tallien* is a wonderfully high-flying tale of two woes, made out of juicy just-right sentences. . . . His 'brief romance' is the real thing: unforgettable."

A writer's writer, Tuten, Director of the Graduate Program in Literature and Creative Writing at the City College of New York, continues to engage, with playfulness and passion, the issues of language, style, politics, and aesthetic and ethical value that have been the touchstones of the highest modern writing.

BOMB # 25, Spring 1989

bruce wolmer How did you come upon the story of Tallien, the historical character?

FREDERIC TUTEN By accident, in the eleventh edition of the *Encyclopaedia Britannica*, which I love going through, reading it like a dictionary. There was an extraordinary brief account of this fellow whom I had never heard of. He was a young radical at the outbreak of the French Revolution who took it upon himself to write and print posters demanding the execution of the King. He was taken up by older more powerful revolutionaries—like Danton and Robespierre—and given the responsibility of supervising the Terror. While he was inspecting one of the prisons where the aristocrats were being held for execution he saw the noblewoman, Therese—fell hopelessly in love, took her out of prison and began living with her. Soon, under her pleading, he was helping her aristocratic friends escape France. I was fascinated by his ascent, and by the intensity of his romance with Therese, the aristocrat. The story of a young man born to servants who climbs his way up the ladder of Revolution—I mean it's a success story. And his fall. Other falls usually led to the guillotine but this was different. His was more protracted. He lives through the Revolution, the Terror, the Republic, and becomes an adjunct to Napoleon. And after all that, abandoned by Therese, he proceeds to stumble into poverty and oblivion. I also love the story of Therese, the story of someone who survives everything, who has a force in life, who is beyond politics and revolutions, who literally just wants to live.

bw Perhaps because of the deliberate use of the contemporary idiom in telling Tallien's tale, as well as some of the action itself, one got a sense that the story might be functioning as some fractured allegory of the 1960s and after.

FT The fact that I don't write about contemporary life doesn't mean I'm any less taken up with it. I find it too limiting to write about contemporary life in contemporary diction. I don't think there's enough flexibility. I can imagine writing about characters who feel passion for one another in a contemporary setting, but I don't, as yet, hear the language for that. But I'm always thinking about a contemporary life vis-á-vis the way it looks in the past. I mean, how it looks in the past is a reflection of what it is today. I'm always talking about present-day life, not only political life but about the quality of passion, the quality of all relationships and love. But in more specific ways, yes, there is a feeling in *Tallien* that if you don't commit yourself politically, you're lackluster. If you do commit yourself, there's danger, and it comes from the possibility of overlooking what truth you see for the sake of ideas. We all know people like that, people who, for the sake of something even larger than the ugliness they see happening, kept quiet, a kind of betrayal for the idea of a higher principle. And I think that Tallien, in the beginning is someone like that. Remember the case of the nobleman Tallien is asked to consider? Tallien doesn't see any criminality or subversion on the nobleman's part, but Tallien allows himself to be silenced for the purported sake of the Revolution. He convinces himself that it's better to allow an execution than not. I think if you read *Darkness at Noon*, Arthur Koestler's novel, you'll see that that's exactly what many Bolsheviks must have felt. Case after case, people kept quiet, hoping that the bastion of socialism would be left to go ahead and become a real citadel of humanism. Meanwhile, the cellars were filled with tortured bodies.

bw *Tallien* strikes me as very much an end-of-the-century book. It is the story of a disillusioning. It's a novel of history and ideas when both seem to be occasions for irony rather than belief. As such, the book raises the whole problem of writing a novel of ideas in a contemporary context. I think that this ties in with your paralleling the story of the narrator's father, who was a labor organizer in the 1930s with that of Tallien—the father being someone who lived in a more innocent period, an age of belief. The contemporary section is captured so well by the almost comically direct proletarian language in that part of the book.

FT Well, that was deliberate. I know that proletarian literature very well, and its diction. I did a kind of parody of John Dos Passos in the *Mao* book. What might have once seemed a language spoken by the working class became a literary convention, and it's the convention of that language that I'm interested in. We hear that in the father's saying, "Why don't you fellas come over to the union hall." To me, it has nothing to do with how the father actually speaks, it's about how

his language echoes the genre of proletarian fiction.

bw But isn't it also a language of innocence?

FT That's right, it's completely innocent. A projection of middle-class writers on the language of a class they largely did not know.

bw What I'm trying to get at is how you write a novel about history and about ideas when the ideas no longer seem connected to . . .

FT To life? *Tallien* isn't a novel of ideas, it's a novel about people who are passionate about ideas in a way that I don't see reflected too much in our contemporary life. And, in that sense, it's an end-of-the-century book, I think you're right. It's a farewell to your generation which was still touched by ideas as mine was. That people could really commit themselves to a way of life, to being a certain kind of person because of their ideas! Today, and this is putting it crudely I know, all that seems to matter is the "idea" of success, of material success. I think that's basically what people believe, not everyone of course, but fundamentally that's what it is. Not the notion of living for an idea, a moral idea, an idea of morality, of an ethical way of life . . . I don't encounter that . . . do you? I guess the issue today would be how much can you grab without becoming vulgar? But I don't think that's really even what people worry about — vulgarity. Good manners don't matter. Good taste doesn't matter. Culture doesn't matter. Those things are just gone. I think there was a time probably, when people might have thought vulgarity was fresh. That vulgarity had a sort of . . .

bw   . . . energy and vitality . . .

FT Yes, and maybe an honesty and purity to it, that it could be excused if the intention behind it wasn't crude. I think none of that applies anymore. And I think this is the case today with language too. I will go back to the idea of language again and again in *Tallien* because the book plays on levels of language. What I want there, what I always want in writing, is that the language has some sense of echo below the surface. And that the language has integrity, even if it's playful or ironic or working off conventions. Somewhere there must be a place where vulgarity doesn't intrude itself. We have to take our stand individually. I can't control the world, the marketplace, or people's behavior at dinner parties or on the battlefields of commerce. But I can try to control the language of my book, and have it so that every line is the best and most honest I can make it. I can go back to that as a notion of language in *Tallien* because I don't just see it as a political novel. End-of-the-century maybe, because it's old-fashioned, my dream of wanting to make something beautiful, wanting to make language beautiful. Trite to say, but beauty is politics and a hedge against vulgarity.

bw **Your work has always been involved in a debate on politics and beauty, aesthetics and ethics, action and contemplation.**

FT I don't know if that's a question or an observation, but as an observation, I'm grateful that you've made it and I'm flattered because I think that's basically the precinct of my work. I'm still interested in ideas of what a work of art is, to whom it's addressed. Does art have obligations, does it have a morality? Is it a free form? Those questions fascinate me. When you speak of *Tallien* as an end-of-the-century book, I don't know if it's exactly in the *fin de siècle* mood, but I guess the last two decades of the nineteenth century would have been the time when people like Ruskin thought about art, and Oscar Wilde and Whistler talked and wrote about it in the ways I mean. Ideas about art and its meaning to the culture. They had meaning to the creation of the art work. And they still do to me. So when Tallien comes back to Paris after the Egyptian episode and he looks at the Boucher painting in Therese's room—you may remember that in the earlier part of the book Tallien had denounced painters like Chardin and Fragonard and Boucher at a speech in the Convention, asking, "What shall we do? Shall we give the Revolution back to the aristocrats and bring back Boucher and Fragonard?"—suddenly that painting is stripped of all class value and it's just, in itself, a beautiful object. Those considerations, I find, may be a bit recondite, a bit archaic, but fascinating. So, too, the notion of beauty, and what is beautiful, who is beautiful. Therese is beautiful to me in the novel.

bw Therese is beautiful but she is also the calculating survivor. She may be a force of nature, of passion, but Therese is also the embodiment of what defeats utopian dreams throughout history—she responds to the sheer weight of circumstance.

FT Therese fascinates me. First of all, she's beautiful, physically. And she knows how to adopt a style of costume. In the prison-cell scene in the book, for example, she completely creates a kind of costume to complement the setting of the prison. So I find her dress reflecting an intelligence, an irony, a wit, which I find beautiful. Tallien absolutely gives up the Revolution because of her. He surrenders. You might say that that's a kind of idiotic male idea: that men fall in love with women and then leave themselves behind. There's a whole literature about that, *Carmen, The Blue Angel* . . . and I must say it's something I understand. Of course, it goes both ways. Gender isn't the issue, the power of beauty is. What I find striking, and why I think I have fallen in love with Therese, is that when you look at the very rare moments when she speaks, it's eloquent without being strained or too self-conscious. And it's ironic.

bw But Therese's irony makes Therese the realist. Unlike Tallien, she doesn't have any belief in the Revolution.

FT Or, worse, any interest. The trick would be to discover how to believe, without having any terrible conse-

quences. To struggle, and to work for what you think is good—that sounds so trite—and to hope that by some ironic circumstance it doesn't backfire or bring mayhem, that's the issue. How do you keep your distance so that those actions which you take in the name of passion, political and social passion, don't corrupt you because you live for principle rather than for persons? The thing about Therese is that she cares only about saving her friends from the guillotine. Therese is saying, "My friends before the Revolution, before ideology." That's the problem in the book, it seems to me. That's Tallien's problem. Personally, I'd rather burn than rot. I'd rather have gone in the direction of commitment, hoping it doesn't lead to disaster and trying to avert it, than feeling predisposed to the cynicism that allows for inaction. And allows you to stay on the sidelines and jeer at the others.

bw What makes these issues all the more provocative, of course, is the central place of the French Revolution in modern history and culture.

FT Absolutely. The French Revolution is the paradigm of how everyone thinks about revolutions from that point. After all, it was, in a way, the model for all following revolutions. Almost everything that ever happened in every revolution afterward happened there.

bw At one point in *Tallien*, Robespierre addresses the Convention on the question of what is an acceptable republican literary style. This, too, is a touchstone for modernity, the conjoining of political and artistic renovation. As Mao reflects in your *Adventures of Mao on the Long March*, "Poetry is revolution without bloodshed."

FT The notion that a new kind of culture should have a new kind of language doesn't seem so farfetched when the French Revolutionaries thought their new culture should have a new subject matter for painting. They were really trying to revolutionize every aspect of their life; it wasn't a matter of just getting rid of the king. They were even concerned with the issue of diction, of finding a revolutionary language for the new literature and poetry. What does literature mean to a culture that is trying to create for the first time a language suitable to its politics? In his "Preface" to the 1855 edition of *Leaves of Grass*, Whitman says that poetry in America will be a different poetry. It won't be bound to feudalistic forms. It will be a poetry born from the language of the masses, of a democratic American society. Look at the 1855 *Leaves of Grass*. You will see it has sinew and it has simplicity. Let's face it, these are strange issues.

bw Why "strange?"

FT I say "strange" as if I don't believe them. What I mean is that I care about these things and I think that no one else raves like this. I find that strange. It's as if these issues don't even matter anymore, and maybe that's because they don't matter anymore. Somewhere, I'm straining to say what I feel about language—it's meaning in politics, its meaning in our political life, in our cultural life—and what I find lacking today in American society, maybe in the French and the English too. What is a beautiful language these days in America? What would it mean?

bw One consistent feature of your work is your use of larger-than-life historical characters—Mao, Malraux, even Tallien in an anti-heroic way. They become for you heroic, aesthetic myths. What is your interest in these figures?

FT When you come to them as a writer, the construction is preordained, the narrative format is there. The characters are like readymades. And then the question is: what do you do with them? What do you invest in them? How do you subvert them or enhance them or alter them? Fiction is all invention anyway. Part of using these historical characters is the very seductive quality, the resonance of who they are. In a certain sense, you don't have to create a character and convince your reader about this character. You have a shell, it shines already, it's luminous. People will notice it. Then, when they come close, they will find features different than what they had expected. That's interesting to me.

bw For example, when one reads the "Letter to Mao from Malraux," the opening chapter of your *Tintin* novel-in-progress, you have Mao meditate sublimely on matters of aesthetics and manners. The historical Mao would never have reached such heights of language and feeling. As you read it, there is a real shiver, it takes on a very extravagant quality.

FT Because you're playing with what you think you already know. When you read that, it's as if the gangster John Dillinger was being described in heroic couplets. There's an incongruity that makes for the ludicrous. But I think less so in the Mao case, because, in fact, he was interested in art, in poetry and what it meant, and he wrote his own poetry. So that I was able to find Mao as a kind of advanced decadent, a kind of Mao/Oscar Wilde figure, and that's how I see him. I like having the format of a ready-made character. I like having the possibility of doing what I want with the language. To have a language that isn't exactly how Americans speak in ordinary life. I'm trying to imagine where I would have the access in contemporary life to do what I like to do with language. I don't know where. Historicity allows me the outlandishness, if you will, or the possibility of a rhetoric that contemporary life doesn't allow. But, of course, there is another reason why I'm so interested in those characters. Malraux, Mao, Tallien, even the narrator's union-organizing father, lived in a moment where each believed they could effect a change in history. That they could literally transform what would happen to humankind. I don't think anyone thinks that today. First we don't think about it, and second we don't think that it's possible. Not in the way they did. I think those are

engaging characters for that reason, in a certain sense they had faith. Their presence in that historical stream made things happen. They changed radically the notion of what culture is, of what society is, of what human conduct is. When you speak of the concerns of contemporary fiction— I'm not too intrigued by them. Not because I want mighty themes at all moments, but because I'm not too interested in characters without high consciousness. That could just be the lack of our times. After all, where could you find characters in contemporary American life of the kind that Malraux creates in *Man's Fate* or those characters in Mann's *The Magic Mountain*?

bw I find *Tallien* a more deeply felt book than *Mao*.

FT Susan Sontag said to me, "What made us think in the seventies that we had to be cool?" And that's really the point, it isn't really that the emotional tenor of *Mao* for me was less intense, the point of *Mao* for me was not to make it *seem* intense. In other words, to have the emotion there but not to make it so apparent on the surface of the page. The aesthetic of the seventies was predicated on irony. We were looking for irony as a mode, the subversion of feeling to create work impervious to banal response. The strategy there was to turn away from heat and emotion, to cool it down, to keep it iced and self-referential. It certainly doesn't allow for what you might find in *Tallien*, a molten quality. I let it out full-stop on the page in

Tallien. I didn't care if it burned on the page. I would have cared a lot in the seventies, I would have turned away from that.

bw So now you're able to deal with familial matters?

FT I never wanted to talk about my family, although people in the past had encouraged it. I remember after *Mao* was published, I was at dinner parties, I talked about life in the Bronx, my father, and my family, and people would say to me, "Why don't you write about that? You know you could really make, if not a commercial book, an accessible book. People would want to read it, it's heartwarming." Part of me rebels against that so profoundly that maybe I went the other way in my earlier work. I thought it was vulgar to write about your family. I'm not interested in that kind of exorcism, or writing as therapy. I guess there was a time for it, there was a moment when that kind of writing seemed fresh. I can't see how it would be fresh today. Those parts in *Tallien* that have to do with my father, the character called Rex, talking to the policemen or talking to people who wanted to break the strike, are not how people spoke in life but in the thirties proletarian novel. What I did in that section was to distance myself with a certain irony by creating a language that was already extant in those proletarian fictions. In any case, I never wanted to write about my parents, and I think, in some ways, that was wrong. Now that they're both dead, I feel better doing it. I think I could finally see my father not just as a father but as a person in history.

bw You say in the book that you would like to have told your father the story of Tallien. If you had, what would you have liked him to learn from it?

FT It's funny, because if you look at my father's character, Rex, he is the one who never sells out. Rex is the one who doesn't become corrupted. He's a fallible human, he leaves his family. He says in the book that he was a Communist but never a Marxist.

bw It's usually the other way around.

FT Yes, but if we treat him as a character in the book, not as a person, that's probably why he stayed intact, because he didn't subscribe to the ideology. Conviction wasn't ideology for him . .

bw It was a form of action . . .

FT And for others who commit to ideology, the danger is that everything can get perverted because of that. But you were asking . . .

bw The lesson . . .

FT I guess it's kind of monstrous that the son says he wishes he could have told Rex the story of Tallien. And what does it really mean to tell Rex the story of Tallien? Telling the story of someone who betrays the revolution, who betrays his principles, to a person who never betrayed his principles. So, in fact, I don't really understand what it would have meant to tell him that, except in some mean way to show him what happened.

bw Is it less of a question of telling him here's someone, Tallien, who betrayed his principles, but rather that time and history betray us all?

FT That's what I mean, in some way to tell him, "look what this led to." Maybe also to tell him something else, it's also telling him how wonderful he is. That he didn't sell out for love, or passion, or fear. That he kept himself intact. I think it was Richard Eder, in the *Los Angeles Times*, who points out that the father, although he's a drunk and leaves his family, is really the only admirable character in the book. That's rather interesting. Rex keeps himself. Everyone else in the book goes off-balance for one reason or another. Actually, Rex is like Therese. They both respond to life, not to ideas. I'm puzzled about the ideas that I would subscribe to: I don't know if I'd be my father or I would be Tallien. But if I were thinking of this book in a psychological light, I'd say it's a novel about the triumph of a father over a son.

bw Your father, the union organizer, and your mother, the pious Italian Catholic woman, actually describe the polarities of the ethical and aesthetic, the active and the contemplative.

FT My father is a romantic figure to me, much more than anyone I've known, and he, in fact, still stays that figure for me. Let's say that my father remotely describes what Whitman would have loved in the American male. He was a gentleman and he was one of the roughs. That balance moves

me still. His example, his presence, the way he was with people, moved me. Easy familiarity. He would be driving the car and stop to ask directions—he had this beautiful Southern accent—and he'd call out to someone strolling by, "Hi, Jim, which way's . . . " And I would say, "Dad, how do you always know these guys are named Jim?" But I never heard about things like dialectical materialism from him. I got that from people in my neighborhood. Especially when I went to City College. And there was the "Red Belt" of the Bronx. There was no Red Belt, really, but the very young, young kids were already doctrinaires by age twelve or thirteen. It was hilarious. Their parents were militant Communists and nobody believed in God. Everything had a scientific explanation. And that's the polarity in me, the polarity between a scientific rationalism and a kind of religious exultation, that spiritual, mystical thing that my mother represented and whose incarnation was the Italian church. Because in the Bronx there was the Italian church one went to if you were Italian, and then there were the Irish churches. Irish churches were very different, they were Anglo places. We didn't go to Anglo places; they weren't as mystical, as idolatrous, although they probably had the same amount of sculpture. So for me there was, on one hand, the lusciousness of the Catholic Church in the Bronx—statues and drapes and robes, velvet veils—very powerful stuff that I could imagine Oscar Wilde responding to. And then there were my peers. Let's call them rationalists, the believers in reason and function. In my mind, they were elements as important as what, probably for most kids, baseball or basketball are.

bw You've written about film for *Vogue* and about art for *Artforum*. What's been the impact of the visual arts, especially film and painting, on your writing?

FT I'm dazzled, besotted by painting. Forgive me the platitude. It's just that I'm shocked by painting. Synthesis in painting, the compression of so many elements of experience, still grips me. Painting mystifies me. All it is, after all, is paint, this sort of glucky stuff, it's just material. And look what beauty comes out of it. I know that Hemingway was influenced by this thing of painting. He talks about Cézanne, hoping one day to reach the kind of level that Cézanne could reach in his painting—Hemingway wanted his own language to reach that certain exceptional plane, or transcendental dimension. I don't know about planes and dimensions of language, but I certainly would like to have painting's compression. It's poetry. In contemporary art, I'm fascinated with David Salle's radical juxtapositions. The *Mao* book has much of that, of the juxtaposing of elements, of parodistic passages with quotations, for example.

bw Are there other artists or film directors that . . .

FT . . . I'm crazy for? Godard because of the structure, Godard because of the episodic, Godard because of the quotations. And also Roy Lichtenstein.

In Roy Lichtenstein there is this extraordinary attention to the formal, the composition of the work whose subject matter is apparently banal. There is this majestic idea of how you can transform what seems so commonplace as subject matter, and really create a painting as unified as a Poussin. Lichtenstein has it both ways; he has the formal beauty of that, and the irony of an attentive disregard for the subject matter.

Someone who I also feel a different affinity with—like me he's an Italian-American, although no one thinks I'm Italian, everyone thinks I'm a New York Jew—is Martin Scorsese. Here's what kills me about him. He understands exactly what linoleum means to immigrant Italians. Probably to Jews, too. Scorsese understands perfectly the sadness of those musty corridors and dreary hallways in the old Italian-American tenements. Scorsese is the Racine of linoleum. But Scorsese also knows about the violence and craziness under the linoleum mat. *Raging Bull* is that kind of truth, especially in the early scenes. And in the *King of Comedy* and *Taxi Driver*, Scorsese comes to the realization that in America—and everyday proves this to be more and more true—you do not have to earn fame by virtue or talent, you merely have to be outrageous to become famous. That's different than Warhol's observation that everyone will be famous for fifteen minutes, it's something else. It means that you can rob a bank and write a book about it and go on television and make a fortune. It means exactly what it means in *King of Comedy*—you can do terrible things—kidnap someone—and it doesn't matter, because once you're thrust into the transcendental sphere, the amoral sphere of celebrity, there's no criminality. In America, there's only success and failure. And Scorsese understands that.

bw Since 1971, you've been working on a novel based on the French comic book *Tintin*. What got you interested in the project?

FT Tintin is the boy reporter of one of the most important and the most beautiful comic books in Europe. They're done by the Belgian artist, George Remi, known as Hergé. It's about Tintin and his dog Snowy, or Milou in the original French, and his sidekick, an older man named Captain Haddock, who's an alcoholic and old seadog. Together they have many adventures all over the world—one in Tibet, two in South America, one in China, one in what was then the Belgian Congo. For a long time I've been working on a novel about Tintin. The novel is set in 1968, for reasons the novel will explain, and it's about Tintin at a point where he's utterly and profoundly bored with his life, and where's he's given up being an adventurous young boy of twelve traveling the world, and is living in a mansion, collecting art, learning to cook, learning to ride horses, learning everything. But not doing anything. That's where the book starts, after the letter from Mao to Malraux explaining how Mao Tse Tung is extremely unhappy because he's reached a point

of stasis in his life, quietude. The revolution is over and the bureaucrats are taking over, and he's bored to death. So there's this parallel between Tintin and Mao in that one way. And Tintin gets a telegram proposing that he have another adventure, this one in Machu Picchu. The book takes place, almost all of it, in Machu Picchu. There's a parallel here for me with Hans Castorp of Thomas Mann's *The Magic Mountain*. Tintin goes to Machu Picchu a naive. Tintin goes out and catches crooks, breaks up criminal conspiracies, but he doesn't have any wider view of what he does, he just does it. His education begins in Machu Picchu with his meeting of some of the characters from *The Magic Mountain*. And it's an education in art, it's an education in politics, it's an education in political theory. And of course, in love. And there begins his transformation.

bw It sounds as if we've come back to politics and aesthetics. Mao, Malraux, Tallien and soon, I hope, Tintin.

FT As long as I can remember, I always wanted to be a writer or a painter. And once I became aware of these kinds of aesthetic and political issues, they've always been burrowed in my life, and I'm torn by them. It's so crazy because, in a way, it's a moral sense. Why do you sit down and write? Why do you do any of these things? Is it self-aggrandizement, is it a lovely therapy, with your aggression in the service of the ego? Is it playfulness? But even in play, what's the mode of address and to whom? I keep raising this issue. Maybe that's why I like to toy with those levels of language in *Tallien*, for instance. I love the idea of writing in a direct and colloquial mode, but where it's spiced with fresh imagery, and then somehow to ascend the plane of it, slowly, and then suddenly you're in the middle of another sphere and you level off. I like that. But I guess I like that in shifts of people's conversation, too. I don't want to hear the same tone all the time. To go back to the issue of politics and aesthetics, how do you write in a way that addresses the notion of how we live as social and political animals? And not to be boring, not to be dogmatic, not to be overtly polemical. The polemics have to come through the tissue of the work, underneath the living body of the work and not the surface of it. Maybe we should ask what that means in America today. It's not just the issues of the Old Left or the New Left, it's really the issue of what it is to be a writer in America and to think to yourself that there's something more to declare than the unhappiness of having been raised in this or that family or to have had some variety of bad love affair. Where is the living umbrella for all we experience, that we can understand, that others will under-

stand, that we shelter ourselves under? I'm doing a little novel now about Van Gogh. Someone asked me about it in regard to *Tallien*, "But what does the Van Gogh story mean?" As if they needed to find some moral to it. They could think there's a moral to *Tallien*: revolution's become corrupted. We all know that. Or you turn your good intentions against yourself, or they turn against yourself, or passion is stronger than ideas. Although one can say all these things, such formulas are not the sum of the novel, nor I hope of the Van Gogh novel. I hope that no one's fiction is reducible to formula. But to go to the idea of political and the social, the idea that an art work has meaning in depth to the culture and is not just a commodity to be produced for a collector, I think of Van Gogh and I think of his *Sunflowers*, corny as they are to us now, or a pair of peasant shoes, or a field — those were political paintings. The address to the political culture doesn't have to be a direct one. How do you do that so it has at once the aesthetic beauty we're talking about, and the aesthetic integrity, and also has a moral integrity? I've been deficient in not doing as much work as I might have but now I feel I don't want to stop. I just want to write all the time.

MELANIE RAE THON   caryl phillips

BOMB # 44, Summer / 1993

I first came upon the work of Melanie Rae Thon in London. A publicity manager at Penguin (U.K.) suggested I might like the work of this "new writer" who had recently published a first collection of short stories, *Girls in the Grass*. I not only liked them, it seemed clear to me that I was witnessing the debut of a serious and powerful voice in contemporary American fiction. The brief biography in the book mentioned that the author lived in Cambridge, Massachusetts. At the time I was teaching at Amherst, so I invited her to come and give a reading at the college. Thereafter, a firm friendship was forged.

I spoke with Melanie in a hotel room in Cambridge. I was midway through a coast to coast reading tour promoting my novel, *Cambridge*. Melanie was anxiously awaiting the imminent publication of her second novel, *Iona Moon*. Her first, *Meteors in August*, had attracted fine reviews on both sides of the Atlantic, London's *Time Out* calling it "beautifully written, serious and thoughtful."

caryl phillips   Graham Greene said that childhood is the bank balance of a writer. You were born and grew up in Montana, and this clearly has informed your stories, some of which are set in the West. Have you defined your subject matter as that geographical milieu?

MELANIE RAE THON   I'll always return to that landscape. No matter how long I live somewhere else, those images are imbedded in ways I can't escape. As much as I might like to think I've worked through a certain period, I've found that some experiences can't be exorcised. Many years later I may return to an old story in a new form. But the next piece I have in mind to write is set in Florida. I'm very interested in moving beyond childhood, both within the body and within the space of the story.

cp   But are you ever really going to be able to go beyond that Western experience? It seems to me that it's the old adage: You can take a person out of a place but you can't take the place out of the person. Writing a novel set in Florida, is that something that's happening naturally?

Melanie Rae Thon, © Marion Ettlinger. Courtesy the artist.

MRT I think it's a natural movement. I don't know how it will work out. I feel a connection with the way so many things collide in Florida, with the extremities of wildlife and landscape, the violence of weather, the collision of cultures. Even though it's radically different from what you would find in Montana, there's a strange parallel.

CP At what point did you know your first collection of short stories, *Girls in the Grass*, was complete as a whole?

MRT I knew it was a collection when I had enough good stories. I made other stories that are not included. The eleven pieces in *Girls in the Grass* emerged over a span of twelve years 1977 to 1989.

CP That route suggests what most people contemplating MFAs in writing may not want to admit. In other words, that it's: degree, writing fiction, master's degree in fiction, then a long slough, slowly putting together a collection of stories. Was it a case of bit-by-bit writing when you had the time and money to write? Is that the traditional development of an American writer or are there short cuts?

MRT I don't know what's "traditional." I didn't find any short cuts. I started my first real story in 1977 and finished it eight years later. It took me that long to hear the true voice. I did other work during that time, but nothing as strong or important to me as "Repentance." I did go through a master's program in creative writing but nothing I wrote during graduate school became part of my published work.

CP Why do you think that happened?

MRT I wasn't working on my true material. But I don't consider that time a waste. I was building many skills: most importantly, I was learning the tolerance for revision, which I really didn't have before that.

CP You said I wasn't going to like anything else of yours as much as that story "Punishment" in *Girls in the Grass*. You've got no reason to worry about that. But I detect in "Punishment" the influence of Toni Morrison and John Wideman and Faulkner. It was the first thing of yours that I read, and it deals with the black experience, it deals with the institution of slavery and the legacy of slavery. But there was no author's photograph on the book. I had no idea whether you were black, Latina, Asian. Your name didn't betray anything to me, at least, of what you were. I had no idea who was the author of this incredibly passionate and lyrical story, partly rooted in the black experience, a story which due to the sources that I sense feeding into it, is technically very daring. Does it concern you or surprise you that I had no idea what kind of person had created such a story?

MRT It's exactly the response that I would wish for. I believe it's important for people to transcend who they are as individuals. That's one reason we write, to get outside of ourselves, to try to understand something beyond our particular experience.

cp What about the influences that I detected? I did sense that lyrical passion of a Toni Morrison, particularly in the black vernacular voice. I did feel, structurally, Faulkner. Was I way off track?

MRT I love all those writers. I had not read anything by John Wideman when I made "Punishment," but since then I've read most of his work, and I identify with his desire to speak in voices much different from his own. Certainly I feel a connection with Faulkner and Toni Morrison because of the lyrical tilt in my writing.

cp Your recent story, "Little White Sister," again flies in the face of those who would argue against this clumsy term I first heard used years ago called "cultural appropriation." I found the story strong and moving and totally convincing. Writing outside of yourself allows writers to deal with some subject matter with a greater panache. Nobody would dare imagine that such writing might in any way be autobiographical, because the voices are so far beyond the person who's created them, at least on the surface. Is there something in either "Punishment" or "Little White Sister" that you do identify as autobiographical?

MRT I thought about that a lot after I made them. Whenever you go outside of yourself—in your writing or your reading—there's a point at which you get pushed back *inside* at the very deepest level. You're forced to recognize things that you really didn't know about yourself. Months after I finished "Punishment," I realized how desperate the white girl is to understand the black woman: that's how I'd entered the story. The white girl identifies passionately with the abuse the slave endures. In fact, she believes the slave has suffered for her sake. She fears her own father, the man who becomes a threat to the slave as well. That was where my life touched the lives of the women in that story—not because I feared my father, but because I understood how dangerous men could become at any time. And those men who enter our lives most intimately are the ones who create the most fear. The story "Little White Sister" kept coming to me in the voice of a black man in first person, which I realized was completely inappropriate. It took me a long time to trust that voice. But every time I tried to write the story from some other perspective, it didn't work and didn't seem as true.

cp Why is it inappropriate for you to write the story as a black man?

MRT I was listening to the outside voices, the ones that say: "What right have you to do this?" I was comforted myself, listening to your voice saying: "Go ahead, do it," but that didn't always work. "Little White Sister" is about a black man explaining why he didn't help a white woman in trouble. He's trying to understand her life just as I'm trying to understand his. So, this man and I were engaged in the same process. When I saw that I said, "Fine, I have the right to make this story."

CP You must have come under some considerable pressure listening to what you termed the "outside voices." Do you still listen to those negative outside voices? Has the process of writing another short story, which has largely to do with a black person's experience, shut down the volume?

MRT Each time I do something different I become a little less vulnerable. If you listen to those voices, you start to wonder what right you have to make any story? Each story is some kind of leap, unless you write only about yourself, exactly as you are at this moment, which is tremendously uninteresting to me. The novel *Iona Moon* is about a white girl. But, people might say I had appropriated that experience as well because the way that Iona grew up is not the way that I grew up. Those voices of censorship become ridiculous. The extrapolation of that kind of thinking is that you can't write as a child, you can't write as an old person, you can't write as somebody of the opposite sex. I move into my material intuitively and if I'm paying attention to that, if the things that I'm writing are things I feel I must understand, then I have a right to explore them. I have a need to explore them and ultimately a duty to do so.

CP When you read Faulkner, did you feel any discomfort or any sense that Faulkner is somehow culturally appropriating the black experience of the South in his novels? I mean, there are a number of academic/critical skirmishes that have focused on Faulkner's perception of the black South. When you read, are you reading it looking at that, or for the structure, or something else?

MRT When I read Faulkner, I certainly don't think of the work in those terms, worrying about whether or not he's done something inappropriate. When I read any writer, I think: Is the story honest? Are the images vivid? Are the people real to me? If those things are true, what do I care who the author is in real life?

CP Let's move on and talk about your novels. *Meteors in August* picks up where *Girls in the Grass* left off. Its first person tone is assured and its world is busy and certainly disturbing. Lizzie's rite of passage takes place in this small Montana town, riddled with racial intolerance and bigotry of a religious nature. Did writing *Meteors* change your view of Montana? Or had you already, as a sort of long-time East Coast resident, looked west with a change of heart? It's such a searing, critical, passionate look at small town Montana; at times I had the feeling that you couldn't be looking back at the place the same way after having written a novel like that.

MRT Writing that book definitely changed me. I don't think I had any sense of how far I was going to go into that experience or what I would see when I got there. The racial "conflict" in Montana is between Anglos and Native Americans. It's a strange situation, because many Native Americans have assimilated completely; but if they are living as Native Americans, they may be marginalized still on reservation land. There are seven reservations in Montana. In the book the communities aren't so segregated. I pressed them up against each other to see what would happen. By doing that, I discovered things I'd always known but hadn't been allowed to acknowledge so explicitly. I can remember, as a child, driving through the reservation and being completely puzzled by the way people lived there, by the poverty. So one of my journeys in the book was to understand the conflict between the Anglos and Native Americans. I couldn't have done that as long as I lived in Montana.

CP Obviously, you looked at this world differently. How did people in this world look at you differently?

MRT It surprised me. Most people didn't identify with the book at that personal a level, which is interesting. My hometown newspaper reviewed the book and one of the questions they posited was, "So, is it about us then?" And the answer within the review was, "No, not really." I pushed things to the extreme in order to see them more clearly, so in many ways it no longer is about my experience or about that town in particular, but I believe that it reveals certain underlying truths. A pervasive aspect of that culture is the violence. The intimate violence of a place where, as Lizzie says, "Everything happens to someone you know."

CP The leap from "Punishment" to the novel isn't really so difficult to make. They follow logically, particularly when one looks at the themes. They seem to be about racial intolerance, religious bigotry, two communities, whether it's black and white at the time of slavery or Native American and Anglo now. These problems seem to be explored time and time again, just in different locales. In all your work, particularly *Meteors in August*, there seems to be a concern with how sex is related to violence, to a certain form of repression. The sex and the religion and the racial aspects all seem to be tightly connected with each other. *Meteors in August* is in all senses of the word an intimate novel. After all, you can't write a whole novel in the first person without having some powerful attachment to the narrator, in this case, Lizzie. I wondered what you felt, as an author, about Lizzie's predicament.

MRT Lizzie sees the way that sexuality destroys her sister Nina. It's Nina's pregnancy by a Native American boy that catapults her into an entirely different life. Her father, who had adored her, rejects her completely. Her mother lets her disappear. For Lizzie, being sexual is tied to the possibility of being destroyed, to the fear of being abandoned by everyone she loves. She sees Nina as both alluring and powerful. Even after her decline, Nina dazzles people. But she's always in danger. The same people who are attracted become potential attackers and aggressors: anyone might betray her, even Lizzie.

cp Your new novel, *Iona Moon*, is set in Idaho. It picks up from two stories in *Girls in the Grass*: "Iona Moon" and "Snake River." Did you know back then that you had unfinished business with this character Iona Moon?

MRT Most definitely. I didn't see it as a novel at that point. I saw it as a series of interconnected stories. The idea to make it into a novel came later. I started writing about one of the people in the book eighteen years ago. So really, I've been imagining this world since I was in my first year of college.

cp You're quite a careful stylist. How you tell a story seems almost as important as the story itself. *Meteors in August* is written in the first person, *Iona Moon* in the third person, as were the source stories for the novel. Are these decisions of form ones that grow naturally out of the characters themselves, out of your relationships with the characters, or do you deliberately plan in advance the perspective you're going to take?

MRT For the most part it happens naturally. Sometimes I come to it immediately. Other times I shift back and forth trying to find the truest way to tell a story. When I first started *Meteors in August*, I didn't feel confident writing in anything but the first person. I need to feel close to one person, to live in her body. But over a period of five years, I found myself becoming extremely frustrated, I wanted to move beyond Lizzie's point of view. I longed for the flexibility and range of the third person. *Iona Moon* weaves between three primary points of view, but other people's voices and thoughts also enter the narrative. Those shifts emerged naturally. They were necessary. I thought the first story was Willy's alone. It was about a boy who had been attacked—sexually—by a teenage girl. When I heard this story, the boy had become a big Montana man, 6'2", and it was hard to imagine him being attacked by anyone, much less a high school girl. He did escape unharmed, and he left her in her truck by the river. But when he heard tires spinning in mud and realized she was stuck, he went back to help. It amazed me. He was so angry. Twenty years later, he was still angry. But he helped her. I wanted to know, who was this boy? I realized I couldn't understand what happened that night without also understanding who the girl was, so I split the story between Iona and Willy to find out how they ended up in that truck together.

cp *Iona Moon* has this wonderful wildness of the maverick, a quality celebrated in American men, but reviled in women. As a poor farm girl, she is treated as desirable and discardable. Is this a fair assessment of her?

MRT Yes. She's desirable because she's passionate. She's not afraid of her own body. She's not afraid of her sexuality. At one point she says, "What sense was there in saving everything up for some special occasion that might not ever come?" She lives in the present and does what she wants—or what's necessary—in any given moment. This quality makes her tempting but also terrifying. It gives her a great deal of power over the boys who are attracted to her. She scares the boys who want her, throws them off balance. I think that's why she's discardable. If she becomes too threatening, they can revert to their moralistic sensibilities; they can think of her as dirty—physically and spiritually. They can escape her by convincing themselves they prefer "nice" girls, girls who have been taught to feel alienated from their own bodies. As Iona says, "Girls who could pull you right up to the edge and still always, always say *no*."

CP The theme of wild yet sensual local girl has been the raw material for a light industry of inferior novels. In your hands it becomes serious and literary. Were you aware of any tension between the history of the subject matter and your intentions as an author?

MRT No, I honestly wasn't. I didn't ever think about it. As soon as I started telling Iona's story, she became absolutely real to me. She was in me.

That's not always true when I write. Sometimes it takes me months to get close enough to my people to hear their voices and understand what's happened in their lives. But with Iona, I felt I knew everything about her—or that I *could* know everything if I was patient enough, if I thought about her and let her remember. So I never considered the possibility that she might be a "type." To me she was unique. As soon as she spoke she was fierce and insistent. She couldn't be anyone but herself.

CP I'm going to put you on the spot here. A good portion of your life has been taken up with teaching, which you're not only good at, but you obviously like. In what ways has the teaching affected, fed off, your writing? Some people teach as a pain-in-the-backside job to get money, other people love to teach. Your fellow Montana writer, Norman Maclean, fantastic at teaching, would have written more if it hadn't been for teaching. It's a balance, one suspects, between writing and teaching.

MRT I'm certainly in the group of writers who love to teach. Being rigorous in the way that I look at other people's writing, being forced to understand how ideas and language converge makes me capable of doing more in my own work. I grapple with ideas in a more sustained and conscious way. When I was teaching "The Artificial Nigger" by Flannery O'Connor, I was struck by the moment at the end, a fleeting moment, when Mr. Head and his grandson are both "saved" by this image of the artificial nigger, the lawn jockey that they encounter in Atlanta. In that moment of grace there is a miraculous transformation: they can forgive each other. But as they journey home, we see them regressing into their old patterns. They've witnessed a miracle, experienced this sacrifice outside themselves, but they haven't been changed in any permanent way. It's a very Christian idea, that Jesus—or the artificial nigger—had to die in order for these people to be spared. But, in Flannery O'Connor's interpretation, Jesus has to die again and again. I think that's one of the ideas that was working for me in "Punishment." I had a vision not of a single death that allows us to be merciful and humane, but of sacrifices innumerable and endless.

cp How does that connect with teaching?

MRT Being forced to articulate that about O'Connor's story made me understand something about myself and my beliefs. It made me want to explore the idea in my own way.

cp Are there any contemporary American writers that you particularly admire?

MRT I wouldn't limit that to American, or contemporary writers. I was influenced by Thomas Hardy and also by Emily Brontë. Both of those writers took on huge subjects. They weren't just looking at individuals and their passions, but also at the society and the landscape in which those people

lived. I've always wanted to make big stories. I was tremendously influenced when I read *A Death in the Family* by James Agee, because of the lyricism and the release from structure. I know he died before he had a chance to finish the book, so we can't ever really know his final intentions. But the fact that the book works, despite breaking all the rules, is tremendously liberating to me. Certainly my writing changed when I read "Tell Me A Riddle" by Tillie Olsen. She compresses a novel's worth of material into only forty pages.

cp What do you, after all these years, know about writing?

MRT The only thing I know for sure is that it takes a tremendously long time to find and explore the truth. I'm still scared. Even when things seem to get easier for you in circumstantial ways, there is no way to make the internal process easy.

cp You know that?

MRT I'm certain of it.

cp John Cheever said in 1979, "Endeavoring as a serious writer is quite a dangerous career," and though it seems the pendulum is swinging in your direction, what do you see lying ahead? Has it been dangerous?

MRT It's been dangerous but I can't imagine living any other way. When I'm in the middle of making a story, I feel completely separated from what most people would consider to be a normal life. There's always a risk: how far will I go, and how long will it take to come back. But the alternative is to willfully ignore what's in front of me. I can't. To live that way would be like being dead.

CP There is an aspect of writing where you turn that around. The danger, perhaps, is that you can't see what's in front of you and you have to discover it all the time.

MRT Maybe that is the problem.

CP Most people are quite happy not to have to grope towards certain questions, answers, resolutions, or truths. It's a dangerous thing.

MRT This goes back to what we were talking about earlier when you asked how it changed me to make *Meteors in August*. The impetus for me to make a story or a novel is that I believe I see things that others don't see or don't wish to see. I have to speak about what I've witnessed. But once I'm inside a story, I begin to see things that I didn't know were there. That's the scary part. You never know what any piece will force you to face.

ARIEL DORFMAN jenifer berman

Ariel Dorfman is obsessed with giving a voice to those who cannot speak: the dead, the missing, those whose lives are interrupted by history. Like many of his characters, Dorfman's own life was interrupted when he was forced into exile from Chile after General Augusto Pinochet's coup ousted the socialist government of Salvador Allende. Grounded in Chile, but addressing all diasporic communities, Dorfman explores life on the frontier, a fluctuating space between past and present, the physical and the psychic. With an elegance and dignity that distinguish both his prose and his person, Dorfman is a shrewd storyteller whose bold forays into fantasy coexist with the gruesome realities of his country. His voice is prolific, fueled by an abounding energy that enables him to balance writing a novel, adapting a screenplay, traveling to Thailand, Scotland, Berlin and back researching his latest film project, and teaching. Well known for his book of cultural criticism, *How to Read Donald Duck* (1971), Dorfman has also written three novels, a collection of short stories, and a book of poems. His plays include *Widows* (coadapted for the stage with Tony Kushner), *Reader,* and the much acclaimed *Death and the Maiden,* which won the Olivier Award for best play in London and was adapted for film by the author and directed by Roman Polanski. In his soon to be published novel *Konfidenz,* he attacks an undulating current of truth and desire, deceit and self-propagation—almost entirely in dialogue.

jenifer berman You were forced to leave Chile in 1973, and most of your previous writing has dealt with Chile's torturous political history. Now you say you are getting away from Chile. What do you mean by that?

ARIEL DORFMAN For many years I have been struggling with a problem that many exiles have: How are you faithful to your country while, in fact, you are writing for people who have not been your fellow countrymen for a long time? Chile has been and always will be a source of inspiration for me. It forms the backbone, the inspira-

Ariel Dorfman, © Thomas Victor. Courtesy Viking.

tion, and the challenge of everything I write. The experience of inventing that country—in a way that makes sense to myself in exile—has been very central to everything I've done. I do feel that one of the reasons one is in exile is to keep alive what the country is. A certain freedom of expression that is no longer allowed under the dictatorship back home. I'm obsessed with the country—writing it. The poems come out of that need, as well as the stories of *My House Is on Fire*. It's only when I began *Widows* that I slowly drifted away from the sense that I have to write about the country. I started examining the deeper dilemmas of Chile, not in a realistic vein, but through an allegorical approach. So I took a step toward a certain universality of my experience and of Chile's experience. In *The Last Song of Manuel Sendero* I took one further step and confronted exile as a real problem. But even in the first works, there is the sense that though it is Chile, it is not a local Chile, it's a Chile of the imagination, a Chile of the mind.

jb **The reception to your work in Chile, especially in response to *Death and the Maiden*, was mixed, if not very critical, whereas you were lauded with praise abroad. Are you writing for Chile?**

AD In some way I am always writing for that imagined community of my fellow countrymen. I'm always asking questions about how the nation can be healed, retold, or modified—how it can be explored—as if this nation

were incomplete until writers had found the way of best imagining it, of really challenging it with their literature. That never disappears entirely. At the same time, I'm constantly trying to go beyond the provincial interests of that community. And there's a tradition for that in Latin America. When Pablo Neruda writes *Residence on Earth* and he writes it in Sri Lanka, he writes it in Thailand . . . he's indicating that you can write about your land by exploring other places. This grows from the tension between what we could call the cosmopolitan and the local, the regional and the universal. Or in more contemporary terms, the global market and the local readers. All these tensions riddle my work. I'm constantly trying to figure out how you can be true to an experience which in fact very few people in the world would understand, such as having most of your friends disappear or be tortured, and at the same time finding a way of telling that story so other people in other places can read their own lives into that. *Death and the Maiden* is the first work of mine in which I finally manage to do that in a way which is entirely satisfying. That's what may explain its enormous success around the world. In Chile, the people found it not to be allegorical at all, but realistic, and found themselves hurt or wounded by the brutality with which I show their lives. Not the brutality of the torture, it's hardly mentioned, but what I show in *Death and the Maiden* is the stark, painful Chilean transition to democracy.

jb It's been said that through your writing you attempt to give a voice to the dead. Can you discuss this?

AD First of all, to go into exile is to go into the country of the dead. It is to lose everything that made your life meaningful. It is to be cut off. And in fact there are many tribes that consider when a person is banished from a tribe, that they die in some way, and to return is a resurrection. I believe that I have had that experience of death, I lost those things that gave meaning to my life. You're outside a culture, outside a place where everyday things are at your fingertips. You have to reinvent yourself.

But I've always been obsessed with having the dead speak, and that's something that comes from before the coup. You do not need to have people murdered to want to make them speak. If you can't make the dead speak, then how do you speak to the future when you will be dead? So I have an intimation that somebody in the future is listening to me as I speak right now, especially as I write. I'm trying to listen to the voices of those who were not able to accede, who went through life without leaving traces, especially in the written language, of who they were, what they tried to be, what their dreams were.

jb What sparked that obsession?

AD I don't know. It's a feeling of transience on my part. I have a sense of unreality constantly around me. I'm a very sensual person, very optimistic, very vital. And yet, at the same time, I have the very strange certainty of not being quite here. Of being already dead. I've always wondered what it would be like to be dead. And in the course of Chile's history, it turned out that death was not a common experience that happened to everybody, but to certain people prematurely, selectively, unfairly, as terror, as punishment for having transgressed, dared to find a voice. We had dared to think of a world that was free, that was equal, a world that did not have the terrible injustices that characterize most of humanity. Because of that, we were condemned either to death or to flee in order to stay alive, but to die in the sense of having our country killed for us. That, of course, has enhanced my sense of death. It was a very anguishing question that I continued to ask in all my work, including *Death and the Maiden*. Paulina's problem is, how does she tell her story when everyone thinks she's dead, and she thinks she's dead, too? Then at one moment, she understands she is not dead, she's only being treated as if she were dead.

jb Certainly in *Death and the Maiden*, and very often in your work, you address the issue of reconciliation, of the conflicts between personal justice and national reconciliation. Can you grapple with this reconciliation unless you're willing to forget?

AD From my point of view and my sense of what literature and living are about, my general tendency is toward peace and reconciliation, living harmoniously with one another. However, you cannot do this based upon lies, based upon the suppression of feelings, the suppression of experiences of a part of the population, or a part of your personality. In other words, you cannot reconcile with someone who has done you a terrible damage unless you both begin to live in the same country, in the same territory. You can't reconcile if you belong to two separate and warring nations. When one part of the nation, or one part of your being achieves victory over the other, in those circumstances, reconciliation becomes a very difficult process. So before we focus on reconciliation we need to face the issue of truth. The problem is, there is precious little justice in the world, and therefore you are stuck with a very complicated situation: how to keep on living as a survivor, how to keep on living in a world where there is not that justice. There are damages done to people and to countries that can never be dealt with totally. When you've been through traumatic experiences like the one I'm talking about in Chile, there's a part of us that cannot entirely heal. There is a zone, a forbidden zone, where it is better not to venture. "An overdose of the truth," as Gerardo says in *Death and the Maiden*, "can kill you." On the other hand, the struggle for that truth, to go as far as one can go in searching for this truth, should never be abandoned.

jb Your work, especially your new novel *Konfidenz*, is steeped in ambiguity. Both the narrator and Leon are unreliable. To what effect do you play with this ambiguity?

AD I'm torn between two sentiments here and in my work as well. On the one hand, there's a deep longing for stability, for what I call the anchor, for a country, for wholeness, a desire for integrity. In the characters and in the language there's a desire for integrity. On the other hand, there is this ghost sense of the world, which has to do with the fluctuation of the personality of the stories. It's as if we are inhabited by a narrative voice that we don't find entirely reliable. In all my work there is a certain masculine figure who manipulates the characters, who tries to tell their story in his words, who tries to possess them, to appropriate them. And the characters themselves are always fighting to tell their own stories. This sensibility antecedes the coup, but it must have been incredibly accentuated by the feeling that all of a sudden these all too real paternal figures have the ultimate power to decide our world.

I believe that as human beings we have certain zones that are not touched by this manipulation. There is a spark of rebellion, the possibility of an alternative future, an alternative vision of the narrative, which is what I explore. You have narrators telling a version of reality, and you're not quite certain if that version is correct or not. Ambivalence is the major instrument the writer has to destabilize the readers' conventional views of the world. I love challenging the readers, I love their being unsure. Because I do think we live in a time of surfaces, collages, pastiches. Literature can make ambiguous what seem to be dangerously clear truths.

jb You've said that in politics the best way is often indirection. Do you believe that the best way in art is also indirection?

AD Well, I don't make much of a distinction between real politics and art. I've always thought that one's writing is deeply political. Not in the sense that it's partisan or that you're trying to convince somebody of something, but much of the most interesting writing engages the major dilemmas, certainly the moral ones, of the community. And language contains and very often hides the solution to those dilemmas. Indirection for me was a way of dealing with the fracture of my world, of Chile. This also predates the coup because even during the revolution in Chile, it did not seem as if the clash of the old and the new could be narrated frontally. *Hard Rain*, which I had already begun work on before the coup, addresses this ambiguity. If you try to speak directly about what is happening to you, you may fail. The way is to circle the object, circle the experience so the experience speaks through the residue, through the cracks. In *Konfidenz* I come to that as a full narrative method.

jb In *Konfidenz* Leon doesn't really have a voice, and in the end he's silenced. Silence and longing show up in many of your works silence in captivity, silence in exile, silence in death, longing for what cannot be or for those whom one cannot have.

AD I do feel my life has been filled with a sense of loss. *Konfidenz* could also be seen as a very strong critique of political utopias in our time, their failure, the need to dream something to replace them and keep hope alive. It's deepest desire is a call for somebody to tell Leon's story: probably a woman to complete that story. Leon, at the end of his life comes to the conclusion that only if the woman takes over and possesses a voice of her own will she be able to tell his story. You said Leon doesn't have a voice of his own. You think he's a chameleon?

jb Leon gives up his voice to Suzanna at a very early age, at twelve to be precise, and then he gives his voice to the resistance, and then he gives it to Barbara. He never keeps it for himself. He's given up a sense of personal direction.

AD How interesting. I never saw it like that, but I think you may be right. You know, I've hardly spoken about this novel. The others I have given a great deal of meditation to. Perhaps my "hero" has given up. But let's remember he's given his voice up to structures he has built in his head. He's not giving it to things outside him, but to entities like the resistance or Suzanna, a woman he has built from inside his dreams. The reason for this crisis—a story, tension—is because both the resistance and the real incarnation of the woman of his dreams, Barbara, refuse to cooperate, they belie what his construction of them has been.

jb But Barbara does teeter on giving herself up to this construct of Leon's mind.

AD She does. And we're not sure if she does or she doesn't at the end. All of this is also constructed by a narrator who is himself in a situation which is the worst condition any narrator can find themself in: he really doesn't know how to save these people. In a way, he doesn't know how to narrate them. He's just a camera, testifying about them. He's an almost mute witness to what is happening.

jb *Konfidenz* is a much more personal work. First of all, seventy percent of it is written in dialogue. But it seemed a far more intimate work than what you've done in the past. Was that intentional?

AD I think it deals with interpersonal relationships in a much more anguished and mature level than previous work. I do believe I'm touching on an intimacy between those characters, in those characters and with those characters which is different from the distance I've kept with other characters in other novels. I do believe you're right, that *Konfidenz* marks a phase in my work that is dealing with a world where we must build our relationships with one another in a very intimate, cavernous space. An intimate cavern of reality.

jb Why all dialogue?

AD Two reasons. One, let's call superficial or anecdotal, comes out of working in theater and cinema for the last three years. The idea of having a camera there watching this was intriguing. It was not unlike the position I was in, and had never been in before, which is

watching other people rehearse or rewrite your words, and you can't do anything about it. During the period in which I was writing *Konfidenz*, I was in the midst of production on the movie, *Death and the Maiden*, and watching all the productions of the plays. And that influenced me. A deeper reason was not knowing who these people were. From the very start I felt that they were shadows or actors who were speaking certain lines in front of me. I was unable to gauge what was really in their minds, what masks they had put on, what their real stories were.

jb Do you know where the work is going prior to writing it?

AD Never. There's only one work of mine that I've known how it ended, which is *Widows*. I knew it would begin with a captain saying, "That old bitch," and I knew that at the end that old bitch would be gone, but all the other women would be in her place and a body would appear out of the river and the widows would take the corpse toward the soldiers, who would either kill them or. . . . I had no idea how to get from that first phrase to the last idea. Outside of that I have never known, ever, where anything is going, only that first phrase. I have an atmosphere, and a general idea of what I want to explore. One of the reasons I write is to find out what it is that interests me in that first phrase. I want to unravel the experience hidden there. *Konfidenz* took me entirely by surprise, more by surprise than other works. I knew there was a certain experience during the first years of my exile from Chile when I was the intermediary between the people who left the country and the people who stayed in the country. I had that experience, and I knew it touched that. But I had no idea where it was going.

jb   What sparks that first line? The idea for *Death and the Maiden* came from your car breaking down when you were living in Washington, D.C. Do these random, freak events hold a greater significance for you? Are they symbolic?

AD   I don't think that these events are random or freak. Certain things happen to you at a certain moment, and you either understand their meaning then or twenty years later you find their meaning.

jb   Are you a fatalist?

AD   Yes. I'm an optimistic fatalist. We live in a universe where everything has a hidden meaning. It's almost as if every object is a sign of something else. And especially experience. There's a reason why certain experiences happen to you, and if you can discover the meaning of that—such as, why was there a coup in Chile? We understand the socioeconomic and political reasons why there was a coup. But what is the meaning of it in human terms? Very often you have an experience and you keep it in your head for a long, long time and then something sparks a fire. You become the one person who can explore the meaning of that. But very often you

have to wait twenty years. I could not have written *Konfidenz* seventeen or eighteen years ago when the experience itself happened. Not the experience of *Konfidenz*, but the core: what happens if you have power over a person, over a man, and you fall in love with—or you were already in love with—that person's lover? What happens in those circumstances? I didn't answer that question until almost twenty years had passed. In 1975 I would not have been able to go into the ambiguity of the politics. Pinochet was in power and we were fighting him very hard. It was very difficult for us—like many people in the novel—to critique our resistance leaders, the people who were able and capable of betraying us at a certain moment. I wouldn't have dared, for my own sanity, to have asked the questions I ask in *Konfidenz*. These questions were very painful ones.

jb   What were those questions?

AD   I really wouldn't want to tell you that.

jb   Okay, let me then ask you about free will, or self-empowerment. Leon decrees he was born at the age of twelve when Suzanna came to him in his dream. And in *Manuel Sendero* the fetuses refuse to be born. Does one have the ability to choose when they are born?

AD   There's a fate awaiting the character, and that has to do with that tragic sense of life I feel. You choose your fate. I've always felt we control so little of our lives, but we do control how we react to that destiny, to what is chosen for us. So I'm always focusing on people in very extreme situations who react in very extreme ways. And one of the ways in which they react is through their fantasy.

jb Very often in your work you set up a dichotomy between fantasy and hyperreality.

AD There's a constant appeal to the imaginary. I believe strongly that if there is salvation, if such a word exists or has a meaning, it's in that capacity to create an imaginary world which gives an alternative meaning to the fate that has been imposed upon us. In as much as we can express that imaginary, we can commune with others who are constructing their own imaginaries in a similar distance. Then, we can create solidarity. Solidarity of the imagination. My work is infused with the notion that what happens to somebody is very often less important than the way in which the person reacts in his or her imagination. There is a way of telling the story differently, if only we can find it. And I'm always asking how you can join the visionary and the practical, the person who lives history without great fantasy and the person who's shut up in the fantastic world and is creating these images. Or, in the prose sense, how can you join a very colloquial language with an enormously metaphorical, rich, perhaps baroque vocabulary? These are two parts of my personality. In fact, I fluctuate between two conditions all the time. I'm exiled and at the same time, I'm obsessed with my country. I feel

very much alive, while at the same time I'm a ghost. I love the mass media, and I detest the mass media. I live the contradiction. Fortunately, I'm a writer. Otherwise, I'd probably be in an asylum.

jb Do you consider yourself a cultural ambassador?

AD I am in a way. A bit less than before, but life has given me a rather strange bridge position. I am entirely bi-lingual and bi-cultural. I do belong to two worlds, and these are the two worlds of the Americas.

jb You were born in Argentina, raised in New York, and then you finally settled in Chile. You said you have fanatical feelings toward your country. To what degree was a feeling of cultural identity imposed upon you, or did you actively look for it?

AD I looked for it. I left Argentina when I was two, and I went through a very traumatic adaptation in the United States, which I don't want to go into now because I'm writing about it. I tried to become a typical American boy, which I wasn't. And then I had to leave for Chile when I was twelve years old and I found myself trying to remain loyal to the American child I thought I was. It was only gradually as time went by that I fell in love with Chile and with my wife to be, Angelica. I was seduced by the country. And then I lost the country. And I went abroad into exile. I spent a great part of my exile pining for that country, but pining for it in a very special way, now a much more sophisticated way. And the years go by and I've gone back to Chile, and I've not really found myself belonging entirely there. I have discovered that perhaps I must admit the fact that I am a man in between. That I am a man who lives on the frontier between places. A fluctuating place is an interesting place to live. And perhaps I have all my life lived on the frontier trying to deny it. Trying to deny life on the margins or periphery of something. But that's a very stimulating, creative place to be.

jb Your work appeals on such a universal level to diasporic communities, and it addresses the need to create a psychic homeland in an immediate environment when one has had to, or been forced to, or chosen, to give up a physical homeland.

AD I would agree with you absolutely. Since Pinochet ceased to be the dictator in Chile five years ago and comforted himself with being head of the army, I am free to go back to live in my country or not live there. Since that moment five years ago I have begun to feel accompanied by many similar experiences of diaspora, in the sense of saying: Look Ariel, it's time you didn't try to mold yourself or conform yourself into one version of who you are, but you are as plural and as multiple as many people around the world. Your story is in one sense very unique and in another sense it is the story of so many others who have to cross the borders, who have to work with the ideas of cultural identity clash, and assimilation. I have to live

these problems. And I feel myself inhabited now by these dilemmas, more than by the dilemma of what does it mean to be Chilean, but by what it means to live the border crossing in this age of ours. *Mascara* and *Konfidenz*, and even *Death and the Maiden*, I've written in a way in which readers can find their own stories, even if it's not immediately identifiable with their local circumstances. I really feel the story of *Konfidenz* has happened innumerable times to innumerable people in innumerable places. And history interrupts their dialogue, it does not allow their dialogue to continue. Which is what happens in our life stories. We try to create an imaginary story and then all of a sudden history, or the historical circumstance, comes and breaks open that reality which we try to create like a womb or an intimate experience.

jb That's certainly what happens in *Death and the Maiden*, the hazy boundaries of trust between Paulina and Gerardo and Miranda.

AD The problem of trust is very central in *Death and the Maiden*, *Manuel Sendero*, and *Konfidenz*. In my literary evolution I go from the epic to the intimate. Before the coup we seemed to inhabit a time of revolution when we were going to change everything. There was a sense that reality was ours for the taking, that all we had to do was imagine a different future and it would immediately come true. Gestate out of ourselves. But as the years go by the epic question of the country, or of the world, becomes a question of how do I trust one other person in the world, and with that one person create a community with which to confront the horrors of our time? And more and more the question is: how do I trust somebody else? How do I believe somebody else? How do I know if the story they're telling is the truth? How do I know if their mask is not hiding something terrible? This has to do with my meditation about the public and the private. Our privacy has been invaded to the point that I think we hardly have any privacy. Everything has been appropriated from us. That's the feeling I have constantly. And it has to do with another thing you mentioned, which is the degree to which you collaborate or not, with power. Because the only way in which

you can change the world is if you are born, if you do engage with the world as it is. At the same time, if you give of yourself too liberally, if you don't keep some part of yourself intact, you may not have anything with which to change the world once you have engaged it. And this problem of trust, which has a lot to do with betrayal, is crucial. *Konfidenz* is a study in betrayal, and therefore, it's a study in loyalty. Is it possible to love and be loyal in times such as ours? It's not about our times, really, but it is, of course. These are the central questions we have to ask ourselves: how can we believe somebody else, how do we know who that somebody else is? When all the constructs have failed us, how do we continue to dream?

GRAHAM SWIFT patrick mcgrath

BOMB # 15, Spring 1986

Graham Swift, when I first met him in the winter of 1985, in a cold house in Fulham, had published a story collection, *Learning to Swim*, and three novels: *The Sweet-Shop Owner*; *Shuttlecock*; and *Waterland,* which was short-listed for Britain's Booker Prize, and won the Guardian Fiction Award. *Waterland* is a beautifully written, eccentric, profound and funny book, at once a family saga, a mystery, a meditation on history, and a treatise on, among other things, eels. It immediately established its author as one of the most original and elegant of the younger English writers.

Since then Graham Swift has written three more novels; *Out of This World*; *Ever After*; and *Last Orders*, which won the Booker Prize in 1996, and is an extraordinary and sensitive exploration of the minds and hearts and memories of four seemingly ordinary Englishmen as they carry the ashes of a dead friend down to the coast to throw into the sea. Less antic, and formally more austere than *Waterland, Last Orders* is a major work of a mature humanistic imagination, and has been justly celebrated for its depth and wisdom and sympathy.

But all of that was yet to come when I enjoyed the first of what would turn out to be many merry meetings with Graham Swift. This is the part of the conversation we had before going down to the pub.

patrick mcgrath You make the point in *Waterland* that history moves in circles, or even spirals, our disasters worsening every time round. Have you been accused of fatalism?

GRAHAM SWIFT Not in any deeply offensive way. I tend to shrug that off anyway because novels aren't statements, they aren't prophecies or philosophies, they're stories, and there is a great deal more going on in the novel than simply speculation about the fate of the world. I wouldn't be a novelist if I wanted to be a philosopher, and I hope that what my novels give readers is an experience, not something from which they can extract messages. I also ought to say that, bluntly, I don't actually say those things. You can call this sophistical if you like, but it's my character who says these things, it is Tom Crick who holds these views, and he says many contradictory things; he's a highly intelligent man but he is in a state of personal crisis and his once-cherished and fairly coherent views of history are being challenged, and so he's voicing in the novel different views of history, of progress, the fate of mankind and so on.

pm Yet Tom Crick carries moral authority in the novel. It is he who speaks, it is he who controls the narrative.

GS He does exercise a great deal of authority. There is a tendency, I suppose, to take what he says as the last word on things, but against that there is the plight of this man who is heartbroken and reduced and lonely. And what becomes of this man? What becomes of Tom Crick? I think he's a very sad, a very desolate figure, for all of his intellectual powers.

pm Tom Crick's half brother Dick is a fascinating figure. He is inarticulate and retarded, it's implied that he's half-machine, that he's half-fish, half-eel, even half-vegetable, a potato-head; and he works with silt, which is another of those half-and-half things, water and land; and it's into the silt that he makes his final dive.

GS I'm not sure that I know, and if I did I wouldn't say, what happens to him at the end. When he dives into the river, you could interpret that as an act of despair, a return to nothingness and

so on, but it is also, I hope, a sort of escape, so there is some sort of feeling of liberation. I am, it would seem, interested in inarticulate characters, characters who become silent, inert, vegetable; I think it may have to do with this question of whether knowledge is good or bad: is it good to know the truth, or is it harmful? Are there situations where it is best not to tell, or not to know? Or not to remember? Dick Crick is a character who among his many *semi* attributes has an ability not to remember. He lives in an amnesiac world, and whilst we pity him in some ways, can we be sure that because of this faculty, or nonfaculty, he's not better off than we are? Henry, his grandfather, goes off to fight in the trenches and comes back without a memory: there's a great deal of irony in the book about recalling things or not recalling things. History is constantly confronting this basic choice: why should we summon up the past? Why should we remember anything, whether it's personally or collectively? Does it do us any good? Does it hinder us? And I don't attempt to come down on one side or the other, to resolve the issue, but I suppose you could say that Dick is a peculiar embodiment, among many other things, of this paradox.

pm What is the thing beneath language that Dick has access to?

GS I'm not sure that I know. It could simply be nature. Dick seems to be much more a part of primitive nature and its primitive cycles than any other character in the book, yet after all human nature does stand apart from nature, and I wouldn't want for one moment to share in that romantic view that going back to nature is a good thing. On the other hand, a complete loss of contact with nature— an inability to see that human nature, even if it is a peculiar and separate phenomenon, is after all part of nature—is I'm quite sure a bad thing.

pm Nature is at its wildest, the old, wild Fens, provides the setting for one of *Waterland*'s most horrific scenes: the abortion that Martha Clay, an alleged witch, performs on Mary Metcalf. It is evil, and results in septicemia and barrenness for Mary. Yet Martha Clay is as close to nature as Dick Crick.

GS The reactions I've had to that chapter have been interesting. It is a horrible scene, some people find it almost impossible to read. I've never felt that. I was very conscious of wanting to construct a scene that was very sinister, strong but with a fairytale feeling, for it incorporates so many almost supernatural things; and even for Mary and Tom, the only way they can see it is as something out of a fairytale, in the gruesome sense of fairytale. And I suppose there is no sense of there being any positive outcome. Given that Tom and Mary do want to get rid of the child, one could imagine an outcome where the abortion is successful, if any abortion is; but from the beginning you do have the sense that everything is going to go wrong. Oh, without a doubt it is a central episode in the book.

pm Is the nature which Martha Clay, the alleged witch, inhabits, the nature to which Dick Crick is connected in his inarticulacy?

GS I would be reluctant to make these schemes, but if Dick somehow has this contact with nature which the other characters don't have, I wouldn't put Martha Clay in the same category. Her realm is superstition rather than nature, and there's a great deal in the novel about superstition and its vices and virtues. And like many other things in the novel, superstition is paradoxical. I tend to see things in terms of paradox. Superstition, when it creates an event like the abortion scene, is undoubtedly a bad thing, all the potions and the sheer crudeness, the unmedical nature of it all, this has disastrous consequences. But in another sense, in other areas of the novel, superstition, in terms of a need for something extra, is a benign thing; even telling stories is a kind of superstition, an imposing of extra structure on reality, and it's something very much needed by these people who happen to live in a landscape which almost says to them, look, reality is flat and empty. Insofar as superstition is creative it's perhaps not a bad thing.

pm How was the idea of *Waterland* born?

GS I think I started with the scene that opens the books, with a picture in my head of the corpse in the river, the floating corpse, and then certain things started to emerge around that, to do with location, setting, other characters, time. So it began as a kind of detective thing, classic case of a dead body and whodunit? The other crucial moment in the gestation was when, having evolved the narrator figure as the boy who lived in the lockside cottage—one of the people who discovers the dead boy—I felt for some reason that this was back in the forties in wartime. But I wanted it to be seen and told from a much later perspective, the 1980s. So the question is, naturally, what becomes of this boy Tom in later life? Then, when I made him a history teacher, there was a little—not so little—there was an explosion of ideas. I thought of all sorts of possibilities, all sorts of things that I could bring in, which was very exciting. I think that is when I said, well, alright, it is a novel and I can now start it. But we're talking about a process which maybe went on for a year before words got put down on paper.

pm At what point did you decide to include a natural history of eels?

GS Well, there's always a large element of serendipity, and also, even though we're talking quite seriously about the book, there is an element of fun. One does have fun when one is writing, although the issues at stake may be very grave; and the construction of a novel can be enormous fun. I didn't know as much as that chapter makes clear, but I knew a fair bit about the eels before I started writing *Waterland*. Because I'm a fisherman, I know a bit about fish; and eels have always fascinated me. An incredible lifecycle they have, the mystery of it!—and the

extraordinary psuedoscience through the centuries, trying to find out how the damn things breed. And I thought, well, this is a wonderful little story in its own right and wouldn't it be great to have the opportunity to sort of just fling it into the middle of some larger work; and the opportunity arose. I found generally that in writing the book I evolved a sort of form, or nonform, in which I could be totally digressive, I could have chapters in which the subject matter was virtually nonfiction, was no longer narrative; and the eel fitted superbly into that scheme, because after all the Fens are a region which abounds in eels, and the eel has always had metaphorical overtones, like the landscape. And it suddenly seemed to me that the life cycle, the natural history of the eel, seemed to say so much about history generally, and about our attempts to discover the origin of things. And all of that was quite apart from it being just an incredibly intriguing and amusing subject.

pm You mentioned that *Waterland* was much more ambitious than anything you'd attempted before. Were you referring to this integrating of nonnarrative, nonfictional material into the story?

GS Yes, I think that was part of it. I suppose, too, I rather relished in anticipation a slight perplexity on the part of the reader—where the reader comes to the end of one chapter, and then finds a chapter about eels, or beer, or something, apparently not connected to the narrative; and the reader would think, well, what the hell's going on? I rather delighted in that prospect.

pm Will you do it again?

GS I don't know. I think every book dictates—somehow mysteriously—its own terms. It says to you, well, you can get away with that or you can't. And in any case, it's never a good policy to repeat a pattern.

pm Do you think it's alright for middle-aged men to run off with small female antelopes?

GS Well, they don't.

pm Uncle Walter did in your short story collection *Learning to Swim*.

GS It was alright for him. I might be wrong in saying they don't. There might be a case somewhere. I'm very fond of that story, "Hoffmeir's Antelope," I suppose because of the antelope. It was a fairly early story, a story which wrote itself. One invents a totally unknown, totally specious species, and that's just good fun.

pm There's another story in *Learning to Swim*, "The Hypochondriac," in which a doctor projects his clinical knowledge onto a young man, unaware that he is also projecting his own denial of pain; and then to his immense surprise the young man dies. There's a failure of medical knowledge, of scientific thought.

GS It's a concern which is not unrelated to this business of, is it better to know or not to know. It's an illusion that knowledge is always coupled to

authority. Knowledge doesn't bring authority, and authority doesn't necessarily imply knowledge. The doctor in that story is a good example of someone who feels that they have knowledge, and indeed they do, but of a very limited kind, in fact. The crisis of that story is really a man's discovery that he has no authority; neither over people, nor, as he once thought, over his own experience, his own life. There's a great deal in the story about how he's dealt with his own marriage, in terms of "I know what I'm doing, I can deal with this, my knowledge and my clinical cool will hold things together." But it is blown apart, by an incidence of the supernatural, because the patient, who is the cause of all this, who does die, reappears for one moment. Of course such an event is quite outside the doctor's range of experience. And he breaks down.

pm It's a lovely delicate ghost, a Jamesian ghost. It just flickers for a moment.

GS Not really a haunting at all.

pm Ghosts appear here and there in the short stories, and there's an important ghost, Sarah Atkinson's, in *Waterland*. Yet the earlier novels manifest no such magical or supernatural elements. Why is this?

GS They were there inside waiting to get out, and they did in *Waterland*. But it's very hard to talk about the construction of a novel in terms of actual decisions to do this or that. Sarah does become a ghost, she returns supernaturally and she dives, as Dick dives, she returns to the water. She began as a solid, flesh-and-blood character who was the young wife of this very solid commercial man; and then I got to the situation where she is knocked unconscious, literally senseless; and remains so.

pm She hits her head on a writing desk.

GS Yes, falls and knocks her head against a desk. I see no significance in the writing desk. [*laughter*] She is another inarticulate character and for the remainder of her life she says virtually nothing. It's as though she passes into ghostliness, almost within her own lifetime, because the people in the town turn her into this curious, angelic, saintly figure, who is invested with strange powers, or so they believe. Then when she dies, almost inevitably you know she's going to come back, she's going to continue to have an influence. But I don't think there was ever a moment where, before writing, I said, well, this is what the character is going to do. You just see possibilities. Some of them you pursue, and you fall flat on your face. Sometimes the pursuit is fruitful.

pm Two of the observers of Dick Crick's plunge into the silt are American serviceman. It is sunset. Overhead, bombers are flying off to their targets. Is this an implication of Americans in some final apocalyptic moment, in some sort of final global plunge?

GS No, I haven't seen it that way, but I don't see why you shouldn't. I thought you were going to say, "Can you use the presence of the Americans in some way to indicate a sort of New World?" Americans from the New World who have come into this old and in some ways inbred and failing English world—there was possibly an element of that. And I don't suppose I chose entirely by accident the state where these Americans come from: Arizona, the dry zone; and there they are in the wet Fens. One mustn't forget too that historically it's quite accurate, there were many American servicemen based in East Anglia at the time.

pm Do you really see the retarded Dick Crick as an individual?

GS Very much so, very much the character fiddling with his motorbike. I don't see him as a sort of cypher, symbol, representation—he's certainly very there. Some of the little things he keeps in his bedside cupboard.

pm A bird's nest?

GS Oh, he has little bits of animal skulls, and a pathetic sort of thing he made out of a tin for his mother on one of her birthdays.

pm There's a fish hanging over the bed.

GS I do like the concrete. Novels should be this mixture of the intensely concrete and the world of ideas.

pm Many stories are told in *Waterland*, and one of the funniest is the story of Jack Parr's suicide attempt. Jack is a railway signalman, and decides to end it all by sitting on the rail-

way lines. So he sits there doggedly all night, while unbeknownst to
him his wife is in the signal box,
throwing switches and making
telephone calls, and lights are
blinking all over the eastern Fens
as expresses and goods trains are
rerouted to avoid the unhappy
man.

GS He's asleep by this time, and he never
learns about the subterfuge. And is
actually convinced when he wakes up
that he's been saved by a miracle. And
nobody breaks his illusion.

pm He goes on the wagon and stays
on it. Many events in *Waterland* are
seen to have two explanations,
often one logical, the other super-
stitious. A live fish dropped into a
woman's lap will make her barren,
it's said; and this is precisely what
does happen to Mary.

GS Yes, you can imagine some of the old
people in the Fens maintaining
staunchly that the reason for all the
trouble was the eel, the fish in the lap.
There's a parallel in some ways
between superstition and the way fiction works, the way fiction can produce these rather magical moments,
which aren't entirely impossible,
aren't entirely beyond belief. I think
it's important for fiction to be magical, just as it's important for fiction to
embrace the real world, to look really
hard at the real world.

pm Real world?

GS Whatever the real world is.

pm Now, this feeling for magic is

quite new to the English novel.

GS Yes, that's true, it's not at all a recognizable English tradition. The phrase
everybody comes up with is *magic realism*, which I think has now become a
little tired. But on the other hand
there's no doubt that English writers
of my generation have been very much
influenced by writers from outside
who in one way or another have got
this magical, surreal quality, such as
Borges, Marquez, Grass, and that has
been very stimulating. I think in general it's been a good thing. Because we
are, as ever, terribly parochial, self-
absorbed and isolated, culturally, in
this country. It's about time we began
to absorb things from outside.

pm What about France?

GS I think there's always been a cultural
antagonism between us and the
French anyway, but I think also the
French may have held this view, and
justifiably so, that English fiction of
the immediate postwar period, up to
the sixties and early seventies was terribly bound up in its own Englishness,
middle-class suburbs and so forth, and
that it just didn't travel. But they're
more interested in English writers
than they used to be.

pm Have they warmed to *Waterland*?

GS Quite. I was asked to go over there, be
around for a few days and so on. It
was entered for some prize they have
for novels in translation. It was short-
listed but it didn't win.

pm Who amongst your contemporaries do you particularly enjoy?

GS Well, I actually like very much a writer who's originally American, Russell Hoban, who wrote *Riddley Walker*. He seems to me to be completely his own man as a writer. I think he's got a real touch of genius. Then there's a writer who's originally Japanese, Kazuo Ishiguro, and he's about to publish a second novel. His first was called *A Pale View of Hills*, and it is simply amazing. He's a remarkable writer in an understated, very quiet, unextrovert way. There's Timothy Mo, who is also about to publish a new book. His second novel was called *Sour Sweet*, which is a lovely book about the Chinese community in London. Some of these writers I know quite well as friends. One of the pleasures of having written a successful book is that you do get more opportunity to meet other writers. For a long time, really until *Waterland*, I knew virtually no other writers; not that it changed anything fundamentally. In some ways you can argue that knowing other writers is a disruption, a distraction. You can become more concerned about how other people write, which is not necessarily good for your own work. I think in the end writing is a lonesome business. You have to go away by yourself to do it, whether you've got hundreds of friends or not. Nothing will ever change that.

pm Would you like a glass of beer?

GS Yes please.

pm There's a book by a French writer, Michel Tournier, which I think might be to your taste. It's called *Friday, or The Other Island*, and it's a sort of postcolonial rewrite of Robinson Crusoe. The relationship of Crusoe and Friday grows increasingly uneasy—Friday blows up the gunpowder supply and runs away—and Robinson becomes increasingly distraught. His one solace is a peaceful little patch of ground in a very obscure part of the island, which he becomes closer and closer to, this patch of black earth, until finally he's regularly inseminating it, he's making love to the earth. Then, to his delight, he begins to see these beautiful white flowers appear—he has successfully inseminated the earth! And as things get worse and worse with Friday, so Robinson comes to spend more and more time in his secret place. Till one day he goes up, and there amongst his white flowers is a *black* flower—and this is a major crisis.

biographical notes

Paul Auster by Joseph Mallia. *BOMB #23, Spring 1988* Paul Auster was born in Newark, New Jersey in 1947. He received a BA and an MA in Comparative Literature from Columbia.

Auster's first full length prose work, *The Invention of Solitude*, was published in 1982. Auster was the editor of *The Random House Book of Twentieth-Century French Poetry* (1982) and has translated the work of Blanchot, Mallarmé, Sartre, and Joubert, among others. Between 1982 and 1984, Auster wrote three novels that comprise *The New York Trilogy*. *City of Glass* appeared in 1985, and *Ghosts* and *The Locked Room* in 1986. Since then, Auster has published five other novels, *In the Country of Last Things* (1987), *Moon Palace* (1989), *The Music of Chance* (1990), which was nominated for the PEN/Faulkner Award for fiction, *Leviathan* (1992), and *Mr. Vertigo* (1994). *Disappearances: Selected Poems* was published in 1988; a collection of Auster's essays, *The Art of Hunger*, appeared in 1992. Auster's *City of Glass* is the first novel in Avon's Neon Lit graphic novel series edited by Bob Callahan and Art Spiegelman. *Hand to Mouth*

(1997), Auster's most recent book, is comprised of an autobiographical essay, a detective novel, a baseball card game, and three plays.

Auster, with director/partner Wayne Wang completed two movies for Miramax. The first, *Smoke,* starring Harvey Keitel and William Hurt, was an original screenplay loosely based on an Auster short story commissioned by the *New York Times*, "Auggie Wren's Christmas Story." The second, *Blue in the Face*, was a spontaneous *Smoke* spin-off filmed in three days and set in the same Brooklyn smoke shop with Harvey Keitel, Michael J. Fox, Roseanne, Lou Reed and Lily Tomlin. Hyperion's Miramax Books subsequently published *Smoke & Blue in the Face*. Auster makes his directorial debut in the upcoming film *Lulu on the Bridge,* for which he also wrote the screenplay, and which stars Harvey Keitel and Mira Sorvino. Auster lives in Brooklyn with his wife and two children.

Russell Banks by Pinckney Benedict. *BOMB #52, Spring 1995*

Russell Banks was born in 1940 in Newton, Massachusetts. He has published twelve books of fiction, including four short story collections. His books have been translated into ten languages, and two—*The Sweet Hereafter* and *Affliction*—have been adapted as films, directed by Atom Egoyan and Paul Schrader, respectively. His best-known novels include *Continental Drift, Affliction, The Sweet Hereafter*, and most recently, *Rule of the Bone. Cloudsplitter*, a historical novel based on the life of abolitionist John Brown, was published in March 1998. Banks has taught at various colleges and universities including the University of New Hampshire, Massachusetts Institute of Technology, New York University, Columbia, and most recently Princeton, where he is Howard G.B. Clark University Professor in the Humanities. He has received numerous awards and prizes, including the O.Henry, Pushcart, and Best Short Story Awards; a National Endowment for the Arts Grant; Merrill and Guggenheim Fellowships; the John Dos Passos Prize; the American Book Award, and a Literature Prize from the American Academy and Institute of Arts and Letters. He is married to the poet Chase Twitchell, and currently lives in a small Adirondack town in upstate New York. He is the father of four grown daughters.

Pinckney Benedict grew up on his family's dairy farm in the mountains of southern West Virginia. His stories, interviews, and nonfiction have appeared in a number of magazines and anthologies including *George, BOMB, Ontario Review, Story, Wigwag, Southern,* Italy's *Grazia,* Japan's *Gunzo, New Stories from the South*, and *The Oxford Book of American Short Stories*. He has published two collections of short fiction, *Town Smokes* and *The Wrecking Yard*, and most recently a novel, *Dogs of God*. All three were named Notable Books by the *New York Times Book Review*. They have been or will soon be published in the United Kingdom, France, and Germany. His awards include Britain's Steinbeck Award (he was the first recipient), the *Chicago Tribune*'s Nelsen Algren Award, a James Michener Fellowship from the Writers' Workshop at the University of Iowa, inclusion in the Pushcart Prize XXI anthology (he is a contributing editor to the Pushcart series), and two of the Henfield Foundation's Transatlantic Review Awards. From time to time he has appeared as an essayist on National Public Radio's "All Things Considered." He has taught on the Creative Writing faculties at, among other places, Oberlin College, Warren Wilson College, Davidson College, Breadloaf, and Princeton University. He is an associate professor in the English Department at Hope College in Holland, Michigan.

Sheila Bosworth by Guy Gallo. *BOMB #39, Spring 1992*

Sheila Bosworth is the author of the novels *Almost Innocent* (1984) and *Slow Poison* (1992) and of the dramatic monologue *Angel Mama*, produced in New Orleans and at the National Institutes of Health in Bethesda, Maryland as part of World AIDS Day (1994). Her work has appeared in various magazines and journals, including *A World Unsuspected: Portraits of Southern Childhood, Southern Living, The Double Dealer Redux* ("Women in the Fiction of Walker Percy"), and *Icarus*. She was born and raised in New Orleans, educated at Tulane University, and now lives in Covington, Louisiana.

Guy Gallo was born and raised in New Orleans and has lived in the Northeast since escaping soon after high school. He began his career as a playwright: *Failing* (1977), *Rain in Lent* (1979) and *Peter and Wendy* (1981). He then took a hectic sojourn in the land of film, writing several screenplays, including *Under the Volcano* (1984) and *The Adventures of Huckleberry Finn* (1985). He has recently returned to playwriting with *Antigone in Desire* and *The Shallow End*, and is currently revising a novel entitled *The Pointed Heart*. His relationship with *BOMB* began in 1990 when he was interviewed by Betsy Sussler. He wishes now to express his gratitude for the magazine's support and friendship.

Lucie Brock-Broido by Carole Maso. *BOMB #53, Fall 1995*

Lucie Brock-Broido was born in Pittsburgh, Pennsylvania. She received her MA and BA from Johns Hopkins University, and her MFA from the School of Arts at Columbia University. She has been awarded fellowships in poetry from the Guggenheim Foundation, the National Endowment for the Arts, the Witter Bynner Prize from the American Academy of Arts and Letters, the Massachusetts Cultural Council, the Hoyns Fellowship from the University of Virginia, and was a fellow in poetry at the Fine Arts Work Center in Provincetown. From 1988–1993, she was a Briggs-Copeland poet at Harvard University, where, in her final year, she served as director of the Creative Writing program. She has also taught at Princeton College and in the writing seminars at Bennington College. She is currently an associate professor in the Writing division of the School of Arts at Columbia University, where she also serves as Director of Poetry. Her poems have appeared in numerous literary magazines and journals, including the *New Yorker*, the *New Republic*, *Antaeus*, *Parnassus*, *Boulevard*, the *New York Times*, the *Agni Review*, the *Harvard Review*, the *American Poetry Review*, and the *Paris Review*. She has published two volumes of poetry, *A Hunger* (1988), and *The Master Letters* (1995), both with Alfred A. Knopf. She currently lives in New York City and in Cambridge, Massachusetts.

Carole Maso is the author of *Ghost Dance*, *The Art Lover*, *AVA*, *The American Woman in the Chinese Hat*, and *Aureole*. Forthcoming books include *Defiance* and *Beauty is Convulsive*. She teaches at Brown University where she directs the Creative Writing program.

Peter Carey by Robert Polito. *BOMB #54, Winter 1996*

Peter Carey was born in 1943 in Bacchus Marsh, Victoria. He is married to the theater director Alison Summers, and lives with their two sons in New York City, where he teaches at Columbia University. His books include the short story collections *The Fat Man in History* (1974) and *War Crimes* (1979) which won the New South Wales Premier's Award. His novels: *Bliss* (1981) won the Miles Franklin Award, a National Book Council Award, and the New South Wales Premier's Award; *Illywacker* (1985) was shortlisted for the Booker Prize; *Oscar and Lucinda* (1988) won the Booker Prize and numerous other awards, and is now a movie directed by Gillian Armstrong and starring Ralph Fiennes; *The Tax Inspector* (1991); *The Unusual Life of Tristan Smith* (1994); and *Jack Maggs* (1988). He has also written a memoir, *A Letter to Our Son* (1994), and a childrens book, *The Big Bazoohley* (1995). His screenplays include *Bliss* (with Ray Lawrence) and *Until the End of the World* (with Wim Wenders).

Robert Polito is the author of *A Readers Guide to James Merrill's The Changing Light at Sandover* (University of Michigan Press, 1994); a book of poems, *Doubles* (University of Chicago Press, 1995); and *Savage Art: A Biography of Jim Thompson* (Knopf, 1995), for which he received a National Book Critics Circle Award in biography and an Edgar from the Mystery Writers of America. He edited *Crime Novels: American Noir of the 1930s & 1940s* and *Crime Novels: American Noir of the 1950s* (Library of America,

1997). The recipient of a fellowship from the John Simon Guggenheim Foundation in 1997, he is a contributing editor at *BOMB*. He directs the Writing program at The New School in New York City.

Ariel Dorfman by Jenifer Berman. *BOMB #50, Winter 1994*

Ariel Dorfman, born in Argentina in 1942 and a Chilean expatriate, is the Walter Hines Page Research Professor of Literature and Latin American Studies at Duke University and is a regular contributor to the *New York Times*, the *Los Angeles Times*, the *Nation*, the *Village Voice*, and many other papers worldwide. His books include the novels *Widows* (1983), *The Last Song of Manuel Sendero* (1986), *Mascara* (1988), *Hard Rain* (1990), and *Konfidenz* (1995), the short story collection *My House is On Fire* (1990), and the poetry collection *Last Waltz in Santiago and Other Poems of Exile and Disappearance* (1988). His play, *Death and the Maiden*, won the Sir Lawrence Olivier Award for Best Play in London (1991) and was produced in over fifty countries, winning numerous other awards. He cowrote and coproduced the screenplay for the film *Death and the Maiden*, directed by Roman Polanski. He is a member of the Academie Universelle des Cultures in Paris, and has received many honorary degrees. He has been a human rights activist for many years. His books have been translated into over thirty languages, and his latest is *Heading South, Looking North: A Bilingual Journey* (1998).

Jenifer Berman is the Senior Editor of *BOMB* Magazine. Born in 1968 in Washington, D.C., she graduated from the University of Michigan in 1990 with degrees in English Literature and Art History. In New York, among many freelance projects, she has also worked as an assistant editor at Farrar, Straus and Giroux, taught art education at the Museum of Modern Art, and compiled research for the Andy Warhol Film and Video Project at the Whitney Museum of American Art. Her film work includes writing, producing and codirecting two short films, *Dear George* and *7:30*; her writing and reviews have appeared in *New Digressions*, *WORD*, *Los Angeles Reader*, *Arena*, and *BOMB*. She lives in New York City where she is currently writing her first novel.

bell hooks by Lawrence Chua. *BOMB #48, Summer 1994*

bell hooks (a pseudonym derived from her great grandmother's name) is a fiercely contentious social critic, writer, and feminist intellectual. She was born in Hopkinsville, Kentucky. hooks received her BA from Stanford University and her Ph.D. from the University of California, Santa Cruz. She has taught at Yale University and at Oberlin College, and as of 1993 is Distinguished Professor of English at City College in New York City.

hooks is the author of a number of books including *Ain't I A Woman* (1981), which *Publishers Weekly* called one of the "20 most influential women's books in the last 20 years"; *Feminist Theory* (1984); *Talking Back* (1989); *Yearning* (1990), which won the Before Columbus Foundation's American Book Award; *Breaking Bread* (with Cornel West, 1991); *Black Looks* (1992); *On My Mind* (1995); a poetry collection, *A Woman's Mourning Song* (1993); and the first volume of her memoirs, *Bone Black* (1996); and *Wounds of Passion(1997)*, the second volume of memoirs (Henry Holt).

Lawrence Chua (born 1966, Penang, Malaysia) is a writer whose work has appeared in *Rolling Stone*, the *Nation*, *Vibe*, the *Village Voice*, *Artforum*, and many other publications. He is the author of the novel, *Gold by the Inch* (Grove Atlantic Press), and an editor of the anthology *Collapsing New Buildings* (Kaya). He is the recipient of awards from the New York Foundation for the Arts, the National Endowment for the Arts, and the New York State Council on the Arts. He was the managing editor of *BOMB* Magazine from 1993 to 1996.

Suzannah Lessard and Honor Moore by Betsy Sussler. *BOMB #57, Fall 1996*

Suzannah Lessard was born on December 1, 1944. She studied English Literature at Columbia University, where she received her BA in 1969. In 1970, she joined the writing staff of the *Washington Monthly*, where she remained for three years, and is a contributing editor to this day. After a year of freelancing, she joined the staff of the *New Yorker* in 1975, where she worked for twenty years, writing Profiles, Reflections, Reporter at Large articles, and many of the anonymous Notes and Comments, as well as what became her book *Architect of Desire: Beauty and Danger in the Stanford White Family*. In 1995 she left the *New Yorker* to finish her book, and then embarked on a new one, a meditation of the American landscape (mostly the manmade landscape) as a text of our history, our present, and future, as we slide toward the millennium. She publishes in the *New Yorker*, the *New York Times Sunday Magazine*, *Mirabella*, the *Washington Monthly*, and *Architectural Record*.

Encouraged and inspired by the feminist movement, **Honor Moore** began writing poetry in the early 1970s, publishing in such magazines as *American Review*, *13th Moon*, and *Amazon Quarterly*. At the suggestion of Mary Silverman and Lyn Austin of the Music Theater Group, she adapted poems about her mother's death from cancer for the theater; *Mourning Pictures* was produced by Austin and Silverman in Lenox, Massachusetts, and then on Broadway in 1974. In 1988, Moore's collection of poems, *Memoir*, was published by Chicory Blue Press; recent poems have appeared in the *Paris Review*, the *American Poetry Review*, *Ploughshares* and the *American Voice*. She is the recipient of poetry fellowships from the National Endowment for the Arts and the Connecticut Commission on the Arts, and in playwrighting from the New York Council on the Arts. In 1981, "My Grandmother Who Painted," the essay with which she began her work on her grandmother, was published in *The Writer on Her Work*, edited by Janet Sternburg; for twelve years Moore worked on Margarett Sargent's biography, researching and writing the book and curating a retrospective of Sargent's paintings and drawings. In 1996, Viking published *The White Blackbird: A Life of the Painter Margarett Sargent by her Granddaughter*, and *Margarett Sargent: A Modern Temperament* was mounted at the Davis Museum and Cultural Center at Wellesley College; a related exhibition was shown at the Berry-Hill Galleries in Manhattan in September, 1996. In July, 1997, *The White Blackbird* was published in paperback by Penguin. Moore is now working on new poems and an untitled prose work inspired by the work of Marguerite Duras.

Betsy Sussler was educated at Newcomb College in New Orleans, and the S.F. Art Institute. She cofounded *BOMB* magazine in 1981 and has been its publisher and Editor-in-Chief ever since. Some of her many interviews for *BOMB* include: artists Sarah Charlesworth, Keith Sonnier, Robin Winters, James Nares, and Cindy Sherman; writers Nancy Lemann, Gary Indiana, Suzannah Lessard and Honor Moore; actors Eric Bogosian, Richard Caliban, and Al Pacino. City Lights published a compilation of *BOMB* interviews edited by Sussler in 1992.

In the late 1970s, Sussler wrote and directed several independent features, most notably *Tripe* and *Menage*, which she screened at the Bleecker Street Cinema and The New Cinema in New York, and the Corcoran Gallery of Art in Washington, D.C. She wrote for and acted in Rosa von Praunheim's German feature, *Red Love*. From 1978–82 she acted with the theater group NIGHTSHIFT in Melbourne, Sydney, and New York. Plays include: Marguerite Duras' *The English Woman*; Fassbinder's *Pre-Paradise Sorry Now*; and Joe Orton's *Ruffians on the Stair*. In 1991 she won a NYFA Fellowship in playwrighting for her first feature length screenplay *Cane River*; her second is *Nod's End*. She has just completed a novel, now titled *Station of the Birds*.

James Merrill by Thomas Bolt. *BOMB #36, Summer 1991*
James Merrill was born in New York City on March 3, 1926, and lived in Stonington, Connecticut. He was the author of twelve books of poems, which won him two National Book Awards (for *Nights and Days* and *Mirabell*), the Bollingen Prize in Poetry (for *Braving the Elements*), the Pulitzer Prize (for *Divine Comedies*) and the first Bobbitt National Prize for Poetry awarded by the Library of Congress (for *The Inner Room*, 1988). *The Changing Light at Sandover* appeared in 1982 and included the long narrative poem begun with "The Book of Ephraim" (from *Divine Comedies*), plus *Mirabell: Books of Number* and *Scripts for the Pageant* in their entirety; it received the National Book Critics Circle Award in poetry for 1983. *Late Settings* appeared in 1985. In addition to the one volume edition of his narrative poem *The Changing Light at Sandover*, he also issued two selected volumes: *From the First Nine, Poems (1946-1976)* (1982), and *Selected Poems, 1946-1985* (1992). He is the author of two novels, *The (Diblos) Notebook* (1965, reissued in 1994) and *The Seraglio* (1957, reissued in 1987) and two plays, *The Immortal Husband* (first produced in 1955 and published in *Playbook* the following year), and, in one act, *The Bait*, published in *Artist's Theater* (1960). A book of essays, *Recitative*, appeared in 1986, and in 1993 a memoir, *A Different Person*. His last book of poems, *A Scattering of Salts*, was published in 1995, following his untimely death on February 6 of that year.

Thomas Bolt's first book of poems, *Out of the Woods*, was selected by James Merrill for the Yale Series of Younger Poets. Bolt's poems have appeared in the *Paris Review*, *BOMB*, and *Southwest Review*, and on the Internet's Zembla website. His awards and fellowships include the Rome Prize for Literature of the American Academy of Arts and Letters, the Peter I. B. Lavin Younger Poet Award of the American Academy of Poets, and a 1997 Artist's Fellowship from the New York Foundation for the Arts.

Bradford Morrow by Jim Lewis. *BOMB #51, Spring 1995*
Bradford Morrow is the author of four novels: *Come Sunday*, *The Almanac Branch* (finalist for the PEN/Faulkner Award), *Trinity Fields* (Los Angeles Book Award finalist), and most recently *Giovanni's Gift*, as well as a collection of prose poems, *A Bestiary*, which was illustrated by eighteen artists, including Kiki Smith, Eric Fischl, Joel Shapiro, Vija Celmins, and Richard Tuttle. He is founding editor of the literary journal *Conjunctions*, which since 1981 has published over 750 writers and artists. With Patrick McGrath, Morrow coedited the anthology *The New Gothic*. He is completing work on a novel, *The Prague Sonatas*, as well as a collection of essays, *Meditations on a Shadow*. He lives in New York City.

Jim Lewis is the author of two novels, *Sister*, and *Why the Tree Loves the Ax,* published by Crown in February of 1998.

Walter Mosley by Thulani Davis. *BOMB #44, Summer 1993*
Walter Mosley is the author of five critically acclaimed mysteries starring the character Easy Rawlins. The first, *Devil in a Blue Dress*, published by W. W. Norton in 1990, was nominated for an Edgar. The TriStar film, *Devil in a Blue Dress* (1995) was produced by Jonathan Demme and directed by Carl Franklin. *A Red Death* and *White Butterfly* were also nominated for several awards. *Black Betty* and *A Little Yellow Dog* were *New York Times* bestsellers. The prequel to the Rawlins' series was published in January 1997 by the independent Black Classics Press, Baltimore, Maryland. *Gone Fishin'* will be published in paperback by Pocket in 1998. W. W. Norton published Mosley's blues novel, *RL's Dream* in 1995, which was a finalist for the NAACP Award for Fiction and won the 1996 Black Caucus of the American Library Association's Literary Award. W.W. Norton also published another non-Easy Rawlins novel in 1997, *Always Outnumbered, Always Outgunned: The Socrates Fortlow Stories*, of which

one story was an O.Henry Prize winner. Mosley has written a screenplay version which is in production with HBO and Palomar Productions for 1998, directed by Michael Apted and starring Lawrence Fishburne. In 1996 Mosley was named the first Artist in Residence at the Africana Studies Institute, New York University. Since that residency, he has continued to work with the department, creating an innovative lecture series entitled "Black Genius." Designed as a "public classroom," these lectures will include speakers ranging from Spike Lee to Angela Davis. Mosley founded PEN American Center's Open Book Committee, which has just created, with CUNY, a new publishing certificate program. Mosley also serves on the board of directors of the National Book Awards, The Poetry Society of America, and the Manhattan Theater Club. He lives in New York City.

Thulani Davis is a published poet, playwright, librettist, and novelist. Her works include the libretto for the opera, *X: The Life and Times of Malcolm X* by Anthony Davis, and the libretto for another Davis opera, *Amistad*, which premiered in Chicago in the fall of 1997. She has written nine plays, edited twenty-two anthologies and published two books of poems, *Playing the Changes* and *All the Renegade Ghosts Rise*, as well as the accompanying text for *Malcolm X: The Great Photographs*. Her first novel, *1959*, was nominated for the *Los Angeles Times* Book Award and her most recent novel is *Maker of Saints*, (Scribner, 1996, Viking Penguin, 1997). *Into the Light*, a collection of African American family photographs forthcoming from Bantam Books is her latest book project. Her play *Everybody's Ruby* premiered at the Public Theater in New York in 1998. Ms. Davis is a Grammy winner, a teacher of writing at Princeton University and Barnard College, and an ordained Buddhist priest. She lives in Brooklyn, New York, with her husband.

Michael Ondaatje by Willem Dafoe. *BOMB* #58, Winter 1997

Novelist and poet **Michael Ondaatje** was born in Sri Lanka. He left at the age of eleven to go to school in England, and came to Canada in 1962.

Ondaatje's *The Collected Works of Billy the Kid* (prose and poetry) won the Governor General's Award for poetry in 1970; *Coming Through Slaughter*, about the American jazzman Buddy Bolden, won the Books in Canada First Novel Award in 1976; his fictionalized family history, *Running in the Family*, was published in 1982. His novel, *In the Skin of a Lion*, was published in 1987 to international acclaim. It was the winner of the City of Toronto Book Award and the first winner of Ontario's Trillium Book Award. It was also shortlisted for the Governor General's Award and the Ritz Hemingway Prize.

Ondaatje's films include *Sons of Captain Poetry*, on the work of bp Nichol, and *The Clinton Special,* about Theatre Passe Muaraille's *The Farm Show*. His stage version of *The Collected Works of Billy the Kid* has been performed in Canada and the U.S., as well as in Britain. *Coming Through Slaughter* has also been produced for the stage.

Ondaatje's last novel, *The English Patient*, was published in 1992. It won Ondaatje the Governor General's Award as well as the Booker Prize (the first and only such award for a Canadian). *The English Patient* is now available in thirty-two countries, in thirty languages. The film adaptation of this novel was released in 1996 and won nine Academy Awards. Mr. Ondaatje lives in Toronto.

Willem Dafoe has appeared in over two dozen films. He made his screen debut in 1980 in Kathryn Bigelow's *The Loveless*, followed by Walter Hill's *Streets of Fire* and William Friedkin's *To Live and Die in L.A.* He went on to earn an Academy Award nomination for Best Supporting Actor for his performance in Oliver Stone's *Platoon*.

Among Dafoe's diverse film roles are Martin Scorsese's *The Last Temptation of Christ*, Alan Parker's *Mississippi Burning*, Oliver Stone's *Born on the Fourth of July*, Robert Young's *Triumph of the*

Spirit, David Lynch's *Wild at Heart*, Wim Wender's *Faraway, So Close* and *White Sands*, and Paul Schrader's *Light Sleeper*. Dafoe also played opposite Madonna in *Body of Evidence*, costarred with Harrison Ford in *Clear and Present Danger*, portrayed T. S. Eliot opposite Miranda Richardson in *Tom and Viv*, and costarred in *Speed 2* opposite Sandra Bullock. He will also be starring in Abel Ferrara's *New Rose Hotel* and Paul Schrader's *Affliction*. He recently played Caravaggio in the Oscar winning film *The English Patient*, based on Michael Ondaatje's novel.

In addition to his film work, since 1977 Dafoe has been a core member of the internationally acclaimed theater company The Wooster Group. He performs in all of the theater and media pieces with The Wooster Group at The Performing Garage in New York City, and tours with the group throughout the world. Recently Dafoe played Yank in The Wooster Group's production of the Eugene O'Neill play *The Hairy Ape*. His other Wooster Group productions include *Brace Up!*, *Fish Story*, and *The Emperor Jones*.

Caryl Phillips by Graham Swift. *BOMB #38, Winter 1992*

Caryl Phillips was born in 1958 in St. Kitts. Shortly thereafter, his parents emigrated to Leeds, England, where he spent his youth. He was educated at The Queens College, Oxford. Phillips began his literary career as a playwright and turned to fiction with his first novel *The Final Passage* (1985), which won the Malcolm X Award for Literature. His other published works include one book of non-fiction, *The European Tribe* (winner of the 1987 Martin Luther King Memorial Prize), a collection of essays which recount his journeys through Europe, and the novels *A State of Independence*, *Higher Ground*, *Cambridge*, *Crossing the River* (shortlisted for the 1993 Booker Prize), and *The Nature of Blood*. He has written numerous scripts for film, radio, and television as well as theater, and has taught and lectured throughout the world. Most recently, he edited an anthology *Extravagant Strangers: A Literature of Belonging*. Phillips' awards include a Guggenheim Fellowship, the 1992 *London Sunday Times* Young Writer of the Year Award, and the James Tait Black Memorial Prize. He currently divides his time between London and New York City.

Padgett Powell by Victoria Hunt. *BOMB #55, Fall 1996*

Padgett Powell was born in Gainesville, Florida in 1952 and by accident lives there again now, teaching at the University of Florida. He attended college in Charleston, South Carolina, flunked out of college in Tennessee, went back to college in Houston to meet women, and wrote there, as a Masters thesis under the late Donald Barthleme. His first novel, *Edisto* (1984) was nominated for the National Book Award. He has since published four more books of fiction: *A Woman Named Drown* (1987), *Typical* (1991), *Edisto Revisited* (1996), and *Aliens of Affection* (1998). He has received the American Academy and Institute of Arts and Letters Prix de Rome and a Whiting Writers' Award. His introduction to *The Adventures of Huckleberry Finn* appears in the Signet Classics edition of that title. He currently is sojourning in France and Turkey.

Victoria Hunt was born in 1956 at Fort Lee, Virginia, an army brat who grew up on the road until her father settled in Sweetwater, Tennessee. She was a high school dropout who worked as a waitress, a dry-cleaning clerk, and a forklift driver, before enrolling at Georgia State University when she was twenty-seven years old. After taking eight years to complete her BA in English, graduating summa cum laude, she attended Florida State University where she earned her Ph.D. in 1996. Her work has appeared in the *African-American Review*, the *Southern Quarterly*, *Art and Understanding*, and elsewhere. She is currently at work on a novel, *Cutting Pictures to Fit*, and a collection of interviews with gay and lesbian writers from the South. She teaches Creative Writing at Mississippi State University.

Francine Prose by Deborah Eisenberg. *BOMB* #45, Fall 1993

Francine Prose is the author of nine novels, two story collections, and most recently a collection of novellas, *Guided Tours of Hell*. Her stories and essays have appeared in the *New Yorker*, the *New York Times*, *Antaeus*, and other publications. The winner of Guggenheim and Fullbright fellowships, two National Endowment for the Arts grants, and a PEN translation prize, she has taught at the Iowa Writers Workshop, the Breadloaf, and Sewanee Writers' Conferences. A film based on her novel *Household Saints* was released in 1993.

Deborah Eisenberg is the author of a play, *Pastorale*, a monograph, *Air: 24 Hours, Jennifer Bartlett*, and three collections of stories, the most recent of which is entitled *All Around Atlantis*. She has received numerous awards and honors, including a John Simon Guggenheim Fellowship, a Whiting Foundation Award, and an Award in Literature from the American Academy of Arts and Letters. She lives in New York City and teaches at the University of Virginia.

Sapphire by Kelvin Christopher James. *BOMB* #57, Fall 1996

Sapphire is the author of *American Dreams*, a collection of poetry, which was cited by *Publishers Weekly* as "One of the strongest debut collections of the nineties." Her novel *Push* won the 1997 Book of the Month Club Stephen Crane Award for First Fiction, the Black Caucus of the American Library Association's First Novelist Award 1997, and in England, the coveted Mind Book of the Year Award. *Push* was named by the *Village Voice* as one of the top twenty-five books of 1996 and by *Time Out, New York* as one of the top ten books of 1996. Sapphire was born in 1950 in Fort Ord, California. She currently lives and works in New York City.

Kelvin Christopher James was born in Trinidad, circa 1950, and emigrated to New York circa 1975, where he found work at Harlem Hospital. He holds a B.Sc. from the University of West Indies, and a doctorate in Science Education from Columbia University. His short stories have appeared in *Quarto*, *Between C & D*, *BOMB*, the *Portable Lower East Side*, *Callaloo*, the *Literary Review*, the *Massachusetts Review*, and anthologies such as *A Junky's Christmas* (England), *Les Jungles d'Amerique* (France), *Children of the Night: Best Short Stories by Black Writers* (USA), and *Leave to Stay* (England/New Zealand.) In 1989, he was awarded a New York Foundation for the Arts Fellowship in fiction. Villard Books of Random House published *Jumping Ship and Other Stories* in 1992, and then *Secrets*, a novel, in 1993. *A Fling with a Demon Lover* was published by HarperCollins in 1996. In 1996, Kelvin was granted a National Endowment for the Arts fellowship in literature. Since 1992, through the Board of Education, Kelvin donates about $3,000 to New York City high schoolers for his annual writing awards. He is now at work on a novel entitled *The Poisoner*, based in nineteenth-century Dahomey.

Graham Swift by Patrick McGrath. *BOMB* #15, Spring 1986

Graham Swift was born in London in 1949. His stories first appeared in *London Magazine*. He is the author of six novels: *The Sweet Shop Owner* (1980); *Shuttlecock* (1981), which received the Geoffrey Faber Memorial Prize; *Waterland* (1983), which was nominated for the Booker Prize and won *The Guardian* Fiction Award, the Winifred Holtby Memorial Prize, and the Italian Premio Grinzane Cavour; *Out of this World* (1988); *Ever After* (1992) which won the French Prix du Meilleur Livre Etranger; and *Last Orders* (1996), which won the Booker Prize and the James Tait Black Memorial Prize for fiction and was an international bestseller. He has published a collection of short stories, *Learning to Swim* (1982) and coedited (with David Profumo) *The Magic Wheel: an Anthology of Fishing in Literature* (1985). *Waterland* was made into a film (1992) starring Jeremy Irons. Swift's work has been translated into over twenty-five languages.

Patrick McGrath is the critically acclaimed author of *Blood and Water and Other Tales* and the novels *The Grotesque*, *Spider*, *Dr. Haggard's Disease*, and *Asylum*. His work has been translated into more than a dozen languages. His screen adaptation of *The Grotesque* was produced by Xingu Films and released in 1997 under the title *Gentlemen Don't Eat Poets*. He has been a contributing editor to *BOMB* for many years.

Melanie Rae Thon by Caryl Phillips. *BOMB #44, Summer 1993*

Melanie Rae Thon's most recent book is the collection of stories *First, Body* (Houghton Mifflin, 1997). She is also the author of two novels, *Meteors in August* (1990), and *Iona Moon* (1993), and the collection of stories *Girls in the Grass* (1991). In 1996, she was named by *Granta* as one of the "Best Young American Novelists," and she has received grants from the National Endowment for the Arts, the Massachusetts Artists' Foundation, and the New York Foundation for the Arts. Two of her stories appeared in the recent editions of *Best American Short Stories* (1995 and 1996). Born in 1957 in Kalispell, Montana, Thon did her undergraduate work at the University of Michigan, and her graduate studies at Boston University. She now teaches at Ohio State University in Columbus.

Frederic Tuten by Bruce Wolmer. *BOMB #25, Fall 1988*

Since the publication of his interview in *BOMB*, **Frederic Tuten** has written the novels *Tintin in the New World* (1993) and *Van Gogh's Bad Cafe* (1997), both published by William Morrow and Company. His *Tallien: A Brief Romance* and *The Adventures of Mao on the Long March* have been reissued in paperback by publisher Marion Boyars. His *Tintin in the New World* is also available in paperback, published by Riverhead Press.

He has retired from his position as professor at the City College of New York, though he continues to teach Creative Writing in its graduate program. He received the DAAD award to spend a year writing fiction in Berlin, 1997–98.

Bruce Wolmer, Editor in Chief of *Art & Auction* magazine since 1994, has written about art, literature, and politics for publications in the U.S. and abroad.

Luisa Valenzuela by Linda Yablonsky. *BOMB #35, Spring 1991*

Luisa Valenzuela was born and currently resides in Buenos Aires, Argentina. Most of her work has been translated into English: the short story collections *Open Door* and *The Censors*, and the novels *Clara*, *He Who Searches*, *The Lizard's Tail*, *Black Novel* (with Argentines) and *Bedside Manners*. In spring 1998 Valuenzuela's latest collection of short stories, *Symmetries*, will be published by Serpent's Tail. She has spent a good many years living abroad in Paris, Barcelona, Mexico, and New York. From 1979 to 1989 Valenzuela lived in New York City. Since 1982 she has been a fellow of the New York Institute for the Humanities. She has been a Guggenheim Fellow (1983), a Fulbright Fellow (International Writers Workshop–Iowa, 1970), a Writer in Residence at Columbia University and at New York University. In 1991 Knox College, Illinois conferred her an honorary degree. She is a member of the Academy of Arts and Sciences, Puerto Rico.

Linda Yablonsky is the author of a novel, *The Story of Junk*, published in 1997 by Farrar, Straus, & Giroux. A contributing editor to *BOMB*, she also writes a monthly column for *PAPER* magazine and regularly contributes art criticism and artist profiles to *Time Out New York* and *Out*. Her essays have also appeared in the *New York Times*, *Elle*, *Artforum*, and *Art in America*. Her short fiction has been included in anthologies, *The New Fuck-You* (Semiotexte) and *Low Rent* (Grove/Atlantic). She appears in an HBO documentary, *Addicted*, which first aired in summer 1997, in a segment based on her story "Diary of a Nicotine Queen." Born in Philadelphia in 1948, she graduated from NYU in 1970 with a degree in English Literature and Theater and went on to write for La Mama Plexus, an experimental theater group. At the same time, she was an assistant editor and house copywriter for Viking Press. After a long hiatus from writing, during which she became a professional chef, she returned to literature and in 1991 created NightLight Readings, a monthly writers-in-performance series currently based at The Drawing Center in New York. She has been awarded residencies at Yaddo and the MacDowell Colony and is a member of the PEN American Center. She is now at work on a new novel.

Edmund White and Alain Kirili. *BOMB #47, Spring 1994*

Edmund White was born in Cincinnati in 1940. He has taught literature and creative writing at Yale, Johns Hopkins, New York University, and Columbia, was a full professor of English at Brown, and served as executive director of the New York Institute for the Humanities. In 1983 he received a Guggenheim Fellowship and the Award for Literature from the National Academy of Arts and Letters. In 1993 he was made a Chevalier de l'Ordre des Arts et Lettres. He was awarded the National Book Critics Circle Award and the Lambda Literary Award for *Genet: A Biography* (1994). His other books include: *Forgetting Elena*, *Nocturnes for the King of Naples*, *States of Desire: Travels in Gay America*, *The Burning Library*, *A Boy's Own Story*, *Caracole*, and *The Beautiful Room is Empty*. His latest book is *The Farewell Symphony*. He lives in Paris.

Alain Kirili has been showing his artwork internationally since 1972. His most recent shows include, in 1992: Galerie Carée, Villa Arson, Nice; Galerie Daniel Templon, Paris; Musée d'Art Moderne, Saint-Etienne; Galerie Saint-Séverin, Paris; Centre d'Art Contemporain, Vassivière en Limousin; in 1993: École des Beaux-Arts de Nantes; *Baptism by Steve Lacy for the Sculpture of Alain Kirili*, Thread Waxing Space, New York; Daniel Templon, Paris; in 1994: Sainsbury Centre for Visual Arts, University of East Anglia, Norwich; in 1996: Daniel Templon, Paris; Centre d'Art Contemporain, Castres; in 1998: Marlborough Chelsea Gallery, New York. *Celebration* (1997), a book published by Christian Bourgois, records with photographs the collaboration sculpture/jazz that Kirili did over the past five years with Cecil Taylor, Steve Laly, Sunny Murray, Archie Shepp, Evan Parker, and others.

John Edgar Wideman by Caryl Phillips. *BOMB #49, Fall 1994*

John Edgar Wideman received a BA in English from the University of Pennsylvania and a B.Phil. from Oxford University in 1966. His books include *A Glance Away*, (1967), *Hurry Home* (1969), *The Lynchers* (1973), *Hiding Place* (1981), *Damballah*, a collection of short stories (1981), *Sent For You Yesterday* (1983), *Brothers and Keepers* (1984), *Homewood Trilogy* (1984), *Fever* (1989), *Philadelphia Fire* (1990), *The Stories of John Edgar Wideman*(1992), *The Homewood Books* (1992), *Fatheralong: A Meditation on Fathers, Sons, Race, and Society* (1994), and *The Cattle Killing* (1996). He has received a grant from the National Endowment for the Arts, a MacArthur Award, a Lannan Literary Fellowship, a PEN/Faulkner Award, and the American Book Award. He has taught at the University of Pennsylvania, the University of Wyoming, and presently at the University of Massachusetts. He lives in Amherst, Massachusetts.

Jeanette Winterson by Catherine Bush. *BOMB #43, Spring 1993*

Jeanette Winterson was born in Lancashire, England and adopted by Pentecostal evangelists. She read English at St. Catherines College, Oxford. Her first novel, *Oranges Are Not the Only Fruit* (1985) won the Whitbread Award and was adapted by her for BBC Television in 1990. The series won international prizes, including a BAFTA for best drama, the Prix Italia, the Prix d'Argent (Cannes), and the ACE Award Los Angeles. Her other books include *The Passion* (1987), which won the John Llewelyn Rhys Award, *Sexing the Cherry* (1989), *Written on the Body* (1992), *Art and Lies* (1994), *Gut Symmetries* (1997), and *The World and Other Places* (1988), a short story collection. She has also written a comic book, *Boating for Beginners* (1985), a collection of essays, *Art Objects* (1995), and is currently working on a screenplay of *The Passion* for Miramax Films. In 1989, she was awarded the E.M. Forster Award from the American Academy and Institute of Arts and Letters. She lives in London and Gloustershire.

Catherine Bush was born in Toronto, Canada, in 1961, and received a B.A. in Comparative Literature from Yale University in 1983. She is the author of the novel, *Minus Time* (Hyperion, 1993); published in Canada, the U.S. and the U.K., short-listed for the 1994 SmithBooks/Books in Canada First Novel Award and a City of Toronto Book Award, and currently being adapted for film. Her non-fiction has been published widely in the *New York Times Book Review*, the *Village Voice Literary Supplement*, and many other publications. She is currently working on a second novel, *Radar Angels*, and teaches in the Creative Writing Program at Concordia University in Montreal.

Tobias Wolff by A.M. Homes. *BOMB #57, Fall 1996*
Tobias Wolff's books include the memoirs *This Boy's Life* and, most recently, *In Pharaoh's Army*; the short novel *The Barracks Thief*; and three collections of short stories, *In the Garden of the North American Martyrs*, *Back in the World*, and most recently, *The Night in Question*. He has also edited several anthologies, among them *Best American Short Stories 1994* and *The Vintage Book of Contemporary Short Stories*. His work has been translated widely and has received numerous awards, including the PEN/Faulkner Award, the *Los Angeles Times* Book Award, and the Rea Award for the Short Story. He teaches at Stanford University.

A. M. Homes is the author of the novels *The End of Alice*, *In A Country of Mothers*, *Jack*, the short story collection *The Safety of Objects,* and the artists book *Appendix A*. Her work has been translated into eight languages and has been much anthologized. Homes' fiction and nonfiction regularly appears in many magazines including: *Artforum*, *Blind Spot*, *Elle*, *Esquire*, *Harpers Bazaar*, *Mirabella*, the *New Yorker*, the *New York Times Magazine*, *Story*, *Vanity Fair*, *Vogue*, the *Los Angeles Times*, the *Washington Post*, and the *Village Voice*. Homes has been the recipient of numerous awards, including a National Endowment for the Arts Fellowship, a New York Foundation for the Arts Fellowship (1988), a James Michener Fellowship and the 1993 Deutscher Jugendliteraturpreis. Born in Washington, D.C., A.M. Homes is a graduate of Sarah Lawrence College and The University of Iowa Writers Workshop and currently teaches in the Writing programs at both Columbia University and the New School in New York City.